GABRIEL MARCEL
ON
RELIGIOUS
KNOWLEDGE

Neil Gillman
The Jewish Theological Seminary
of America

University Press
of America™

Library of Congress Catalog Card Number: 80-5061

For Sarah

iii

ACKNOWLEDGMENTS

For permission to reprint selections from a variety of works by and about Marcel, and on other issues covered in this volume, the author wishes to thank:

The Editor of the Aristotelian Society, for "Gods" by John Wisdom, Proceedings of the Aristotelian Society, 1944-1945, © 1945 The Aristotelian Society, London, England, reprinted by courtesy of the Editor of the Aristotelian Society.

Dacre Press/A & C Black (Publishers) Limited, London, England, for Being and Having, by Gabriel Marcel.

Duquesne University Press, for Presence and Immortality, by Gabriel Marcel, © 1967 by Duquesne University.

Farrar, Straus and Giroux, Inc., for Creative Fidelity. Reprinted with the permission of Farrar, Straus and Giroux, Inc. From CREATIVE FIDELITY by Gabriel Marcel. Translated from the French with an Introduction by Robert Rosthal. Copyright © 1964 by Farrar, Straus and Giroux, Inc.

Librairie Armand Colin, for "Les Conditions dialectiques de la philosophie de l'intuition," Revue de métaphysique et de morale, XX (1912).

Lyle Stuart, Inc., for The Philosophy of Existentialism by Gabriel Marcel. Copyright © 1956 by Philosophical Library, PHILOSOPHY OF EXISTENTIALISM published by arrangement with Citadel Press, a subsidiary of Lyle Stuart, Inc.

TABLE OF CONTENTS

PREFACE

An earlier version of this study was presented to the Faculty of Philosophy at Columbia
University in 1975 in partial fulfillment of the
requirements for the degree of Doctor of Philosophy
in the Department of Philosophy. I have now
revised and updated that work, utilising material
by and about Marcel that has been published in the
intervening years.

In trying, retrospectively, to trace the
evolution of my interest in Marcel and in the so-
called "problem" of religious knowledge, I am
struck by what Marcel would have called the "mysterious" convergence of concerns that I am now able
to see in my work. I was born and raised as a Jew
in French Canada. My undergraduate studies at
McGill University in Montreal kindled my interest
in philosophy and introduced me to the literature
and civilization of twentieth-century France, the
matrix out of which Marcel emerged and to which his
work is a response. My studies of the classical
texts of Judaism at the Jewish Theological Seminary
of America in New York City during the early
fifties taught me about a people who exemplified
fidelity at its most tenacious and who articulated
multiple visions of the transcendent but grounded
these in the everyday. Finally my doctoral studies
at Columbia University convinced me that for the
believer, the epistemological issues are inescapable.

My studies at the Seminary with the late
Abraham Joshua Heschel who is so close to Marcel on
so many important issues, left me with a basic
sympathy for this style of philosophy along with a
certain wariness of many of the problems that come

in its wake. My readings in the secondary literature on Marcel revealed that with the exception of
Paul Ricoeur and some of his colleagues in France,
students of Marcel tend either to be uncritically
eulogistic or to attack him from an ex parte (e.g.
Thomist) perspective. What was missing, especially
in English, was a serious attempt to take Marcel's
thought on its own terms, uncover its primary impulses and internal stresses, and evaluate it
according to its coherence and faithfulness to its
own stated purposes. My purpose, then, has been to
expound and appraise this philosophy, hoping that
what would emerge would be neither unqualified
praise nor blanket condemnation but rather a finer
appreciation of why he took the positions he did
and how those initial options shaped the final outcome of his philosophical quest.

Thus, for example, I have tried to stress
the evolution of Marcel's thought on a number of
central issues from the 1910-1914 years through to
the seventies. I have carefully separated the expository and evaluative sections of each chapter,
and at critical points in my analysis, I have com-
pared Marcel's thought with that of other philos-
ophers--Martin Buber, Abraham Heschel and Paul
Tillich--who share his basic assumptions but treat
a particular problem in a different way. It
remains my conviction that in the long run an approach of this kind will be more helpful to the
next generation of Marcel's students for none of
these issues has been settled once and for all, nor
are they likely to be in the near future.

I was introduced to Marcel's writings by
Professor Albert Hofstadter, formerly of Columbia
and now at the University of California, Santa Cruz,
and by the late Professor Daniel Day Williams of
Union Theological Seminary. Fortuitously, both of
these men were to guide my research--Professor
Hofstadter when I began my work and Professor
Williams when I returned to it after a hiatus of a
number of years. Upon Professor Williams' untimely
death, Professor Arthur C. Danto undertook to guide

my work to its completion. I am indebted to these
three scholars for their direction and for the many
contributions they made to my thinking. In addition, mention should be made of Professor Richard
F. Kuhns Jr. who offered numerous suggestions and
of Professor Robert D. Cummings whose advice at a
number of critical points in the course of my
studies proved invaluable. I must add, of course,
that whatever inadequacies this work may contain
are mine alone.

It has been my good fortune, during the
years of my doctoral work and thereafter, to study
and teach at the Jewish Theological Seminary of
America. Professor Gerson D. Cohen, Chancellor of
the Seminary, has been unstinting in his support
and encouragement of my scholarly efforts. He made
it possible for me to be relieved of my adminis-
trative and teaching responsibilities at the
Seminary, without which this work could not have
been brought to fruition. Professor Louis Finkel-
stein, Chancellor Emeritus of the Seminary, gave me
my first opportunity to teach philosophy and has
been a source of inspiration and guidance for close
to three decades. The stimulus of hours of conversation with my teachers, now colleagues, and my
students at the Seminary have helped sharpen my
perception of many of the issues covered in this
study and of many others as well.

Professors Seymour Feldman of Rutgers
University and Elliot Dorff of the University of
Judaism in Los Angeles, friends of many years, read
extended portions of this study and shared their
insights with me. Professor Eugene B. Borowitz of
Hebrew Union College-Jewish Institute of Religion
generously helped clarify some of the issues
covered in Chapters V and VI. I acknowledge, with
gratitude the support of the Seminary's Herbert H.
Lehman Fellowship program, the National Foundation
for Jewish Culture and the Danforth Foundation's
Kent Fellowship program.

Ms. Ruth Sussman of the French Department

at Barnard College helped me decipher and translate some of the more obscure passages in Marcel's French. Ms. Helen Hudson, Editorial Assistant at the University Press of America dealt, with unfailing graciousness, with the many questions that arose during the preparation of the manuscript. Mrs. W.T.H. Jackson, who typed the original dissertation, was kind enough to undertake to type this revised version as well. Ms. Amy Lederhendler reviewed the entire manuscript prior to publication. I acknowledge their help with gratitude.

It is my deepest regret that my mother did not live to see the publication of this book. Her love of books and of learning served as a model from my earliest childhood. My father's abiding concern throughout these years has been indispensable; I am pleased that he is able to share in the joy of this accomplishment. My children, Abby and Debby, tolerated with their customary good humor the demands which their father's studies made on time which otherwise would have been spent with them. Finally, I cannot find the words to acknowledge what I owe my wife, Sarah. She has enabled me better to understand what Marcel was trying to teach us of the way one human being can be "present" to another--and what difference this presence makes.

Hanukkah, 5740
December 13, 1979
New York, N.Y.

KEY TO ABBREVIATIONS

BH   Being and Having (Etre et Avoir, 1935*)
CF   Creative Fidelity (Du Refus à l'invocation, 1940)
DW   The Decline of Wisdom (Le Declin de la sagesse, 1954)
EBHD   The Existential Background of Human Dignity (1963)
ECVQE   En Chemin, vers quel éveil? (1971)
HV   Homo Viator (1945)
MBI   The Mystery of Being. Vol. I (Le Mystère de l'Etre, Vol. I, 1951)
MBII   The Mystery of Being. Vol. II (Le Mystère de l'Etre, Vol. II, 1951)
MJ   Metaphysical Journal (Journal métaphysique, 1927)
MMS   Man Against Mass Society (Les Hommes contre l'humain, 1951)
PF   Philosophical Fragments 1909-1914 (Fragments philosophiques 1909-1914, 1962)
PI   Presence and Immortality (Présence et Immortalité, 1959)
PM   Problematic Man (L'Homme problématique, 1955)
SEAR   Searchings (Auf der Suche nach Wahrheit und Gerechtigkeit, 1964)
TPE   The Philosophy of Existentialism (1949)
TWB   Tragic Wisdom and Beyond (Pour une sagesse tragique et son au-delà and Entretiens Paul Ricoeur-Gabriel Marcel, 1968)

*Publication date of original version.

xiii

CHAPTER I

MARCEL AND THE TRADITIONS OF PHILOSOPHY

Introduction

A monograph on the concept of mystery in the thought of Gabriel Marcel reaches the following conclusions:

> . . . one cannot enter thus into himself without discovering that he is not a "subject" after all but is personally and positively related to his own existence. Unfortunately, Marcel often continues using the word "subject" in a way which does not help to make this clear: and several of his interpreters fall into the same confusion. The point is that introspection opens out upon an intuition of being who one is; but this, as James Collins explains, is a "blindfold intuition, a non-self-conscious apprehension of existence in the existent thing." Here again the language is probably unfortunate; but all of us are victimized by philosophical language at this point, and neologisms sometimes do more harm than good.[1]

The apologetic tone that haunts this statement is all too familiar to anyone who has tried to expound the thought of Gabriel Marcel, for in the

---

[1] Roger Hazelton, "Marcel on Mystery," _The Journal of Religion_, 38 (July 1958), 161-162. The reference to James Collins is to his _The Existentialists_ (Chicago: Henry Regnery, 1952), p. 136.

course of a prolific career that spanned six
decades, Marcel produced a philosophical _oeuvre_
that is distinguished by a richness of imagination
and an acuteness of perception, while remaining
frustratingly ambiguous and incomplete.

Marcel philosophizes in the olympian tradition of nineteenth-century continental philosophy,
disregarding many of the commonly accepted traditions of philosophical investigation. He is
customarily studied as a representative of the
existentialist and/or phenomenological schools of
philosophy, but in each case, he insists that his
own thought was fully formed well before he encountered that literature. Only rarely--Jean Paul
Sartre is one notable exception--does he enter into
an extended give-and-take with a real philosophical
adversary. His preferred mode of exposition is the
philosophical diary--a collection of disconnected
excursions into various topics, unequal in length
and highly tentative as to conclusions. He stresses
his aversion to any systematic presentation of his
thought and insists that this is not a personal
idiosyncrasy, but rather that it is wedded to the
substance of his thought which invalidates from the
outset all abstract and conclusive overviews of any
philosophical issue. Whatever the reason, the
result engenders a sense of betrayal in one who
attempts anything resembling a conventional exposition of his thought.

It should not be surprising, in the light of
this, that Marcel was very much not a "professional"
philosopher. He taught philosophy for relatively
short periods of time, mainly early in his career.
He maintained himself by serving as drama critic for
Les Nouvelles Littéraires and as an editor for a
French publishing house. Marcel considered it fortuitous that his early research could be carried on
in this untrammeled way, free from the more disci-
plined (and inevitably critical) structure of the
classroom. It also, however, contributes to the
highly idiosyncratic style of his work, and is the
source of many of the difficulties involved in

studying it.

A superb illustration of these difficulties involved in a study of Marcel's thought emerges in his discussion of the issue which is the central focus of this work: the place of knowledge in religion.

John Herman Randall Jr.[1] suggests that the intellectual history of the West exhibits three main positions on this issue.

The first maintains that religion teaches a body of truths about man and his world stemming from a revelation which comes to be identified with an acceptable philosophical scheme. Religion then is identified with a body of knowledge which is to be evaluated by the same criteria that serve for any body of knowledge, for ultimately knowledge is one. This position is best exemplified in the enterprise of eighteenth-century rational theology.

The second maintains that religious knowledge inhabits a realm of its own, inaccessible to the usual methods of inquiry or testing. It feeds on distinctive experiences which are "religious" in nature and which can be dealt with adequately only by an equally distinctive epistemology oriented solely to this privileged realm. Thomas Aquinas and Immanuel Kant are most frequently associated with this position, though their characterizations of religious knowledge differ widely.

Both of these positions have run into difficulty. The first places religious knowledge at the mercy of whatever is claimed by the reigning philosophical school to constitute authentic knowledge, constantly forcing the believer to redefine

---

[1]John Herman Randall Jr., The Role of Knowledge in Western Religion (Boston: Starr King Press, Beacon Hill, 1958).

the content of his tradition. The second has suf-
fered from the stubborn refusal of those other
bodies of knowledge--science in particular--to
remain within the boundaries assigned to them by
religion.

In reaction to these difficulties, the third
position has maintained that whatever else religion
may do for man--and that can be considerable--it
does not offer him anything that can be considered
knowledge. Religion does affect the way man uses
the knowledge he has, but it should not itself be
identified with any explicit epistemological claims.
Duns Scotus in the Middle Ages and George Santayana
and Randall himself among contemporary thinkers are
identified with this position.

Now it is completely in character that
Marcel cannot be easily fitted into any of these
three broad categories. He would seem, at first
blush, to be most easily identified with the second
of the positions because of his division of the
realm of knowledge into "sacred" and "profane"
knowledge, each requiring a distinctive epistemology. But the domain of sacred knowledge includes
just about all of the knowledge yielded by philosophy, with scientific knowledge alone excluded.
But this identification of religious and philosophical (primarily metaphysical) knowledge suggests
that Marcel might be identified with the first of
the three positions. But here again, Marcel is not
at all clear as to the relationship between metaphysics and religion and how the vocabulary of the
first is to be translated into that of the second.
Finally, as we shall see, it would not be too difficult for a contemporary philosophical analyst to
show that Marcel does not make a convincing case
for the fact that so-called sacred knowledge is in
fact knowledge at all, thus identifying him with
the third position. Hence the ambiguity which must
be emphasized at the outset.

The key to this ambiguity and the central
issue which will emerge throughout this study is

the adequacy of Marcel's delineation of the situation "which I am" in such a way as to avoid any hint of dualism, whether of body and mind, self and world, self and other, self (world) and being or self (world) and God. Our questions will be: can this aversion to dualisms be maintained? If so, at what cost to the clarity, accuracy and general usefulness of his philosophical views?

The first two chapters of this study will introduce Marcel's philosophical framework--first, three of his central philosophical assumptions, and then his earliest writings which reveal his distinctive positions in the process of being created.

The central issue will emerge clearly in the two central chapters. Chapter three will explore Marcel's discussion of the polarities which the situational structure is designed to integrate: the self, the world, the other, and being--and will show how Marcel is driven by his antipathy to dualisms to force the two primary dimensions of the situation, "incarnation" and "intersubjectivity," into a single mould. Chapter four will pursue Marcel's discussion of the epistemological circuits which bind together the polarities of the situation. It will show how the organizing themes of "mystery," "blinded intuition," "secondary reflection," "participation" and "sacred knowledge" are attempts to reconcile significant differences in the way in which men know different aspects of reality.

Finally, the two concluding chapters will focus on religious knowledge itself. Chapter five will explore Marcel's mature discussion of religious faith and God, his description of the way in which his metaphysics and ontology prepare the way for religious faith and his religious epistemology. Chapter six will appraise this material and will show how Marcel's attempts to clarify the nature and appropriate place of knowledge in religion reveal a basic tension between two antithetical impulses in his thought which can, in retrospect, be traced throughout his entire discussion of the situation.

Our conclusion will be that only according to the second of these impulses can Marcel be credited with having yielded anything resembling knowledge.

We will conclude, then, that Marcel's epistemology is ambiguous and incomplete. But throughout the course of this study we will be struck again and again by the richness of Marcel's philosophical imagination and the extraordinary perceptiveness of his philosophical eye. The very ambiguities which dot his epistemological writings are themselves the source of its genuine suggestiveness, especially on the issue of religious knowledge; he has marked out certain paths and defined a method of philosophical exploration which his successors may undertake to follow--hopefully with greater clarity and precision.

Marcel's Philosophical Assumptions

A detailed study of any one aspect of the thought of a philosopher can only benefit from a preliminary sketch of some of the broad assumptions which underlie his work as a whole. A sketch of this kind is even more useful for a thinker such as Marcel whose conceptual scheme and philosophical vocabulary border on the idiosyncratic.

We begin, then, with brief discussions of three of these assumptions: Marcel's view of the impetus for philosophy, his philosophical method and his delineation of the data for philosophy, suggesting only in a preliminary way, the import of these discussions for the study to follow.

The Impetus for Philosophy

Marcel claims that philosophy begins with a certain disquiet within the philosopher which he calls "metaphysical uneasiness" or "metaphysical

need."[1] It resembles the state of a man suffering
from a fever and trying to find a comfortable position in bed, or the discomfort of a musician as he
awaits the harmonious resolution of a discord.[2]
More specifically, metaphysical need is ". . . a
kind of . . . appetite for being"[3] or, in another
context, a "need for being"[4] or, in still another
context, "a need for transcendence,"[5] where being
(or transcendence) is ". . . what withstands . . .
an exhaustive analysis bearing on the data of experience and aiming to reduce them step by step to
elements increasingly devoid of intrinsic or significant value."[6]

     Marcel tries to be more specific about the
nature of this primitive need. The most revealing
of these attempts links this sense of disquiet to
the very contingent position the individual finds
himself occupying in time and space.[7] In short,
metaphysical disquiet is a sense of human contin-

_____

     [1]MJ 288, 290, 293; MBI 7. The French is
respectively "l'inquiétude métaphysique" and "le
besoin métaphysique." Marcel, more frequently,
substitutes "exigence" for "besoin" doubtless
because it captures more precisely the intensity of
affect. Marcel's historical and phenomenological
study of uneasiness is in Part two of PM 67-144.

     [2]MJ 290; MBI 7-8.

     [3]MJ 288.

     [4]TPE 13.

     [5]MBI 39.

     [6]TPE 14. On "transcendence," see MBI
46-48.

     [7]See his quotation from Pascal in EBHD
11-12.

gency or finitude, and philosophy is the ". . . gathering together of processes by which I can pass from a situation which is experienced as basically discordant . . . to a different situation in which some kind of expectation is satisfied,"[1] i.e. by dispelling the disquieting sense of contingency.

Marcel insists that the need for being is not to be identified with curiosity, even "transcendental curiosity." Curiosity launches an inquiry which yields first an hypothesis, and ultimately a solution--effectively eliminating the curiosity. In an inquiry of this kind, the focus is on the objective of the inquiry and both the inquirer and his inquiry are subordinated to the discovery of the solution.[2] To put this another way, in an inquiry motivated by curiosity, there is a sense of equilibrium at the center (the subject who is conducting the inquiry) but an uncertainty in regard to the object on the periphery. To experience metaphysical unease however,

> . . . is to be uncertain of one's centre,
> it is to be in search of one's equilibrium
> . . . . My curiosity is more liable to
> become uneasiness the more the object which
> arouses it forms part of myself, the more
> closely this object is incorporated into my
> own interior edifice. At the same time
> uneasiness is the more metaphysical the
> more it concerns anything which cannot be

---

[1]MBI 8. Marcel suggests that "metaphysics" refers to reflection trained on what he will call "mystery," i.e. on issues relating to my "interior edifice" (HV 138). But since so many of the traditional branches of philosophy, e.g. epistemology, ontology and ethics also deal with "mysteries," Marcel often uses "philosophy" as synonymous with "metaphysics."

[2]MJ 288, 292.

separated from myself without the annihilation of this very self.[1]

    The various strands of these discussions
converge in Marcel's claim that the "only," i.e.
the umbrella, metaphysical question is: What am I?[2]
for the philosopher, in contrast to the inquirer,
is the stage, not the subject of his research.[3] In
one of his many programmatic statements, he claims
that his central philosophical concern was ". . .
to discover how a subject, in his actual capacity
as subject, is related to a reality which cannot,
in this context, be regarded as objective, yet
which is persistently required and recognized as
real,"[4] i.e. to being. In Marcel's technical terminology, the self is the paradigm of a "presence"
which can never be an "object" and the unease is
precisely "metaphysical" because it is directed to
the heart of my "interior edifice."

    This distinction between "presence" and
"object"--and the correlative distinction between
"mystery" and "problem"--have become synonymous
with the work of Marcel. They are indeed the
primary categories in his epistemology and will be
discussed at length below. But it is well-nigh
impossible to make any progress with Marcel without
some preliminary appreciation of the import of
these distinctions.

    An "object" is any aspect of reality which
is totally distinct from or external to a subject;
a "presence" in contrast, is integral to the

---

[1] HV 138.

[2] Ibid.

[3] TPE 18.

[4] Ibid. 127. "Objective" in this context
means external to the self.

identity of the subject. Hence an object can be "had," manipulated or transmitted to another subject without affecting the integrity of the subject; a presence, if treated "objectively," risks the annihilation of the subject. Any "insular" aspect of the so-called "external" world can properly be treated as an object; my self, being and reflection itself are the paradigmatic instances of presence. My body stands in an intermediate state; it can be understood as a body, hence as object, or as my body, integral to who I am, hence as presence. As a corollary to this, a subject confronting an object, is impersonal or anonymous--hence universally interchangeable; a subject confronting a presence is singular and unique.

Finally, objects raise "problems"--issues which are in principle solvable by anyone with mastery of the necessary techniques, and the solutions thereby obtained can be shared and are more or less permanent contributions to our fund of knowledge. In contrast, presences suggest "mysteries" which can only be acknowledged or evoked, not solved, and the acknowledgment takes the form of personal testimony. Hence the public verifiability of the solutions to problems, and the "objective" unverifiability of the witness' testimony.

In attempting to deal with metaphysical unease, then, the metaphysician must contend with the fact that he is not transparent to himself;[1] nor are any of the realities which touch upon his "interior edifice." In none of these can he stand as an onlooker in juxtaposition to an object. Marcel habitually contrasts the stance of onlooker with that of witness. The onlooker can be anyone at all; he is interchangeable and he can efface himself before what he is contemplating. In contrast, the presence of the witness is indispensable; this man,

---

[1]MJ 290. "Transparency" is a quality of an object whereas a presence is "opaque" (PI 184-185).

in all <u>his</u> singularity, must be present. The metaphysician is a witness and his research is his
"testimony." Marcel insists that our inescapable
mode of belonging to the world is as a witness.[1]

    Marcel acknowledges that the need for being
which gives rise to philosophy can be either
acknowledged or silenced. The latter stance emerges,
for example, when philosophy is seen as beginning
with methodological scepticism which is simply
scientific detachment exaggerated into philosophical
method. Alternately, it can be silenced by a nihilism, an arbitrary act of refusal which claims to be
the expression of a positive theory of thought about
the self and the world.[2] Marcel's writings, further,
abound in descriptions of our present "broken
world"[3] which reduces the human being to a set of
functions or of statistical data, systematically
discrediting all needs of this kind.[4]

    But he insists that methodological scepti-
cism, systematic refusal and the sense of the
"broken world" are all second-level phenomena; they
are a form of reaction, ". . . a kind of recoil
which can only take place when our deepest being has
somehow been split by an ontological mistrust so
deep-rooted so as to be almost a <u>habitus</u> of the
soul."[5]

_____

    [1]<u>TPE</u> 97. On the witness and his testimony
see ibid. 91-97; <u>BH</u> 210-212; <u>MBII</u> 129-131.

    [2]<u>TPE</u> 15.

    [3]<u>Le Monde cassé</u> is the name of one of
Marcel's dramas.

    [4]See, for example, <u>TPE</u> 9-13; <u>MBI</u>, chapter 2,
and his description of "the barracks man" in <u>PM</u>
18-20.

    [5]<u>BH</u> 213.

This claim requires some clarification. At times, Marcel seems to be suggesting simply that at the very outset, the philosopher makes an initial "wager," either acknowledging the need for being or silencing it, and in making this initial wager, he is totally free. In this context, Marcel claims that however possible, in theory, it may be to deny the need for being--i.e. however free this denial may be from internal contradiction--it is nevertheless not _dictated_ by our experience of reality.[1] Experience is neutral and we must then study why an individual will take one option over the other. The role of the will then becomes a central epistemological issue.[2]

More characteristically, however, he detects even in the heart of inveterate pessimism a wish that man could find a way out of his finitude, i.e. that there would be some way to resist the reductionist analysis bearing on value and significance[3] and he calls that very aspiration itself a degree of

---

[1]_MJ_ 323-324; _TWB_ 227-228.

[2]_MJ_ 289. This interpretation is suggested by Marcel in response to a charge of "wishful thinking" directed by Paul Ricoeur to the second interpretation to be described below. Marcel's point here is that under this first interpretation the task of the philosopher is to expose the "pessimistic" approach as the postulate that it is which leaves one free to adopt the "optimistic" stance as equally justified (_TWB_ 227-228). However this first interpretation is clearly a fall-back position; he is much more in sympathy with the second where experience is seen to _favor_ the "optimistic" conclusion. The extent to which this approach is indeed "wishful thinking" will be a central issue in our final appraisal of Marcel's thought at the conclusion of this study.

[3]_TPE_ 14.

participation in being, however rudimentary.[1] In
this vein--which is the dominant one in his work--
Marcel claims that at the very beginning of our
awareness of reality there lies a primitive affirmation of being within or through us, an affirmation
of which we are the stage rather than the subject,
and one that is presupposed by our awareness of the
need for being--for I, who ask the question about
being, am.[2]

The nature of this primitive affirmation
constitutes a major topic in Marcel's epistemology
and will be considered at great length below. However, from this point of view, reality is far from
neutral and to silence or to refuse the need for
being is precisely the second-level phenomenon of
reaction mentioned above. The option remains: we
are free to acknowledge or to reject being, but
experience clearly favors the former.

Marcel's philosophical writings can be
characterized as an exploration of how and why men
choose either one of these options, and the implications of that original choice. The polemical
side of his work--his philosophical critique of
rationalism and scientism and his social critique of
a predominantly technological approach to man and
society--is a scrutiny of the grounds for contemporary man's refusal to accept his natural orientation
to the ontological. As an alternative, he proposes
a series of "approches concrètes," detailed phenomenological probings into certain fundamental human
experiences--faithfulness, hope, and love are the
central ones--which support man's need for being.[3]

---

[1]TPE 14.

[2]Ibid. 18.

[3]TWB 227. Marcel's "What Can be Expected of
Philosophy" (ibid. 3-15) is his most comprehensive
statement on the impetus for philosophy and its
relevance to the human enterprise.

Toward the end of his life, Marcel acknowledged that his thought can be understood as "a metaphysics of light and a sociology of shadows."[1] In a more prosaic vein, using the title of one of his books, it can be said that his work traces man's path as he moves from refusal to invocation of being.[2]

Marcel's Philosophical Method

The key to understanding the evolution of Marcel's philosophical method lies in a record of his memories from childhood preserved in "An Essay in Autobiography."[3] He contrasts his exasperation with his early schooling which he calls a palladium to the spirit of abstraction[4] with his delight at his summer holiday experience.

> The holidays were to me each time an oasis
> in my waste land. Every year we went away
> to the mountains, always to some different
> place . . . . My greatest joy in my child-

---

[1]TWB 253. The phrase is Ricoeur's.

[2]Du refus à l'invocation.

[3]The paper, in the original French, is included in Existentialist chrétien, "Collection Présences" (Paris: Plon, 1947), and in English, in TPE 104-128. Cf. SEAR 93-100. The first third of ECVQE is a storehouse of information on Marcel's early years. See also Madeleine Sabine's recollections, "Mon cousin Gabriel" in Entretiens autour de Gabriel Marcel (Neuchâtel: Editions de la Baconnière, 1976), pp. 263-278. See also, in the same volume, Marcel's "De la recherche philosophique" and the discussion following (pp. 9-52) for his later reflections on philosophical method.

[4]TPE 113

hood was to discover, to explore, to imagine
more than I could see, to plan other journeys
. . . . My predilection for the inaccessible
and the unknown went with a disdain . . .
for whatever is within the reach of all.
There was a lot of vanity in all this, a lot
of snobbery, but there was also something
else: a childish horror of what has lost its
freshness, the ingenuous and absurd notion
that what is distant in space is also the
untrodden, the undefiled . . . whereas the
familiar and the nearby has been distorted
and polluted . . . .[1]

This passage is replete with allusions to some of
Marcel's central philosophical assumptions: his
view that philosophy is an exploration of the implications of experience, his willingness to
explore the more remote areas of experience such as
telepathy and parapsychology, his insistence that
the proper philosophical stance toward the world is
one of child-like wonderment, his disdain for conclusions that are "in the reach of all," and his
"snobbish" appeal to the "connoisseur" with the
"ear" for philosophy who alone can share his philosophical quest. Marcel himself is aware of the
implications of these early memories:

I think I am right in seeing in this predilection something of the metaphysical
concern to discover the intimate at the
heart of the remote, a concern . . . to
wrest from it the spiritual secret which
destroys its power as barrier . . . . The
world seemed to me then, as now, an indeterminate place in which to extend as
much as possible the region where one is
at home and to decrease that which is
vaguely imagined or known only by hear-
say, in an abstract and lifeless manner

---

[1]TPE 114-115.

. . . . The categories I strove to establish later . . . give meaning to these
distinctions and bring out their philosophical basis; but if I felt the need to
establish them, it was because I needed
to understand and to give shape to my own
immediate experience.[1]

In retrospect, Marcel is grateful that this childhood experience was allowed to proliferate ". . .
without submitting it to the control of thought"[2]
and he urges the student of philosophy to resist
the desultory "greyness" which he claims overlies
philosophical education today and to preserve the
freshness of spirit of the explorer in virgin territory.[3]

    Marcel sees his own work as largely an
"explicitation" of immediate experience.[4] He is
convinced that he can remain creative as a philosopher ". . . only for so long as my experience
still contains unexploited and unchartered zones."[5]
The nature of the philosophical "search" is best
expressed by the French verb "reconnaître" which
suggests three separate meanings as expressed in the
English "reconnoiter," "recognize" and "acknowledge." Marcel suggests that these represent three
distinct moments in philosophical reflection.
Philosophy begins with an act of "reconnoitering"
for at the outset, the territory (experience) is
totally strange and the traveler is quite lost.
Gradually however certain signposts are "recognized"

---

[1]TPE 115-116; cf. TWB 217-219.

[2]TPE 116.

[3]EBHD 9-10.

[4]TPE 128.

[5]Ibid.

and they lend assurance of the route to be followed
for the satisfaction of immediate needs; this route
becomes an axis for further explorations on either
side. Finally the explorer can "acknowledge" with
confidence a wide variety of orientations to different parts of the territory.[1] The same three
moments in the process of "reconnaître" are at work
in our relations with other people.[2] This is the
model for philosophical method. It is exploration
in its purest form, with no prejudgments as to what
one will find; everything that comes into view is a
gift.[3]

    If philosophy is an act of exploration,
Marcel's emphasis is on the activity itself rather
than on any results which may emerge. He is uncom-
fortable with the implications of the phrase "to
have a philosophy" as if philosophy were a possession which one can dispose of.[4] He is contemptuous
of the tendency to teach philosophy as a set of
answers to be memorized for an examination.

    In Marcel's own philosophical writings,
substance has been wedded to form. He is most comfortable with two forms of expression: the diary
and the drama. The former--published in three
volumes of extracts--is literally a work-book, a
collection of tentative, disconnected excursions
into various philosophical issues, which, with its
false starts, its internal dialogue and persistent
self-criticism, its detours as well as its slowly
but progressively cumulative character, is a perfect
illustration of what Marcel means by the phrase
"philosophical exploration." Even the two most

---

[1]MBI 139-141.

[2]Ibid. 141.

[3]EBHD 5-6.

[4]PI 16; CF 14-15.

systematic presentations of his thought--the two
volumes of <u>The Mystery of Being</u> and <u>The Existential
Background of Human Dignity</u>--are actually a series
of extended journal entries. The internal dialogue
and self-interrogation of his philosophical writings
suggest the way in which his dramas--over twenty of
which have been published--complement his more
technical philosophical work. Both are examples of
what he calls "la pensée pensante" rather than "la
pensée pensée."[1]

    In Marcel's view, the philosopher must
emphasize the process of discovery over its results
because the mind cannot ". . . objectively define
the structure of reality and then regard itself as
qualified to legislate for it";[2] instead, the exploration of reality has to be ". . . pursued
<u>within</u> reality itself to which the philosopher can
never stand in the relationship of an onlooker to a
picture."[3] The philosopher is unfaithful to reality
whenever he attempts to proceed from ". . . conclusion to conclusion towards a <u>Summa</u> which . . . needs
only to be expounded and memorized paragraph by
paragraph."[4] The work of philosophy remains a
". . . perpetual beginning again" for ". . . in the
real world . . . the stage always remains to be set;
in a sense everything always starts from zero."[5]

    Because the philosopher is not an onlooker
vis-à-vis reality, philosophical conclusions can
never have "objective" validity, but neither are

----

    [1]The distinction was originally Blondel's
(<u>TWB</u> 24, <u>CF</u> 13).

    [2]<u>TPE</u> 127.

    [3]Ibid. 128.

    [4]Ibid. 124-125. Cf. <u>TWB</u> 10.

    [5]<u>TPE</u> 125.

they purely subjective. The attempt to define a
view of verification which avoids these two extremes is one of the central issues in Marcel's
thought and will be discussed in detail below. For
the present, suffice it to indicate that he sometimes likens philosophy to the reading of a musical
score.[1] There is no one objectively valid reading
of a score but yet the varying interpretations
given by two competent musicians have much more
than subjective validity. The musician ". . . can
count only on himself, on his own powers of sympathetic intuition. It will be necessary for him to
. . . open himself to this mystery of which he has
before him only a meager sensible and objective
outline."[2] What will emerge is a "creative interpretation," in which the musician, the composer,
and the audience participate together.

        Reality then, like a musical score, does
exercise a certain control over all "creative interpretations" of its content. However the reading is
neither subjective nor objective but "creative"--
and it can only be appreciated by someone with an
"ear" for philosophy. There is a philosophical
audience of "connoisseurs," men who are set apart
by ". . . the levels at which they make their
demands on life and set their standards."[3] To
these, the work of a philosopher is an "aid to discovery"[4] or "a flame awakening a flame."[5] The
philosopher appeals to them to take up their own
equally personal reflection.

----

        [1]Marcel was a composer, musician and music
critic.

        [2]PI 19-20; EBHD 25-26.

        [3]MBI 13-14; TWB 5-6.

        [4]MBI 2.

        [5]TWB 4, 19; MJ xi.

19

But the philosopher--to be true to himself--
must remain on the move, never snugly settled as if
he has reached the end of the road. The title of
one of Marcel's collections of monographs is Homo
Viator and his preferred metaphor for philosophy is
that of "itinerance"--"le chemin sinueux" or "the
winding path"[1]--with its implications of unpredict-
ability and haphazardness, yet at the same time, of
persistence, direction, and an assurance that the
path does lead somewhere.

But whatever the metaphor, the quality
which above all characterizes the authentic philosopher is that of "openness" to the gifts of experience, or, to use the term which Marcel prefers
and which will loom ever larger as we move into the
heart of his thought, that of "disponibilité."[2]
However the term is translated, it signifies the
very opposite of being shut up within oneself, a
stance of detachment or refusal from whatever
motivation. We are then brought back to that original, pre-philosophical or pre-reflective option

---

[1]MBI 4, 133-134 and TWB 252-253. See also
Kenneth Gallagher, The Philosophy of Gabriel Marcel
(New York: Fordham University Press, 1962), p. 159,
note 27.

[2]A translation is difficult. The closest
would be "availability," "accessibility," or "permeability." Patricia Flagg Sanborn quotes Marcel's
personal communication suggesting "spiritual readiness" ("Gabriel Marcel's Conception of the Self,"
unpublished Ph. D. dissertation, Columbia University, 1965, p. 69). However, as will be seen
throughout this study, this hardly captures the
full range of Marcel's use of the term. See e.g.
Joe McCown, Availability: Gabriel Marcel and the
Phenomenology of Human Openness (Missoula, Montana:
Scholars Press for The American Academy of Religion,
1978).

which men take toward reality.

The Data for Philosophy

If the proper stance of a philosopher is
one of openness to experience, the philosopher can
never dismiss part of his data on the grounds that
it is "natural" or "normal" hence taken for granted
on one hand,[1] or that it is "abnormal," hence suspicious or too idiosyncratic to merit sustained
investigation on the other. His method of operation is as follows: "Admitting the hypothesis that
this given phenomenon is real, what are the conditions under which it is able to be real? When I
have determined those conditions by analysis do
they not allow me to understand that which in
practice is unintelligible in normal experience?"[2]
An approach of this kind, for example, encourages
him to devote considerable space to the study of
telepathy and clairvoyance. At the very least
these phenomena have the methodological value of
disabusing us of any a priori view of what is
normal and abnormal and this is enough to make them
worthy of attention. They force us to confront the
fact that the universe can not lend itself to an
uncritically rational description.[3]

Marcel has commented on the central role he
assigns in his thought to concrete examples taken
from everyday life. His work is replete with
extended discussions of experiences such as hope,
despair, questioning and answering, fear, parent-
hood, love, death, suicide, promising, the sense of

---

[1]TPE 13, 122; EBHD 13.

[2]MJ 274.

[3]TPE 122-124 and his "De l'audace en métaphysique," Revue de Métaphysique et de Morale, 52e
année (1947), pp. 233-244.

family, hospitality and all of the experiences involved in the religious life. He claims that these
examples force the philosopher to remain in contact
with life which is where philosophy begins and ends
--however rarified the reflection in between may be.
These examples serve as philosophical parallels for
the dramatic situations in his theatre.[1] Marcel
finds revealed in these concrete situations which
he describes in as close detail as possible, the
fundamental structure of our experience of reality.
But it is always the detail which can be described,
not the totality; and the method is that of an
"approche concrète."

Ultimately, what the philosopher must be
most suspicious of is abstraction. Philosophy is
at the furthest remove from an enterprise which
yields theoretical understanding alone. It must
exhibit a hold on life. For it is life as lived--
in all its circuitousness--that provides Marcel
with the impetus for philosophy, with his understanding of the proper method for philosophy, and
with his data.[2]

---

[1] TWB 235-236. Mary Warnock, Existentialism
(Oxford: Oxford University Press, 1970), chapter 7,
devotes considerable space to a discussion of this
feature of existentialist thought. Interestingly,
she suggests that of all the English writers, it is
Coleridge who illustrates best the notion that the
details of the world reveal the structure of
reality. Marcel's earliest philosophical work
dealt with Schelling's influence on Coleridge.

[2] In one of his last published comments,
Marcel reiterates the suspicion with which he views
the "specialist" in philosophy as opposed to the
non-philosopher who, nevertheless, is prepared to
share a rich human experience (Entretiens autour de
Gabriel Marcel, pp. 249-250).

Preliminary Appraisal

A preliminary evaluation of Marcel's thought is in order at this point--leaving a more thorough critique for later in this study.

First, on the evidence available thus far and despite his own hesitations, Marcel stands within the tradition of continental existentialism.[1]

---

[1]Marcel has been reluctant to allow himself to be called an existentialist. This seems to be largely in reaction to what the term came to signify in post-war France and to avoid any possible linking of his work with that of his arch rival, Jean-Paul Sartre. F.H. Heineman (_Existentialism and the Modern Predicament_ [New York: Harper and Row, 1953], pp. 149-151) suggests that Marcel may have been motivated by a wish to avoid the condemnation directed against existentialism by the papal encyclic _Humani generis_ (1950). However if this had been his purpose, he would have been better advised to moderate the anti-scholastic tone of his writings on religion. We will attempt to show that Marcel's hesitation about this label may well relate to fundamental issues of substance and method in his thought. He prefers to be labeled, if at all, a "neo-Socratic" (_MJ_ xiii; _PM_ 60-61; the "Avant Propos" to the French edition of _MBI_ 5). Marcel's published reactions to the existentialist label can be found _inter alia_ in _ECVQE_ 228-231; his "Testament philosophique," _Revue de Métaphysique et de Morale_, 74e année, No. 3 (July-September 1964), pp. 253-262; his "De la recherche philosophique," _Entretiens autour de Gabriel Marcel_, pp. 10-11; and his "La dominante existentielle dans mon oeuvre," in R. Klibansky, ed., _Contemporary Philosophy: A Survey_, Vol. III (Florence: La Nuova Italia Editrice, 1969). Marcel's most sustained critique of Sartre is his "Existence and Human Freedom" (_TPE_ 47-90). See also Maurice Merleau-Ponty, "The Battle over Existentialism," _Sense and Non-Sense_ (Evanston:

His view of philosophy as having a "redemptive" role to play in the life of a human being, his claim that on all significant philosophical issues, the philosopher cannot remain detached and objective but _is_ involved, like it or not, his abhorrence of abstraction and his oft repeated emphasis that reflection must begin with and respond to the concrete and singular in experience--these are themes which return in all of existentialist literature. To be fair to Marcel, we should not question his claim that his readings in this literature came well after he had worked out the main outlines of his thought in reaction to the idealism of his early philosophical training.[1] His distinctive contributions to this philosophical tradition will emerge later in this study.

Marcel's main emphasis is that philosophy is _not_ a purely theoretical or intellectual affair reserved for a special class of philosophical technicians. Rather, it stems from and responds to the most deeply felt need of an individual human being, his unease in the face of his own mortality, and it dispells this unease by providing him with a way into a sense of one-ness with something that far transcends him. This is not to say that philosophy is not a matter of reflection. It is precisely reflection--though a very distinctive kind of reflection--that is the main instrument of philosophy. But reflection ". . . is still part of life . . . it is one of the ways in which life manifests itself, or, more profoundly . . . it is in a sense

---

Northwestern University Press, 1964), pp. 71-82; his "La philosophie de l'existence," _Dialogue_, Vol. 5, No. 3 (1966), pp. 307-322; and Mary Aloysius Schaldenbrand, _Phenomenologies of Freedom: An Essay on the Philosophies of Jean-Paul Sartre and Gabriel Marcel_ (Washington, D.C.: The Catholic University of America Press, 1960).

[1] _TPE_ 120.

one of life's ways of rising from one level to another."[1] Marcel will study concrete life situations to see how reflection exposes and resolves their discontinuities precisely by moving from one level to another.

But it is important, particularly for a study devoted to Marcel's epistemology, to note how considerations of this kind will affect Marcel's appreciation of the role of knowledge in his philosophical scheme. If the impetus for philosophy is not primarily the urge to explain or to understand but rather a much more primitive human need for transcendence, if the mind is viewed as not qualified to define or legislate for reality, if philosophical method is not designed to yield conclusions but is confined to a perpetual re-tracing of the contours of experience, and if, finally, the arch-enemies of this philosophical approach are rationalisms and abstractions of all kinds--we may anticipate, even at this early stage, that the knowledge-seeking dimension of philosophy will occupy a tenuous place in the structure that will evolve. Marcel, of course, constantly protests against the tendency of his readers to accuse him of subjectivism, voluntarism, _fidéisme_ or scepticism; the question, he insists, is not knowledge or no knowledge, but rather what _kind_ of knowledge. On the other hand, the basic impulses that underlie his thought exercise their own inevitable sway. Whether this tension is ever really resolved will be a central question in this study.

Marcel's attempt to play down the role of conclusions in philosophical reflection is also open to question. Obviously his own thought has yielded conclusions in abundance and despite his claim that he must always begin with zero, the fact remains that he does eventually reach similar conclusions on most significant issues. If his

---

[1]_MBI_ 82.

25

objection is against philosophical education rather than philosophy itself, his point, though more accurate, is also more trivial.

He does, however, seem to be making the more important claim that these conclusions must be presented as testimony--without objective validity-- and that they are inextricably tied to the thinker and to his process of thought. If they are accept- able to anyone else, it is because each thinker participates individually in a common order of being and chooses to read that "score" in the same way; the reading is neither objective nor subjective but rather intersubjective--a shared enterprise which is mutually enriching. But neither thinker can encapsule reality and legislate for it because neither has the perspective of an onlooker.

If we find ourselves reverting to metaphor- ical expression more than once in this study, it is because ordinary discourse cannot express the core experience of philosophical reflection. Metaphors have a liberating power and can suggest a different way of relating to the world.[1] Marcel is seeking the same liberation by his use of his preferred forms of expression: the journal and the drama. His work exhibits a narrowing of the gap between his thought processes and their formulation in language. He seems to feel that to move from the former to the latter invariably involves distortion; la pensée pensante has become la pensée pensée. His use of the journal form suggests that writing, speaking and thinking are together constitutive of reflection--all at the same time.[2]

---

[1]On the language of metaphysical discourse, see MJ ix-x.

[2]This is suggested by Eugene Borowitz, A Layman's Guide to Religious Existentialism (New York: Dell Publishing Co., 1965), p. 104.

However, it is helpful in appraising Marcel's work, to distinguish between legitimate methodological claims on one hand and stylistic idiosyncrasies on the other. Marcel tends to confuse the two. It is one thing, for example, to insist that one best catches the primitive freshness of the original experience by exposing the circuitous course of philosophical reflection in all of its shapelessness on the printed page itself. It is quite another matter to repudiate any attempt to step back from this preliminary exploration and conceptualize, with some rigor and discipline, the yield that has resulted. Significantly Marcel <u>can</u> do both; he is the author both of the <u>Metaphysical Journal</u> and of "Existence and Objectivity." That 'he sees in the latter format a form of self-betrayal has nothing to do with the <u>substance</u> of his thought; it relates more to considerations of expository style and favored manner of expression. Needless to say, such considerations should not be decisive.

Marcel insists that he tries to retain a stance of openness to all possible data. Again the point seems exaggerated for it is hard to imagine any philosopher disagreeing. What he may be claiming, however, is that the philosophical process of evaluating all data must take place in the heart of philosophical reflection itself--on the printed page, if need be--and not back somewhere in the thinker's previous training, or in the work books which are to be discarded. Marcel tries to recapture his thought processes in all of their primitiveness--not simply because he is eccentric, but because he believes that this is the only way in which reflection can accurately handle the data of experience in all of its sinuosity.

So much for the assumptions that underlie Marcel's work as a whole. We turn now to his very beginnings as a philosopher, to his earliest attempts to articulate those distinctive positions with which he came to be identified. Our study of these early writings serve a dual purpose: first,

they exhibit his philosophical structure in the
process of being created; second, they reveal that
one of Marcel's earliest concerns was to try to
make religious faith intelligible. It is no
exaggeration to claim that this was one of the
central impulses behind his thought as a whole.

CHAPTER II

MARCEL'S EPISTEMOLOGICAL CRITIQUE

Marcel and Idealism

Marcel's earliest philosophical training was in idealism, the reigning philosophy of the day.[1]

---

[1]Only on rare occasions does Marcel link a philosophical position with which he takes issue to a particular thinker; most often his references to other philosophers are casual asides. This makes it difficult to reconstruct the concrete historical situation in which his thought--particularly these early efforts--can be located. We know that at the Sorbonne which he entered in 1906, he read--among the idealists--Hegel, Schopenhauer, Schelling, Bradley and Fichte--the last with irritation (TWB 219; ECVQE 60-71; TPE 105-106). He frequently acknowledges his debt to Bradley (MJ xii, 94, 171, 190-193; TPE 108; EBHD 21-22, 41; ECVQE 70-71). For his diploma at the Ecole des Etudes Supérieures he had planned a major study of Bradley's thought but the topic was taken by another candidate. He had also been impressed by Schelling and therefore decided to write on Schelling's influence on Coleridge which he saw as the earliest penetration of German idealism into the English philosophical tradition. This earliest of his formal writings (1909) was just recently (1971) published for the first time as Coleridge et Schelling with a new introduction describing how Marcel was drawn to this topic. He was also in close touch with American philosophy; he wrote on Royce and acknowledges that his views on the intersubjective

29

However, he often refers to the ambivalence which
characterized his early allegiance to that school.
He was impressed with the ". . . rigorousness of
their thought and . . . their ability to surpass
and transcend everyday life and all its monotonous
round of trivial and exacting concerns."[1] But
idealism also filled him with suspicion. He traces
this contrary influence to his father and their
mutual love for the theatre. The dramatic mode of
thought forced him to confront the fact of subject-
ness in all its irreducible concreteness. As a

---

experience stem from that thinker (MJ 326, and his
Author's Foreword to Royce's Metaphysics [Chicago:
Henry Regnery, 1956], pp. ix-xii); he writes of
William James with respect and from the early
twenties, he corresponded with Hocking whom he was
to meet in America in 1959 (EBHD 1). The Metaphysical Journal was dedicated to both Hocking and
Bergson. The latter emerges in Marcel's writings
as a figure of major influence whose lectures at
the Sorbonne Marcel remembers attending with great
anticipation (TWB 219; ECVQE 66; EBHD 2, 19). The
opposite is the case in regard to Leon Brunschwicg
who became the dominant figure in philosophy at the
Sorbonne during the second decade of this century
and whose brand of idealism Marcel found more and
more repugnant (HV 137; PI 230-231; CF 4-7).
Merleau-Ponty's "La philosophie de l'existence"
(Dialogue, Vol. 5, No. 3 [1966]) describes the experience of studying philosophy at the Sorbonne
during this period and illuminates the contrasting
influence of Brunschwicg and Bergson on their
students.

[1]EBHD 20. More personal reflections on
these early predilections can be found in ibid. 18-
26 passim; TPE 104-128 passim; TWB 230-232; ECVQE
18-87. The latter in particular, Marcel's last
extended work, is a rich storehouse of autobiographical information and sheds a great deal of
light on Marcel's philosophical education.

result, he developed ". . . an increasingly explicit refusal to abstract from all the concrete detail of my life that detail which made my life my own in all its irreducible originality."[1]

His earliest philosophical efforts were an attempt to reconcile these two contradictory aspirations with the abstraction serving as an interim landing stage from which he could set out to encounter the genuinely concrete.[2] The futility of this endeavor led to his eventual break with idealism but the struggle was to occupy him for two decades, from the earliest still unpublished efforts of his years at the Sorbonne beginning in 1906 up to "Existence et objectivité" which was first published in 1925 and republished as an appendix to the Metaphysical Journal in 1927.[3]

---

[1] EBHD 20; TPE 105-109, ECVQE 21-34 and SEAR 93ff. deal with his early interest in the theatre and with the personality of his father.

[2] EBHD 20-21; TPE 105.

[3] Apart from a number of plays, a great deal of music and theatre criticism, and some unpublished material on philosophical issues, Marcel's writings between these dates include: his 1909 work on Schelling and Coleridge; the selections collected in the volume Fragments philosophiques 1909-1914 (published in French in 1961 and in English in 1965); a paper, "Les Conditions dialectiques de la philosophie de l'intuition," Revue de Métaphysique et de Morale, 9 (1912), 638-652 (untranslated to date); two articles on the metaphysics of Royce originally published in the Revue in 1918 and 1919 and later collected in one volume (1945); and most important, the journal entries dating from January 1914 to May 1923 and published in 1927 as Journal métaphysique. An exhaustive bibliography of all of Marcel's writings is in François H. Lapointe and Claire C. Lapointe, Gabriel Marcel and His Critics, An International

Marcel often disparaged these early efforts, especially the material dating from 1909-1915. He rereads them with exasperation and irritation; he is intimidated by the rigor of his own dialectic and he confesses that he finds it difficult to follow his own train of thought. He sees these efforts as an attempt to overthrow a philosophical system all the while using its own weapons. While his intentions were sound, he acknowledges that he was ill-equipped to carry them out; he is particularly critical of the lack of precision in his philosophical vocabulary.

Finally, he comments on how these earliest predilections for idealism reflected the sense of security which he and his generation shared in the Europe of the first decade of this century. The first world war effectively shattered that security and with it, whatever residue of idealism remained in his thought.[1]

This early material is particularly valuable for a study of the problem of religious knowledge.

Bibliography 1928-1976 (New York and London: Garland Publishing, Inc., 1977), pp. 7-107. Equally comprehensive to 1953 is Roger Troisfontaines, De l'existence à l'être, 2 vols. (Paris: Editions J. Vrin, and Louvain: E. Nauwelaerts, 1953), II, 381-425. A comprehensive, though not exhaustive bibliography of writings by and about Marcel to 1966 is provided by Gerald G. Wenning, "Works By and About Gabriel Marcel," Southern Journal of Philosophy, 4, No. 2 (Summer 1966), 82-96. On the early manuscript material, see Lionel Blain's Introduction to PF 27-32.

[1]Marcel's feelings about these early writings are discussed inter alia in PF 23-25; EBHD 18-27, 35-36; TPE 118-121; TWB 220; ECVQE 80, 97 and SEAR 93-95.

These pages were written long before Marcel's formal conversion to Catholicism (1929), yet they show him trying to make religious faith philosophically intelligible. This theme is accorded more space in the first part of the <u>Journal</u> than any other and although Marcel acknowledges the grave inadequacies of these efforts, his later thought on this subject can not be understood without this background.

The purpose of this chapter, then, is to study this phase of Marcel's thought as providing the foundations--both chronologically and structurally--for the positions with which he later came to be identified. In order to highlight this preliminary stage and the intellectual matrix out of which it developed, we will deliberately restrict ourselves at the outset to two early papers dating from 1910-1912, and subsequently to the 1914-1915 entries in what was later to be published as Part one of the <u>Metaphysical Journal</u>. Whatever judgment Marcel may pass on this material from the perspective of his later years, the importance of this phase of his thought to an understanding of his philosophy is indisputable.

<u>Marcel's Early Critique of Idealism</u>

<u>(1910-1912)</u>

Marcel's earliest encounter with idealism is found primarily in two papers dated 1910-1911 and 1912.[1] Both papers cover the same general

---

[1]The first, entitled "Réflexions sur l'idée du savoir absolu et sur la participation de la pensée à l'être" was published in 1961 in the volume: <u>Fragments philosophiques 1909-1914</u> (English translation, 1965). The second is "Les Conditions dialectiques de la philosophie de l'intuition" (above, pp. 31-32, note 3). This latter one, the one published at the time of writing, is the more

ground and the primary thrust of each is epistemological. Though the language and conceptual scheme
are idealist, their ultimate impact brings them
very close to Marcel's mature thought. They contain manifold anticipations of some central positions in Marcel's epistemology, particularly the
problem/mystery distinction and the act of secondary
reflection. Finally, a portion of each paper tries
to show how his position makes religious faith at
least intelligible.

---

polished, the more tightly constructed and by far
the clearer in its argumentation. It is one of the
ironies of Marcel's publishing history that the
former article is now easily available in the
original and in English, whereas the latter has
never to our knowledge been republished or translated. Hence the relative absence of any reference
to these articles in the secondary literature.
Notable exceptions are: Lionel A. Blain, "Marcel's
Logic of Freedom in Proving the Existence of God:
Reflections on Some Early Notebooks," International
Journal of Philosophy, 9 (June 1969), 177-204; Jean-
Pierre Bagot, Connaissance et amour: Essai sur la
philosophie de Gabriel Marcel (Paris: Beauchesne et
ses Fils, 1958); and Guillemine de Lacoste, "The
Notion of Participation in the Early Drama and
Early Journals of Gabriel Marcel," Philosophy Today,
Vol. 19, No. 1 (Spring 1975), pp. 50-60. In regard
to the 1912 article, see James Collins, op. cit.,
pp. 133-139, his "Gabriel Marcel and the Mystery of
Being," Thought, Vol. 18, No. 71 (December 1943),
pp. 665-693; and Dominique Dubarle, "Un franchissement des clôtures de la philosophie idéaliste clas-
sique: la première philosophie de Gabriel Marcel,
1912-1914," Revue des Sciences Philosophiques et
Théologiques, Vol. 58, No. 2 (April 1974), pp. 172-
212, which deals with the 1912 article and Part one
of MJ. Father Troisfontaines, op. cit. had access
to all of Marcel's unpublished manuscripts and
often summarizes their contents, e.g. I, 117-121 on
the 1910-1911 article.

Both of these articles are an attempt to trace the conditions necessary for a philosophy of intuition, i.e. a philosophy that affirms that being can be reached by intuition as opposed to discursive thought.[1] The key step in the demonstration will be to expose the inherently self-contradictory character of the Hegelian ideal of absolute knowledge as the ultimate abstraction, totally intelligible and totally comprehensive of and identified with reality. Such an ideal would affirm the identity of being and the idea of being thereby excluding the possibility of an intuition of being itself by the mind.

Marcel first uses a "negative dialectic"[2] to show that absolute knowledge is in fact contradictory. Absolute knowledge does not escape the Kantian requirement of subjectivity as a precondition for all objective knowledge--even absolute objective knowledge. How do we understand this subjectivity? Do we posit a kind of sur-being which would be the embodiment of transcendental subjectivity for absolute knowledge? This sur-being is either external to absolute knowledge--in which case the ideal is not comprehensive as it claims to be--or within absolute knowledge--in which case Kant's requirement returns--and we are launched on an infinite regress.

----

[1]Marcel's debt to Bergson is clear and often acknowledged, though in these early works, the Bergsonian influence is muted by the idealist framework of the argument (EBHD 2, 19, 35 and TWB 219-220).

[2]The distinction between the "negative" and "positive" phases of Marcel's dialectic is suggested by J.P. Bagot, op. cit. Both in the early articles and in the Journal, the two phases are carried on simultaneously.

Marcel traces the idealist error to the fact that

> . . . we have hypostatized a requirement
> of thought and . . . have thought it pos-
> sible to isolate and consider by itself
> the pseudo-reality thus obtained. The
> philosophers of absolute knowledge are
> the victims, it seems, of the same illu-
> sion as the naive realists. They think
> it possible to break the link uniting the
> object (here, absolute knowledge) with
> the subject and to treat the object like
> a being, without taking notice that this
> being owes its reality to its participa-
> tion in the subject. Absolute knowledge,
> like matter or life, is still only an
> abstraction, even, as it is true, if it
> is the highest and most concrete . . . .
> Absolute knowledge then seems to be in-
> evitably ideal, and that only inevitably
> relative to a pure subjectivity, from
> which it can detach itself only by an il-
> legitimate abstraction.[1]

Absolute knowledge, then, owes its reality to a thinking subject and hence contains, as the very ground of its possibility, a remainder that is properly speaking unknowable in itself. This re-mainder is the act of thinking which can never be an object to itself, but must rather grasp itself non-objectively as pure subject and in so doing become aware of itself as a mode of being.

This awareness, however, poses a genuine dilemma:

> . . . thought posits its participation in
> being insofar as it is itself a pure subject.
> But what does this amount to? To the fact

---

[1] PF 62-63.

that thought tries to make an object of
itself as pure subject and look at it as
something out there in front of itself,
thus transforming the unknowable into an
object and consequently into an abstraction? In these circumstances, does the
affirmation have any meaning? The reasons
why it seemed that the pure subject (thought
qua pure subject) must participate in being
lose their value as soon as the subject is
transformed into an object, fixed into a
sterile abstraction. Hence the moment the
participation in being of thought as pure
subject is posited, it ceases to be think-
able (because the pure subject is turned
into an object).[1]

Marcel is aware that at this point, we have
reached the ". . . outer limits of idealism, where
we can perhaps pass over to a doctrine of being."[2]
We have used a "later act of reflection"[3] to uncover
the contradiction involved in positing participation, not thereby to eliminate participation in the
first place but rather to point out that this participation itself cannot be an object of thought.
It is rather ". . . the upper limit of reflection,
that is, the act before which all reflection must
cease" for ". . . there is no passage from participation to reflection."[4] Reflection locates itself
between two limits: the first, indeterminate, immediate knowledge or "existence in general" and the
second, participation in being.[5]

---

[1]PF 73-74.   [2]Ibid. 74.

[3]Ibid. 75.   [4]Ibid. 76-77.

[5]Ibid. 78-79. The anticipations of Marcel's
later thought in all of this material and particularly in the two extended selections are readily
apparent. The threefold distinction between immediacy, reflection and participation will reappear

What then do we mean by intuition?

> It cannot be, properly speaking, knowledge;
> what remains is that it is a creation, or
> more precisely, an act of transcendence by
> which thought becomes aware of the distort-
> ing character of all objectification,
> affirms itself as being irreducible to this
> kind of conversion and as being, in this
> sense, if not identical with being (an
> affirmation of this kind would throw it
> back into the world of ideas), at least
> participating in being.[1]

This is precisely the intuition of being the conditions of which we have been seeking to establish.
But it is also what we mean by religious faith--not
as an affirmation that anything exists, for that
too would throw us back into the world of objects
of thought--but rather as the absolutely free participation of thought in being as ". . . the crowning point of a dialectic entirely oriented toward
transcendence.[2]

---

in a much more elaborate way in Part 1 of the Metaphysical Journal. The first of these moments will
grow steadily in importance in Marcel's writings
over the next two decades and will be the central
motif in his first major programmatic statement,
"Existence and Objectivity." This motif, traced
through each of the stages of Marcel's encounter
with idealism affords one of the best opportunities
to follow the course of Marcel's philosophical
development from 1909 to 1925.

[1]Marcel, "Les Conditions dialectiques
. . .," p. 652. Translation mine. Compare his comments on intellectual intuition in PF 82.

[2]Ibid. 106. See also ibid. 80-81, 107 ff.;
"Les Conditions . . .," p. 652.

There is much to comment on here. First the style of the discussion: Marcel's ambivalent feelings about these early writings are amply justified. He is trying to overthrow a system of thought using its own weapons; his vocabulary is imprecise and the argumentation, particularly in the 1910-1911 article is often impenetrable. Yet the thrust of his thought is unmistakable. He begins with a presumption for man's natural orientation toward being itself transcending the limitations of any kind of abstraction, however global. But he is not prepared, as yet, to do what would eventually seem to him to be the only natural thing to do: simply trace this orientation as it emerges in concrete experience. At this point, the idealist in him requires that he use a critique of the ideal of absolute knowledge as a bridge to being itself.

The central enduring theme of Marcel's critique of idealism is here in germ. Idealism has dulled man's orientation to being by reducing being to the idea of being through a global abstraction which is identified as reality. The global abstraction is wrong, both because of its abstractness and its global nature: its abstractness deprives it of contact with the gaps and ambiguities of reality, and its global nature suggests that man can stand outside of reality and legislate for it as a whole. All we can ever have is a partial and oblique glimpse of reality for we are encompassed by it and cannot treat it as an object for thought.

The cardinal sin of philosophy, then, is the tendency to objectify what can in no way be an object for the mind--here, the thinking process as subject.

It would seem . . . that the unknowable as pure subject is only an abstraction, a form about which nothing can be said because it is empty. But, precisely, the pure subject appears abstract only from the moment when it is, as it were, posited as an object before itself. It is this conversion alone that makes it an abstraction, and the fact

that we cannot predicate any determination
of it insofar as it is posited as object
proves precisely that this positing is not
legitimate . . . . Far, then, from saying
that the subject is a pure abstraction,
it must be understood that it cannot be
called an abstraction and that it is in
itself the living source of the concrete.[1]

The nature of the self as that which
supremely resists objectification by thought will
be one of Marcel's central metaphysical concerns.
But his discussion of the nature of the self here
is relatively superficial. It will become considerably more complex in the Metaphysical Journal
where he will try to distinguish at least three different facets of the self: the empirical (objective)
self, the (universal) thinking self of the cogito,
and the individual, concrete subject of religious
faith and love. But again, much of this later
thought is foreshadowed in his claim that it is
through the self as subject of thought that man participates in being. Thinking is a mode of being
and to the extent that thought can grasp itself as
subject we can have an intuition of being.

This participation in being is not knowledge. Marcel does not elaborate on this point here,
but it will remain a central issue throughout his
work and he will eventually claim the opposite. For
the present, he holds that it can only be grasped
in its operation by a "later act of reflection"
which, at the very least, has the negative function
of denying ultimacy to objective reflection. What
relation this act of reflection has, or does not
have, to our body of "knowledge" is unclear.

The theme of "participation" which is so
central to these early writings will disappear
almost completely from Marcel's philosophical

_____

[1]PF 70-71.

40

vocabulary during the period of the _Metaphysical Journal_ though the role it plays will remain omnipresent. It will reappear in the two volumes of _The Mystery of Being_ as will the concept of "secondary reflection" which will be the final form of the earlier "later act of reflection." Marcel will then claim that participation and secondary reflection yield authentic knowledge.

Finally, participation in being provides an opening for religious faith understood not as an act of objective reflection but as an act of participation of the subject in a reality in which he is embedded. The very few words that Marcel allots to this theme in these two papers are frustratingly obscure. However _Philosophical Fragments 1909-1914_ contains a paper entitled "Theory of Participation 1913-1914"[1] which deals entirely with faith as participation and which shows Marcel well along the way toward the positions discussed in the _Metaphysical Journal_. This topic will be discussed in detail below.[2]

For the present, one is tempted to ask just what faith understood in this way as ". . . the crowning point of a dialectic entirely oriented towards transcendence"[3] has to do with religious faith as commonly understood. Marcel here is caught in a bind between the requirements of his dialectical view of knowledge within which he wants to find a place for faith on one hand, and faith as experienced by the believer on the other.

This is one of the many phases of the ongoing struggle with idealism which will be the focus of Marcel's thought throughout this early period.

---

[1] _PF_ 106-125.

[2] Pp. 59-68.

[3] Cf. _MJ_ 39, 41, 44.

Like the others, it will be waged throughout the first part of the <u>Journal</u>; again, the pole of experience will finally win out but only in the closing pages of that work. At this point, if Marcel were to be asked why the crowning point of a dialectic oriented toward transcendence should be called "faith," he would probably answer that by faith he understands that act of reflection which is most radically opposed to objective knowledge with its corollaries of truth or falsity and verification.[1] Faith, like participation in being, and like love, are acts in which the mind is supremely free; they reveal man as free subject and show that his freedom is co-extensive with his status as subject. That there are levels of participation and that there is a distinction between the participatory act in which man grasps himself as subject of knowledge and the participatory act of faith, does not emerge until later in his work. But the nexus between the general problem of epistemology and the problem of religious knowledge is present at this earliest stage in Marcel's work.

In general then, and in a preliminary way, we can conclude that idealism stands indicted for its failure to deal adequately with the three central elements of any theory of knowledge: the so-called "object" of knowledge, the subject of intellectual activity, and the reflective process itself.

Marcel's Later Critique of Idealism

(1914-1915)

The main lines of Marcel's early critique of idealism are carried on in Part one of the <u>Metaphysical Journal</u> but with considerably more

---

[1]Blain, "Marcel's Logic of Freedom," pp. 181-182.

precision and elaboration.[1] This material can best
be understood as an extended commentary to one
brief passage in his 1910-1911 paper referred to
above:

---

[1]Marcel's Metaphysical Journal deserves a
full-length study of its own. It would benefit,
particularly, from a line-by-line exegesis with special attention to the original manuscript and to the
material that Marcel decided not to include in the
published extracts. It contains the kind of material that most philosophers would scrap once they
had arrived at their conclusions. In its present
form, however, it presents formidable difficulties:
the topics are presented in no particular order;
there is no highlighting of resolutions, however
tentative; there is no attempt to discard conclusions which are later revoked. At least Part two is
followed by "Existence and Objectivity" which "dis-
entangles" the conclusions of the 1915-1923 extracts;
Part one has no such summary. It is interesting to
note that most of the secondary literature on Marcel
either ignores this material with the comment that
Marcel was later destined to change his mind, or
quotes it uncritically without reference to its context in the development of Marcel's thought. Apart
from being simply inaccurate, this deprives the
student of a rare opportunity to see at first hand
how the skeleton of a philosophical position is
constructed. There are a few notable exceptions to
this procedure. Father Troisfontaines' massive two-
volume study is one, though it is somewhat more an
anthology of Marcel's thought arranged by theme than
a critical study, and it is often difficult to decipher if the author is quoting Marcel, paraphrasing
Marcel, or speaking for himself. More helpful for
this early material in particular is J.P. Bagot,
op. cit., who provides a structure for the material
in the Journal, and Charles Widmer, Gabriel Marcel
et le théisme existentiel (Paris: Les Editions du
Cerf, 1971). Particularly noteworthy is Jean Wahl's
extended review "Le Journal Métaphysique de Gabriel

Thus it seems that reflexive activity operates between two limits of which one is entirely ideal (absolutely immediate knowledge) and the other is participation in being. Neither the one nor the other can be posited.[1]

The very first entry in the _Journal_ takes up the question of these various "planes of intelligibility" and asks whether it is possible to establish the existence of ontological differences between them. And in his first programmatic statement Marcel confirms that he is preoccupied by the problem ". . . of founding the hierarchy of philosophical thought while avoiding both realism and pure subjectivism."[2]

Negative Dialectic of Intelligibility

This first part of the _Journal_ can be understood as an attempt to trace these three moments in the process of reflection beginning with the pre-intelligible level of immediacy and culminating in the transcending of objective thinking through "participation," though that term does not appear in

---

Marcel," in _Revue de Métaphysique et de Morale_, 37 (1930), 75-112, later republished in the author's _Vers le concrèt_ (Paris: Librairie Philosophique J. Vrin, 1932), pp. 223-269. Finally the student of a work such as the _Journal_ is inestimably helped by the availability of a good thematic index which both the French and the English editions of the _Journal_ do provide. Unhappily, this is not the case for the other two volumes of extracts, _Being and Having_ and _Presence and Immortality_.

[1]_PF_ 78-79.

[2]_MJ_ 2.

the _Journal_ extracts. His critique of idealism will
continue the attempt--in the "negative" phase of
the dialectic--to fix objective thought in an intermediate, essentially transitory, and hence relative
position in the thought process, though traditional
idealism ignores this through the familiar procedures of abstraction and hypostatization. These
errors once exposed, Marcel can proceed--in the
"positive" phase of the dialectic--to show how reflection in its non-objective mode can deal with
some of the issues of metaphysics.[1]

The very first topic to receive an extended
(some twenty consecutive pages) discussion in the
pages of the _Journal_ is existence. It will remain
one of Marcel's central concerns and will serve as
one of the clearest of indices in tracing the evolution of his thought as a whole.

He begins by formulating the question in
this way: "What do we mean by existence when we
attribute it to an object?"[2] Although the term
"object" has not as yet assumed the full technical
sense it was later to assume, this formulation is
not fortuitous for throughout most of the _Journal_--
and contrary to the main thrust of his thinking
from 1925 on--Marcel finds the hallmark of existence

---

[1]Marcel himself has commented on the lack
of precision in the vocabulary of the _Journal_.
This is particularly the case in the various terms
used to refer to the intermediate stage in the
process of reflection, i.e. the stage characterized
by the subject/object model. We will try to use
the term "objective thought" or "objective thinking"
to refer to this stage and "participatory thought"
to refer to intellectual activity in its non-
objective mode.

[2]_MJ_ 14.

precisely in objectivity.[1]

> When I say: Caesar has existed--and I take
> my example from the past because it is
> there that definition seems to be **most** sub-
> ject to discussion--I do not only mean that
> Caesar could have been perceived by me; I
> also mean that between the existence of
> Caesar and my state of consciousness, my
> actual awareness, lies an (infinitely com-
> plex) series of relations in time which is
> capable of being determined in an objective
> way.[2]

Existence, then, is relatedness to a consciousness,
not specifically to _my_ consciousness for then a
hallucination would exist in the same way as a
physical object, but rather to any possible consciousness, which amounts to saying that ". . .
there is only existence for what is objective."[3]
Further, not only is existence linked with objectivity, it is also linked with spatiality for in
regard to the existence of "a consciousness," Marcel
claims that "a consciousness only exists for me in
the measure in which it is revealed to me objectively (that is, through the medium of a body.) I
then proceed to think of this consciousness as a
consciousness by analogy with myself."[4] Similarly,

---

[1]The first explicit questioning of this
identification of existence with objectivity is
dated February 2, 1922 (_MJ_ 281).

[2]_MJ_ 14. Interestingly enough, despite
Marcel's later disavowal of the objectivity of
existence, the passage is quoted without change in
_CF_ (1940) 18-19. The translation there is different from the one used here.

[3]_MJ_ 16.

[4]Ibid.

"I cannot think of myself as existing save in so far as I am a datum for other consciousnesses, that is to say in so far as I am a datum in space."[1] Existence then is identified with objectivity and spatiality. What impressed Marcel above all at this stage of his thought is the public nature of the giveness of that which is said to exist; what is given is that which is at the farthest remove from being "subjective"; hence its objectivity. Much later, Marcel will distinguish different ways in which "giveness" can be expressed, not all of them assimilable to that of an "object."

But this identification of existence with objectivity has to be qualified when Marcel considers his own existence.

There seems to be no denying that I can be a datum to myself otherwise than in space, for instance as affectivity. From there on we have a new mode of existence whose relation to the spatial mode of existence seems singularly difficult to determine. Of course my consciousness cannot be a datum given as a whole either to itself or to other consciousnesses except as a body. But, on another plane of existence, might it not be a datum for itself-- exclusively?[2]

But if a consciousness is a datum for itself exclusively, then it is no longer objective.

The self then exhibits two irreducibly distinct modes of existence: one is the objective (i.e. available to any consciousness) relation of my body as spatial to a consciousness; the second is my internal, hence private and individual sense of my body as feeling. Neither of these can be reduced to the other. If a third content is to be subtended

---

[1]MJ 18.   [2]Ibid.

47

under these two, as a substance is subtended to its
accidents, this subtended content itself cannot be
a datum to consciousness, i.e. cannot be considered
as existing. It is a pure intellectual construct.
". . . Thought needs to posit a subject of this
double becoming, a subject placed in some way at
the intersection of this double becoming. Only
this subject is not existent; it can only be
thought."[1]

To say that this subtended self does not
exist is not to say that it is not real; nor is it
to say that it is not. The relation of existence
to being will be a major theme of Marcel's later
thought but it receives little attention in this
context. Marcel clings to his technical definition
of existence while insisting that there are "realities" which do not "exist." The distinction rests
on the fact that existence belongs to the infra-
objective, pre-intelligible realm of what is immediately given, whereas the "real" is for thought
alone.

Existence . . . is that from which all
thought is able to set out, in the sense
that thought cannot define itself save by
the movement by which it transcends the
immediate datum. Hence existence cannot
at any level be regarded as a demonstrandum,
a point at which we end up.[2]

Apart from being identified with objectivity and spatiality, existence is also the realm
of the true and the false. At this stage of
Marcel's thought, truth is identified with the

---

[1] MJ 22.

[2] Ibid. 32, 1. For earlier formulations of
the contingency of existence and the distinction
between the existent and the real see PF 38-39 and
58-60.

possibility of verification which is possible only
when what is being verified is objective, i.e.
available to any consciousness whatsoever, in fact,
available to ". . . indefinite numbers of substitutions."[1] We can speak of the truth or falseness
only of that which exists; the self (in two of its
aspects) and God (for example), are beyond existence, hence beyond truth and falseness.

    Given this seemingly inextricable connection
between existence and objectivity,[2] how did Marcel's
thought evolve into the diametrically opposite position maintained in "Existence and Objectivity" and
thereafter? The key to this development lies in a
further distinction which Marcel is forced to make
between the pre-intelligible giveness of existence
and a _judgment_ that some _object_ exists.

    Existence cannot be the object of a judg-
ment; strictly speaking it can only be acknowledged.
But thought cannot handle existence as immediate
giveness. It dissociates this immediacy and proceeds to question the relation of the object of
thought to the intellectual act which affirms it.
Marcel handles this dilemma in a way which is characteristic of his philosophical method in the
Journal.

        Here it seems to me essential to note that
        the problem when raised, by the very fact
        of being raised, transforms its terms. It
        is presented in the form of a question bear-
        ing on the relation between distinct terms.
        But the terms are only distinct because the
        problem is raised . . . . The very act by

---

[1]_MJ_ 154, note 2, and 284.

[2]Troisfontaines, op. cit., II, 163 gives
an exhaustive listing of all of the passages in the
Journal where Marcel identifies existence with
objectivity.

which we question ourselves on the basis
of the union of the terms is precisely
that which separates them.[1]

It is _reflection_ that introduces the dualism of a
datum and a thought process which operates on that
datum transforming existence into a predicate. But
the postulate itself is erroneous; existence can
never be an object of thought.

How then can the immediacy of existence be
captured by thought? This is the same question
that Marcel was forced to consider in regard to the
subject as the thinking process in the two earlier
articles. His answer here is similar: Only by an
". . . act by which reflective thought becomes
aware of that which came from itself in the preced-
ing act, and sets about making an abstraction of
it."[2] Reflection is capable of purifying itself of
its objectifying role enabling it to recapture the
immediacy of the existent as given. Marcel calls
this act of self-purification "experience-limit"
and he defines it as follows:

> . . . Experience-limit can only be thought
> by an act of reflection brought to bear on
> the dualism of the judgment of existence
> and of that on which the judgment is made.
> This experience-limit, inasmuch as the
> reflecting subject claims to disentangle
> its objective content, is reduced to a con-
> tact between a body, bound up with a per-
> ceiving consciousness, and an external
> datum. Reflective thought thus posits the
> judgment of existence as being the trans-

---

[1]MJ 24. This is clearly an anticipation of
Marcel's later distinction between problem and
mystery.

[2]MJ 25. This is clearly an anticipation of
secondary reflection.

position of the experience-limit into
the intellectual order (where there are
objects and judgments bearing on these
objects); and this goes for any judgment
of existence whatsoever.[1]

It is evident that Marcel is far from
settled on precisely what he understands by the
term "objectivity" and what significance comes from
attributing it to existence. On one hand, existence is objective because it is available to any
perceiving consciousness whatsoever; this will
become the notion of the object as insular (as opposed to the "adhering" nature of the presence)
hence impersonal, for it is external to any particular subject. Marcel insists on the objectivity of
existence to avoid the problem of hallucinations
and he further emphasizes this by adding spatiality
and truth and falsity through public verification
as hallmarks of existence.

But he then proceeds to qualify this claim
by delimiting the objectivity of existence to the
judgment of existence; existence itself, if one may
refer to it in this way, is prejudgmental as sheer
relatedness to or contact with a perceiving consciousness bound up with a body. It is clear that
as far as Marcel is concerned, the judgment of
existence completely misses the point precisely
because it reduces existence to an object of thought.
What then was the significance of the original identification of existence with objectivity?

Eventually this entire problem will be
circumvented as Marcel narrows his concept of object, identifies existence as a prolongation of my
body, hence as adherence to me, hence as "presence"
rather than "object," and introduces his view of

---

[1]MJ 25. This notion of the experience-limit
harks back to his brief comment on existence as immediacy in PF 78-79.

sensation as the immediate participation of the
subject in the world--what he calls here "experience-limit." Existence becomes the paradigm of
presence, and my body becomes the paradigmatic
existent.[1] The issue of hallucinations recedes to
the background as Marcel insists on the indubitable
nature of the contact with the existing universe.
Once objectivity is no longer at issue, verification and truth and falsity also disappear as further
hallmarks of existence.

Spatiality presents a more complicated
problem. It originally entered into the discussion
because of the role that Marcel attributed to the
body in the relation with the existent. If anything, that role will become more and more crucial
in Marcel's later thought.[2] But whereas Marcel will
go into great detail in distinguishing between a
body and my body and in showing how my body serves
as a model for the existent, the issue of spatiality
is never clarified apart from his denial of the
materialist implications of this position.[3]

Characteristically this earliest discussion
of existence in Marcel's work is explicitly related
to the issue of the existence or non-existence of
God.[4] Marcel was primarily concerned with preserv-
ing the reality of God which he saw as being compromised as soon as one spoke of his existence. It
may well be that much of what Marcel has to say
about existence in general is influenced by his
primary concern with dissociating existence from

---

[1]The locus classicus for Marcel's later discussion of existence as presence is "Existence and
Objectivity" (MJ 319-327).

[2]See, e.g., MJ 332-339.

[3]Ibid. 315.

[4]Ibid. 33-45.

God.

God may not exist, but he is _real_--as is the self. Marcel will go to great length to clarify this distinction, though with results that he finds far from satisfactory.[1] God is an intellectual construct with no reality apart from that conferred upon it by the intellectual act through which it comes to be: in the case of the self, by the _cogito_, and in the case of God, by the act of religious faith.

But if the self and God as "real" seem to be relatively vacuous at this stage of Marcel's thought, the same can be said for existence itself. It is a far cry from Marcel's later understanding of "the existing universe" in "Existence and Objectivity." Here it is beyond characterization and beyond discourse as well. It is available only to a reflection which turns back upon itself in an act of self-purification which purges itself of any trace of objectification--a highly negative version of what would eventually become Marcel's secondary reflection.

But throughout all of the later transmutations of Marcel's thought on the subject of existence, the core notion that existence is the immediate, indubitable, uncharacterizable given to a perceiving consciousness bound up with a body remains constant. In fact Marcel's attempt to refine that notion will serve as the context out of which he will develop his idea of knowledge as participation. The participatory experience of existence will come to serve as a prototype for other participatory experiences, this time on a supra-objective plane of intelligibility.

But his discussion of the way objective thought handles existence is a paradigm of the kind of critical analysis that occurs throughout Part one

---

[1] _MJ_ 133.

53

of the <u>Journal</u>. Objective thought must use the sub-
ject/object model and hence is forced to introduce
dualisms which have no reality beyond the requirements of the thinking process. What results is
either a series of antinomies, or an out and out
dualism, or, what is more common and more dangerous,
a highly abstract and synthetic monism which is
bought at the price of suppressing some of the data.
Reflection can only overcome its hypostatizing tendencies through an act of self-purification, later
to become "secondary refléction." At the very
beginning of the <u>Journal</u> Marcel lists some of the
inadequacies of Hegelian dialectical realism and
raises the question ". . . whether there might not
be a way of defining the conditions under which the
reflection of a thought upon itself could be creative (and not be a mere reproduction or sterile
double)."[1] This marks the direction in which Marcel's
thought will evolve.

Throughout this first part of the <u>Journal</u>
Marcel will show how some of the traditional problems of philosophy such as the nature of time, the
nature of the self, the appearance/reality problem
and the "existence" of God have been created by this
illegitimate abstraction of a moment in the reflective process. Each of these is discussed individually but he traces how this abstraction takes place
in more general terms.

The problem begins with the Kantian distinction between a raw, shapeless, experience-matter
and a pre-existing, form-giving consciousness. This
dualism must be rejected.

. . . the idea of pure thought anterior--
even in a rational sense--to all experience is certainly a pseudo-idea; it is the
product of a schematic and illusory reflection. This amounts to saying that it is as

---

[1] <u>MJ</u> 3.

arbitrary to define experience in function
of categories anterior to it, as to make
thought depend on improperly realised experience. Thought, it must be understood,
is only known and grasped in experience in
the measure in which the experience is
defined as intelligible. Kantian criticism corresponds to the purely transitory
moment in which analysis hypostatized intelligibility and converts it into form.[1]

The reflective moment is precisely this
transitory state which introduces a relation of
exteriority between the form and the matter of
thought thus making possible objective knowledge as
we understand it. It is only by an abstraction
that pure thought is dissociated from the process
thus begetting the notion of a universal dialectic.
But ". . . the idea of a system constituted by the
simple application of an internal principle, merely
by the mechanism of a dialectic, is seen to be contradictory. Such a system can never be constituted
save as provisional and within a constructing experience."[2]

In contrast, Marcel will claim that "intelligibility as I conceive it, is a dynamic relation,
the relation of tension by which the mind is constituted when it organizes its world; it cannot be
realised outside that relation."[3] Mind is not a
"thing that can play its part in an order of juxtaposition."[4] It is rather a "term (of a relation)

---

[1]MJ 75.

[2]Ibid. 103-104. See also ibid. 2-3 for an
anticipation of this conclusion.

[3]Ibid. 104.

[4]Ibid. 109. Marcel also uses "mind"
("l'esprit) in a more restricted sense as the

that suppresses itself as a term" and not "a realised and ready-made faculty to which ideas are
given from without."[1] It comes to be in and through
its ideas; like thought, it is activity. If we
refuse to see it as "exteriority treating itself as
provisional moment, and in consequence appearing as
a phase which implies it but passes beyond it . . .
we remain in a sort of imaginary space which in no
degree symbolises the living, dynamic order which
is thought."[2]

There is then no privileged realm of pure
thought with its own absolute, ontological status.
"Thought, in its interior progress, is led to ask
itself certain questions which at first sight seem
to have a possible bearing on the world and its
conditions but which, on analysis, are shown not
only to be insoluble but even inapplicable on that
plane."[3] Neither the subject (or formal condition
of knowledge) nor the object (or material condition
of knowledge) has any absolute standing, and thought
can proceed beyond this objective plane only by
denying exteriority, i.e. through another kind of
intellectual activity which recaptures the earlier
immediacy of the given.

Positive Dialectic of Intelligibility

This negative phase of Marcel's dialectic
of intelligibility establishes the limitations of

---

subject of thought made individualized and concrete
through the act of faith (ibid. 44). This is
another example of the confusion caused by Marcel's
careless vocabulary.

[1]MJ 102.

[2]Ibid. 105-106.

[3]Ibid. 11.

objective thinking. Idealism, of course makes the
further claim that this mode of thinking is exclusive and ultimate, but the criteria for this claim
are all internal to objective thinking itself and
therefore have been exposed as equally relative.

We are then free to complement this negative phase of the dialectic by a parallel ascending
or positive dialectic which will trace the movement
of reflection beyond the realm of objectivity to
new planes of intelligibility. This will consist
of creative affirmations of the mind which can only
be caught in their immediacy as acts of the mind
which can in no way become objects to the mind.
They will then carry their own warranty of certainty for otherwise they would have to be subjected to verification; at the same time, however,
they will have to be free of arbitrariness.

We have seen how objective thought introduces a dualism between the form and matter of
experience. This creates objective knowledge as we
know it. But this entire body of knowledge itself
depends on a free act of the mind which brings into
being that indispensable--though transitory--moment
of subject/object thought which we are then tempted
to hypostatize. Objective thought, however, has no
way of dealing with the act which makes possible
its emergence in the first place. This moment of
reflection can only be grasped in its coming to be.

When thought reflects on the movement by
which truths are constituted, it recog-
nises the necessity of thinking that movement in function of a purely intelligible
activity. But does this mean that that
activity appears as a factual condition,
as existent? Obviously not. The factual
conditions that govern the search for truth
should be capable of being defined psycho-
logically. We can conceive the possibility
of a psychology of the search for truth
which would take all the subjective factors
into account . . . . Strictly speaking all

57

this can be regarded as object for verification. But the pure activity about
which we are speaking is only capable of
appearing to a reflection that itself bears
on the conditions of the possibility of
the true . . . . It is pure reflection then,
that introduces this activity--which is the
equivalent of saying that it brings it into
being and creates it, because it itself is
the very activity in question and is only
capable of thinking itself as identical
with it . . . . Here the ego seems in some
sort of way to be the intelligible medium
by which freedom effects the transition
from idea to being. But it is clear that
this act of creation is nothing save the
cogito. Thought creates itself when it
thinks itself; it does not discover itself,
it constitutes itself.[1]

    Marcel's conclusion here is essentially the
one reached in his two earlier articles though the
argumentation is much richer. Objective knowledge
owes its reality to a thinking subject ("thought
qua pure subject" in the earlier work) which is unknowable in itself but has to be grasped as subject,
i.e. as act in the process of its coming-to-be.
Thus ". . . the ego seems . . . to be the intelligible medium by which freedom effects the transition
from idea to being." In the words of the earlier
work, this is the ". . . act of transcendence by
which thought becomes aware of the distorting character of all objectification (and) affirms itself
. . . as participating in being."[2]

------

[1]MJ 30-31.

[2]"Les Conditions . . .," p. 652. This
theme of the intuition of being which was the main
point of the two early articles and will return as
the main theme of Marcel's later work, is strangely
absent from Part one of the Journal. For one

This was the main point of the two earlier articles. But in the _Journal_ Marcel devotes considerable space to elaborating what had been a mere afterthought in the earlier works, the transition from the intuition of being to religious faith. His aim is to show that his epistemology opens the possibility for faith and his point of departure is Descartes' _cogito_. The _cogito_ may well free us from the realm of objective knowledge but it does not free us from the realm of universality, for the subject that is created through the _cogito_ is the thinking, i.e. universal subject.

Marcel asks whether the _cogito_ can "surpass" itself and he answers that it does in the act of faith. "It is clear that the individuality that is realised in faith must be beyond the purely abstract universality of the _I think_, it must comprehend it and surpass it."[1] How does this take place?

It cannot take place through any principle of interior necessity for we are in the realm of freedom. Marcel approaches this question, instead, by inquiring into the relation between the thinking self of the _cogito_ and the objective, empirical self of experience, and, by extension, the rest of the world of experience. Since this relation involves the _cogito_ which is a free, unverifiable act of thought, the act which claims to relate the _cogito_ must itself be a further equally free and equally unverifiable act of the mind.

---

significant reference, however, see _MJ_ 97-98. For Marcel's later consideration of Descartes' _cogito_, see below, pp. 83-84. More recently, Marcel has acknowledged that his interpretation of Descartes in these pages may be open to question (_TWB_ 226-227).

[1] _MJ_ 41.

If then the relation of the cogito to the
empirical ego is unverifiable (that is to
say, not susceptible of truth) we posit at
least the possibility of faith . . . .
Faith is the act by which the mind fills
the void between the thinking ego and the
empirical ego by affirming that they are
linked transcendentally; or rather faith
is the act by which the mind is made, the
mind i.e. the mind as a living and active
reality, the mind as distinct from the thinking subject.[1]

Marcel seems to be saying that the act by
which the _I think_ is constituted is highly precarious; because of its universality it stands the risk
of being converted into form--which is precisely
what happens through the operations of objective
thought when confronted with the data of experience.
We seem to be left with these two terms (the self
as intelligible and the self as empirical) which
must be seen as partaking in an intelligible whole.
Faith is the act by which I affirm ". . . a transcendental foundation for the union of the world
and of my thought." Through faith, ". . . I refuse
to think myself as purely abstract, as an intelligible form hovering over a world which is what it
may be . . . ." The latter is properly the domain
of science. Religion, however, ". . . is based on
the very mind itself, that is to say on the individualised thought which has posited an intimate
relationship between itself (as abstract) and its
integral experience, by means of the act of faith."[1]
In this brief remark lies the seed for Marcel's
later extensive critique of scientific method as
applied to the issues of metaphysics and religion.

At this early point in his career Marcel is
seen to be struggling with the attempt to maintain

---

[1]_MJ_ 44.   [2]Ibid. 45.

a view of faith as somehow an act of reflection yet
freed from the limitations of objective thought.
It is a problem that will loom larger and larger as
his career progresses. He consistently uses the
term "religious thought" or "religious reflection"[1]
yet it has nothing to do with the ". . . act by
which a subject determines an object."[2] This is
essentially the same difficulty he faced in his
earlier attempts to characterize the "later act of
reflection" (which is not "knowledge") by which
thought frees itself from objectification and sees
itself as participating in being (in the 1910-1911
and 1912 articles) and it is also the "experience-
limit" by which we grasp existence as immediately
given, in contrast to the "judgment" of existence.
He poses the dilemma in this way:

> . . . when pushed to its furthest extent,
> reflection on religion negates itself.
> Such reflection only achieves the entire
> suppression of the dualism of matter and
> form when it is itself suppressed and is
> converted into belief. For reflection is
> inseparable from some kind of dualism
> . . . . Only in so far as reflection
> achieves a grasp of the intimate solidar-
> ity that exists between itself and for-
> malism in general can it manage to recog-
> nise the relativity of this attitude, to
> think of itself as suppressed and to pass
> over to faith. In this sense faith appears
> as reflection that has reflected itself,
> and as a result has been negated.[3]

But, Marcel continues, this negation can be
the object of a further reflection and so on.

---

[1] EBHD 25.

[2] MJ 41.

[3] Ibid. 50.

There must be a point, then, when reflection absolutely forbids itself to reflect upon itself.
Ultimately faith presents itself with the characteristics of an imperative.

> . . . we do not end up with the contra-
> dictory idea of the unthinkableness of
> faith but with the affirmation that if we
> really dissociate belief from thought
> bearing on it, we are involving ourselves
> in a process without end, we are freely
> renouncing our freedom. In place of the
> dualism of faith and of thought bearing
> on faith is substituted the idea of the
> will to believe, and that will is thought
> to be bound by an obligation.[1]

It is important to spell out the implications of this view of faith. It is in no way based
on a demonstration and it has nothing to do with
the existence or non-existence of anything. Nothing in experience bears on faith--neither for nor
against--nor is faith determined by considerations
of God's essence. In fact, ". . . when I say that
faith bears on God I add nothing to the idea of
it."[2] With Plotinus, we can say that "God _is_
veritably for us only in so far as we participate
in him."[3]

Just as we dismiss any sense of an independent object of faith, so must we dismiss any
sense of an independent subject of faith. The subject is neither datum nor form; it is created by
the act of faith. "Faith appears as the act by

---

[1]_MJ_ 72-73. In another context Marcel understands this negation of reflection in the act of
faith as "grace" (ibid. 50-51).

[2]Ibid. 39.

[3]Ibid. 29.

which a thought, which denies itself as fixed and existing subject, reconstructs itself as (willed and created) subject by participation in God (who seems to be defined as the mysterious medium of this recreation)."[1]

This is the closest Marcel ever gets to defining what, from this perspective, God really _is_. He is not an object of knowledge; he does not exist; he has no essence; he has no reality apart from that conferred by the faith relation as Marcel conceives it, but then neither does the believing subject. We may say that he has a _creative_ role in that he is the _medium_ for the creation of the subject as individualized self--but Marcel hastens to warn us that this creative role should in no way be understood in a causal sense.[2]

Yet Marcel insists that God is "living," "concrete" and "personal"[3] very much as the beloved is to the lover, for ultimately Marcel claims that faith and love are integral to one another. Both

---

[1]_MJ_ 41. Cf. ibid. 31. There, it is the ego that is referred to as the ". . . intelligible medium by which freedom effects the transition from idea to being." Both the ego and God come to be in the participatory experience. Marcel here is groping for some way to characterize the non-objective realities on which participation rests.

[2]Ibid. 35. Marcel's consistent rejection of God's creative role has occasioned a good deal of criticism from the perspective of scholasticism: e.g. Rudolph J. Gerber, "Difficulty with the Creative God in Existential Phenomenology," _The Personalist_, Vol. 51, No. 4 (Fall, 1970), pp. 522-534 and Clyde Pax, _An Existential Approach to God: A Study of Gabriel Marcel_ (The Hague: Martinus Nijhoff, 1972), pp. 96-102. We will return to this in our discussion of proving the existence of God (below, pp. 202-206).

[3]_MJ_ 65.

must be understood as totally beyond objective
knowledge, explanation, justification or any form
of judgment bearing on their truth, falsity or
degree of reality or illusion. Neither is affected
in any way by empirical considerations. The, so to
speak, "real" human being who seems to be the
"object" of love is only that--precisely an "object." But love is not directed to independent
objects, any more than faith is directed to an
independent God. Love--like faith--creates its
beloved in the sense that it

> . . . posits the beloved as transcending
> all explanation and all reduction. In
> this sense it is true to say that love
> only addresses itself to what is eternal,
> it immobilises the beloved above the world
> of genesis and vicissitude. And in that
> way love is the negation of knowledge,
> which can only ignore transcendence.[1]

In each case, the "object"--like the "subject" is
a "construction";[2] there is nothing beyond the
relation.

Again, Marcel struggles with the possibility
that love--like faith--might constitute a form of
knowledge, perhaps the most perfect form of knowledge. But he is still trapped by his one-dimen-
sional view of knowledge as objective and the
suggestion is dismissed as he dismissed the suggestion (in the early papers) that participation in
being is knowledge and as he earlier could characterize only in a negative way the "experience-limit"

---

[1]MJ 62-63. On the relation of love and
faith, see also the earlier "Theory of Participation" in PF, especially 109-116; TPE 20; and Blain,
"Marcel's Logic of Freedom," pp. 186-193.

[2]MJ 63. For Marcel's later evaluation of
this view of faith see inter alia CF 148 ff.

of existence. The categories of knowledge are
absolutely inapplicable to faith and love.[1] Is
there any difference between faith and love?
Ultimately none, because apart from the fact that
God is beloved as he is believed in, any beloved is
such in so far as he is totally divorced from any
kind of objectivity, i.e. in so far as he is individualized subject, i.e. through his own act of
faith, God then makes possible both faith and
love.[2]

Apart from the internal problems raised by
the attempt of idealism to give a unified, objective account of reality as a whole, any such
attempt is doomed because it cannot account for
faith and love. To deal objectively with faith is
to end up in hopeless antinomies.[3] If faith is
possible then a "science of providence" is ruled
out. Once we acknowledge the possibility of a
religious affirmation transcending objectivity,
". . . the impossibility of an objective or notional
determination of the spiritual content of the world
has been demonstrated. From the standpoint of
metaphysical knowledge, the world remains the site
of uncertainty, the reign of the possible, it
remains contingent in relation to religious thought."[4]
In short, ". . . there is no objectively valid
judgment bearing on being."[5]

---

[1]MJ 63-66.

[2]Ibid. 66.

[3]Ibid. 31.

[4]Ibid. 97. This will remain the single
most consistent criticism of both idealist and
scientific rationalism in all of Marcel's later
work. See e.g. BH 176-198; MBII, chapter 10;
CF, chapters 6 and 9; TPE 118-120; EBHD 25-27.

[5]MJ 98. Italics Marcel's.

Looking back at this discussion of faith from the perspective of his later work, Marcel claimed that what he was trying to do was to find a way to safeguard

. . . the reality of God, which appeared to me inevitably compromised from the moment one thinks of his existence; I thought one might speak of existence of only that which falls within the purview of experience . . . . But what was constantly at stake . . . was to safeguard what from then on appeared to me of supreme importance. I mean love, and love understood in the deepest, and least psychological sense.[1]

What he wanted to avoid, above all, are the extremes of subjectivism (fidéisme) and objectivism (realism). Both stem from an excessively objective view of thought. Both separate the act of faith from the so-called "object" of faith. Subjectivism makes this dissociation in favor of the act of faith which then becomes a mere psychological state not bound to any reality. Objectivism makes the dissociation in favor of the "object" of faith, but then this God becomes another "that" on which we make judgments and "of" whom we think or speak.[2]

In contrast, Marcel claims that the act of faith--like every act of participation--is constitutive; it is one with its "subject" and "object"; it creates them and they have no reality apart from the act in which they come to be. The act itself must be grasped in its becoming. Faith, like love, is "a mode of being" or "a personal way of qualifying the world metaphysically." To say that both love and faith are unverifiable is simply to say

---

[1] EBHD 27.

[2] MJ 38-39, 67-68, 85, 153-159, 261-262.

that neither permits the possibility of an indefinite number of substitutions for the terms of the
relation.[1] Each free act of thought can be grasped
by a reflection of a thought upon itself which is
still "creative (and not . . . a mere reproduction
or sterile double)."[2]

But it is doubtful whether Marcel succeeds
in investing these later acts of reflection with
anything more than the essentially negative function of de-objectification. It is one thing to
speak of the act of faith as attachment to a _Thou_
which can never be converted to a _Him_;[3] it is quite
another thing to speak of faith as the transcendental unification of the thinking self and the
empirical self.[4] The fact that Marcel can make
both of these statements is an indication of the
struggle between the conflicting claims of his
idealist dialectic and the evidence of experience
itself. The latter claim is more responsive to
Marcel's preoccupation with his dialectic; the
former catches the experience of faith in the heart
of the believer.

At the end of the first part of the _Journal_
Marcel himself seems painfully aware of his failure
to resolve the subjectivism/objectivism dilemma.
In a brief, poignant entry early in Part two, he
refers to his attempt to show how the lover posits
the reality of the beloved as outside and above
time ". . . but . . . we are up against the problem
of the _Palais de sable_ and it is tragic."[5] This is

---

[1]_MJ_ 153-154   [2]Ibid. 3.

[3]Ibid. 137.   [4]Ibid. 44.

[5]Ibid. 133. See also ibid. 85, 153 and
especially 238 for a continuing discussion of this
dilemma as it emerges in this drama. The phrase
"palais de sable" was originally used as a metaphor for idealism.

the title of a drama which Marcel completed in 1913
and which exposes the hollowness of the central
character for whom religion is equivalent to a
". . . faith which . . . sustains itself through
its own ardor, but is dependent on no transcendental
reality."[1] It is interesting to note that the conclusion of the play suggests a way out of this
dilemma by showing the possibility of a kind of
love very different from the one described thus far
in his work, the love between two concrete human
beings. But here Marcel the dramatist was years
ahead of Marcel the philosopher.

Appraisal

A critical evaluation of the thought of any
serious thinker should be directed only to its most
mature and definitive formulation. Marcel's writings through 1915 do not constitute this definitive
formulation for he was struggling for the first
time with those philosophical issues which were to
occupy him throughout a long career.

Yet Marcel's own verdict that his analyses
to the end of Part one of the Journal are inadequate seems justified. He may have exposed the
difficulties of an epistemology founded on the
subject/object model but he is incapable of fur-
nishing an alternative. His goal was to construct
an epistemological framework which would avoid both
objectivity and arbitrariness and open the possibility of dealing philosophically with love and
religious faith. Yet he is left with a characterization of these experiences as essentially opposed

---

[1]EBHD 32. The implications of this play
for Marcel's thought are discussed in pp. 31-34.
This volume represents Marcel's most consistent
effort to relate his plays to his philosophical concerns. See also his "My Dramatic Works as Viewed
by the Philosopher" (SEAR 93-118).

to knowledge and attainable by an act of the mind which he insists is reflective but which he is hard-pressed to characterize. Thus the "tragic" problem of _Palais de sable_: granting Marcel's assumptions that faith is an intellectual act which is at the furthest remove from an objective or empirically-based judgment, how can this act be characterized positively in such a way as to avoid subjectivism? This will become Marcel's major task. But at this point, we can only agree with his verdict that he was trying to overthrow a system of thought using its own weapons. Ultimately Marcel's own account of faith or love in these pages is dictated by the demands of _his_ dialectic which remains firmly rooted in idealist categories. Faith understood in this way is the "crowning point of a dialectic" but it is also little more than a pale image of faith as experienced. The abstraction will not serve as an interim landing stage on the road to the discovery of the genuinely concrete.[1]

Some years later (1920) Marcel notes with trepidation that he has moved away from idealism.

My evolution in the direction of realism has obviously been accentuated in the course of the last month though I cannot see exactly where it is leading. For I still feel that this realism is ambiguous. Yet I glimpse ahead the whole difficult and new work of

---

[1]For an evaluation of Marcel's early thought on these issues, see Blain, "Marcel's Logic of Freedom," pp. 201-204. On Part one of the _Journal_, see Bagot, op. cit., pp. 72-76, Wahl, "Le _Journal_," pp. 82-84, and Widmer, op. cit., pp. 67-74. Bagot and Widmer emphasize the change in tone in the second part of the _Journal_. Faith as the "crowning point of a dialectic" is discussed in _PF_ 106, and Marcel's youthful hope that the idealist abstraction could serve as a bridge to the concrete is recalled in _TPE_ 105 and _EBHD_ 20-23.

re-thinking, beyond idealism, notions that
we too easily took to be over and done
with. A state of interior anarchy. I am
no longer even capable of stating the
problem.[1]

The turn to realism is at the same time a
turn to experience. Marcel will confront faith as
experienced in all its concreteness and allow it
and other experiences like it to dictate the structure of his epistemology. Hence the pronounced
change in tone, method and substance in all of
Marcel's writings from the early twenties on.

Yet the continuities between the earlier
and later stages are just as striking. The philosophical pre-occupations are the same: the limitations of the subject/object model for epistemology,
the sense that some realities (such as the self) do
not permit of objectification without distortion,
the attempt to characterize a different kind of
("later") reflective act by which the mind can
grasp these realities, the conviction that only
this kind of reflection can deal adequately with
human experiences such as love and faith so as to
retain their intellectual character while avoiding
objectivism and arbitrariness, and finally the conviction that only through these acts of reflection
can the individuality and the freedom of the person
be concretized.[2]

Above all, it is inescapable that though
Marcel's conversion may be years away he is clearly
in the process of creating a philosophical structure in which faith, from the very outset, is

---

[1] MJ 238.

[2] Marcel summarizes the continuities between
his early and later thought in EBHD, chapter 2.
See also Blain, "Marcel's Logic of Freedom,"
pp. 201-202.

destined to play a central role.[1] Whatever Marcel may claim about the neutrality of his thought as regards a specifically religious outcome, faith is in the picture from the very beginning. It is clearly one of his central epistemological concerns and serves as a significant impulse for Marcel's mature epistemology.

Marcel's Critique of Scientism

Marcel's philosophical critique of idealism was largely completed by 1915. His experience working with the Red Cross during World War I was decisive.[2] Anti-idealist criticisms are scattered throughout his later work but the themes are familiar: idealism eliminates the existential dimension, reduces the individual to an abstraction, does not leave room for religious faith and fosters a "spirit of abstraction" which, when absolutized into a stance toward all of reality, either topples into nonsense or stands as a deliberate lie.[3]

To the extent that there is a sustained critical note in Marcel's later work, it is directed against what may be called "scientism," the uncritical faith in the universal applicability of the principles of scientific research. Marcel launches a wide-ranging social and moral critique of the pernicious effects on society and personality of a world-outlook identified with the

---

[1]TPE 109 ff. and SEAR 99 f. confirm that Marcel's interest in religion dated back to his childhood and grew out of his interaction with the members of his family.

[2]TPE 121-122.

[3]This critique can be found inter alia in MBI 49-51; CF 5-21; TPE 105-127 passim; EBHD 22-32 passim and 132 ff.; MMS 114-121.

scientific-technological spirit. But underlying
this theme, there is a more properly philosophical
critique of much of post-Cartesian rationalism to
the extent that it assumes that scientific method
constitutes the exclusive model for intellectual
activity.

Despite occasional lapses to the contrary,
Marcel is not critical of the scientific enterprise
in itself. He acknowledges the fruitfulness and
indispensability of science and he grants that at
the highest reaches of their disciplines, the
scientist and mathematician are aware of the limitations of their methods.[1]

What he is critical of is the extrapolation
of the principles of scientific method for the purposes of metaphysical reflection. The critique of
this view continues his earlier critique of idealism
for Marcel claims that scientism and idealism share
the same philosophical assumptions.[2]

In pursuing this critique, Marcel will contrast science on one hand and philosophy and religion on the other. The contrast is clear to him as
early as the first part of the Metaphysical Journal:

Science as science is absolutely incapable
of liberating itself from the idea of the
world as realised knowledge that we have
to find anew. It is a legitimate mode of
representation and ever one that can be
called indispensable. It only becomes
vicious when it is erected into a metaphysical construction. Now that is precisely

---

[1]MBI 214.

[2]BH 183-184. Marcel never identifies his
enemy as positivism, but much of his critique of
science is, in effect, a critique of that school of
French philosophy.

72

the mistake common to optimism and pessimism, for both alike claim to formulate judgments on the content of the real which is posited as an object of science; that is to say they transpose into the metaphysical order the postulate that consists in positing the real as science[1] which is exclusively valid in the order of science.[2]

The thrust of Marcel's critique will center around the now familiar claim that the very success of scientific method rests in its object-centeredness whereas the realities with which philosophy must deal cannot be treated as objects without distortion. The critique of scientism can thus be seen as an extension of his earlier critique of idealism.

This critique deals first with the implications of science for the knowing subject. The object-centered view depersonalizes the subject as

---

[1]MJ 97. The original is obscure and the translation is awkward. The French reads: ". . . le postulat exclusivement valable dans l'ordre de la science qui consiste à poser le réel comme savoir." The parenthesis in the next sentence of the English translation indicates that the translator is aware of the difficulty. The point seems to be that what is posited as real is the object of knowledge which science attempts to grasp. It is worth noting that this view of science is present in one of Marcel's earliest published notes (dated May 28, 1910) in PF 41.

[2]MJ 97. The references to "optimism" and "pessimism" relate to an earlier discussion (ibid. 88-91) where Marcel identifies "metaphysical optimism" as the "identification of necessity and the good," and "metaphysical pessimism" as the opposite. The context deals with the efficacy of prayer.

does the _cogito_.[1] This depersonalization coincides
neatly with the scientific ideal of detachment
which guarantees the validity, perfectability and
cumulative nature of scientific knowledge but it is
utterly false to the realities of metaphysics where
the subject of the inquiry is at the heart of the
inquiry. The subject of metaphysical reflection is
a witness whose presence is indispensable and whose
conclusions are his testimony.

Second, the nature of scientific reflection
itself is different from that of philosophy.
Science begins with curiosity and ends with a solution which dispells the curiosity. In between lies
a process of inquiry which is likened to a technique, i.e. something that can be transmitted impartially to anyone. It is repeatable at will and
if conducted properly will yield identical conclusions every time. In other words scientific reflection is itself an object; like other objects it can
be isolated, examined and transmitted to others.

Philosophy, however, begins not with curiosity but with a felt need--Marcel's "need for
being"--which stems from the individual human being
in all his individuality and which is resolved by
recapturing the primitive unity of the individual
with a reality which encompasses him but from which
he was separated by the dissociative functions of
objective reflection. To show how this takes place
is the task of metaphysics.[2]

---

[1]How this takes place is described _inter
alia_ in MJ 319-320 and 325-327. See also ibid.
40-45 for an earlier discussion of the subject in
science and in religion (or philosophy).

[2]Marcel's discussion of the proper and improper uses of science can be found _inter alia_ in
MBI, chapters 1 and 10; EBHD 159-169 passim; and
particularly in the three papers appended to _Being
and Having_, pp. 176-236, particularly pp. 183-

Scientism is thus the intellectual heir of idealism. It shares the basic structure of idealist epistemology; hence its inadequacies for dealing with metaphysical issues. Both aim at control; for the idealist, an intellectual control of the object which is pliable to the human understanding; for the scientist, a control which results in his ability to predict the course of nature and mould it to his purposes. This is why Marcel defines applied science as ". . . any branch of learning which tends to guarantee man the mastery of a definite object."[1]

The irony of the scientific enterprise rests in the fact that the depersonalized subject of science--precisely because it has become de-personalized--can easily become the object of another branch of science aiming at the control of man himself. This is the point of departure for Marcel's social critique of scientism which he understands in terms of the myth of Prometheus.[2] A society which confers this power on a branch of learning with such destructive potential deserves the characterization of a "broken world," the title of one of Marcel's plays, and he claims, the most appropriate description of our own world today.[3]

There is a certain ritualistic quality to the critique of science among the existentialists which Marcel has not been able to avoid, especially in his later work. His critique of science does

---

19[1]. See also PM 62-63, SEAR, chapters 2 and 3, and the papers collected in MMS and DW. An evaluation of Marcel's views on science and technology can be found in Gallagher, op. cit., pp. 149-157.

[1]BH 183.

[2]Ibid. 184-185; TPE 30-32; SEAR, chapter 3.

[3]See inter alia MBI, chapter 2.

not advance his philosophy. Marcel saw science as inheriting the intellectual assumptions of idealism whose limitations he had amply exposed; the philosophical passion was spent in that earlier struggle. What remains is the social critique of his later years.

But there is much in the scientific mentality which Marcel could find congenial were he able to look at it more dispassionately. For example, Marcel should have been able to appreciate the sense of openness to experience which is part of the scientific stance toward the world. Further the scientist should be able to identify with Marcel's persistent self-criticism and mistrust of conclusions that claim finality. The difference between science and philosophy may be one of emphasis but if dogmatism is the enemy, there can be a dogmatism both of philosophy and science and the scientist would join with Marcel in condemning both.

The image of science in existentialist literature could easily serve as the topic for a major study in itself. Marcel's contribution to that discussion is neither major nor original. It does serve, however, to confirm and extend his philosophical critique of idealism and rationalism and prepares the way for the epistemological proposals of his mature years.

CHAPTER III

THE SITUATION

Introduction

Students of Marcel's work agree in dating
his mature thought from the year 1915 with the
extracts from his philosophical journal published
at the beginning of the second part of the Metaphysical Journal.[1] The continuities in style and

---

[1]In fact, the Journal records only eleven
brief entries from 1915 to July 1918 when the
entries pick up in frequency until May 1923. The
first major summary of the new directions in his
thought is the monograph "Existence et objectivité"
first published in the Revue de Métaphysique et de
Morale in 1925 and then appended to MJ upon its
publication two years later. There followed: a
second major monograph "Positions et approches
concrètes du mystère ontologique" (1933) which
deals largely with the dimension of intersubjectivity (TPE 9-46); the two further extracts from
his journal, Etre et avoir (1935) and Présence et
immortalité (1959); two major systematic presentations, the Gifford Lectures of 1949 and 1950 published as Le Mystère de l'être (1951) and the
William James Lectures of 1961 published as The
Existential Background of Human Dignity (1963); and
five sets of collected papers: Du refus à l'invocation (1940), L'Homme problématique (1945), Homo
Viator (1945), Les Hommes contre l'humain (1951),
and Le Déclin de la sagesse (1954). The changes in
tone between Part one and Part two of the Journal
are stressed by Bagot, op. cit., pp. 72-76 and

77

substance in the post 1915 material are striking and
in sharp contrast to the material which we have considered thus far. The second part of the _Journal_
contains, explicitly or implicitly, just about every
position with which Marcel has come to be identified; the writings that follow are distinguished
more by the constantly expanding range of data in
which he is able to find philosophical relevance.
The remaining chapters of this study will then,
treat the rest of Marcel's work as a unit and as
embodying his final statement on the issues that
concern us.

         In a programmatic statement, dating from
early in this period, Marcel describes his method
as ". . . plumbing the depths of a given fundamental
metaphysical situation of which it is inadequate to
say 'it is mine,' since it consists essentially in
being me,"[1] or, in another context, ". . . which
makes me what I am."[2] Marcel's mature philosophical
work can be understood as this "plumbing" within
the fundamental metaphysical situation.

         The plumbing must take place precisely
"within" the situation because my situation can in
no way be seen as a spectacle unfolding before me
that I can contemplate and delineate objectively.[3]

Widmer, op. cit., pp. 67-74. Widmer (p. 14, note
10) confirms that the strictly philosophical development of Marcel's thought ended in 1951 with the
publication of _Le Mystère de l'être_; his writings
after that date are largely an attempt to apply his
philosophy to a wide range of social problems.
Again, Lapointe and Lapointe, op. cit., lists all
of Marcel's published writings to 1974.

         [1]_BH_ 20.   [2]_CF_ 26.

         [3]Ricoeur suggests that the situation/spec-
tacle contrast is but one of a number of similar
divergences between Marcel and Husserl ("Gabriel
Marcel et la phénoménologie," _Entretiens autour de
Gabriel Marcel_, pp. 53-61).

In fact, that moment in which I recognize my situation as indeed making me what I __am__ is the pivot about which my life revolves as I move, again to use a favorite metaphor, from discordancy to resolution.

Marcel understands this situation as consisting of two dimensions which serve as gateways to yet a third. The two primary dimensions are that of incarnation--or my presence in the existent universe through my body--and intersubjectivity--or my presence to other persons in love. These two dimensions in turn reveal a third and more ultimate dimension, that of being.

Marcel's disdain for system makes it difficult to study individual themes within these dimensions in isolation. The epistemological issues which are the central focus of this study are usually presented "at work," embedded in a discussion of one or another dimension of the situation. However, for the sake of clarity this study will first trace Marcel's understanding of the contours or polarities of the situation and in the chapter to come, extract the more purely epistemological elements implicit in this earlier discussion.

We will discover, as we proceed, that Marcel uses this theme of "the situation which I am" as a means of integrating a wide variety of data which he understands in terms of one unified conceptual scheme. As noted, his main purpose is to avoid any semblance of dualism within the situational structure. Our task will be to discern the motives behind this impulse and the philosophical gains which he hopes to realize thereby. At the same time we will have to specify the difficulties which Marcel has to accept in order to achieve these gains.

The Dimension of Incarnation

Marcel begins his study of incarnation with existence because existence is "préalable"--

79

absolutely "prior,"[1] hence, the most legitimate point of departure for philosophical exploration. Existence is also beyond doubt; to deny or even question existence is either to engage in deliberate negativism--denial by decree--or in mere wordplay.

> Propositions of the type "Nothing exists" . . . need not be construed as internally self-contradictory but rather as empty and meaningless. Indeed, I cannot deny the property of existence to "all things" . . . without presupposing a certain idea of existence and such an idea is here by definition without content or application. The above propositions possess the semblance of meaning only because I am careful not to explain the nature of the indeterminate idea of existence which I have refused to ascribe to this, that, and the other particular. Thus to assert "something exists" is to maintain that it is meaningless in principle to deny existence, that such a denial is wholly verbal, and an unwarranted extrapolation of meaningful particular propositions such as "A does not exist" . . . .[2]

At the outset of his career, Marcel had identified existence as absolutely immediate knowledge, the lower limit of the reflective process. "Existence and Objectivity" unpacks this earlier notion, but with the unpacking comes a far richer appreciation of what is given in existence. It is not only the primary "donné," but also "donnante,"

---

[1] TWB 221.

[2] CF 15-16; MJ 320-322; MBI 89-90; TWB 221. For an earlier version of this claim, see MJ 32. It is this kind of emphasis that led Marcel to identify his thought with "the philosophies of existence" (PM 25-26).

the vehicle of any further given and the model for
those participatory experiences which will be
central to his epistemology.[1]

What then is the nature of this primary indubitable? What is "given" in existence? "What is
given to me beyond all possible doubt is the confused and global experience of the world inasmuch
as it is existent."[2] It is not that _this_ or _that_
exists, nor is it existence in general, but rather
"the existent universe" where existence and the
existent are indissolubly united; the very indubitability of existence which renders it a fit
starting point for philosophy rests on this unity;
otherwise existence would be another predicate which
may or may not be applied to an object.[3] The same
considerations account for the fact that the affirmation of existence is not a judgment of any kind;[4]
there is no inference, no "_ergo_" whatsoever; the
"_sum_" is prior to any inference. Similarly, to deny
existence on the basis of judgment is equally illegitimate. The denial of existence--as with its
affirmation--is done by fiat. Both are beyond proof
or verification and both bear their own warranty of
certainty.

These two claims--that what is given is
"the existent universe," and that the acknowledgment
of the existent universe is prior to any kind of
inference about particular existents--go hand in
hand. Indeed, Marcel insists that even to say that
existence is "given _to_ us," suggesting a dualism of
subject and object, is a distortion:

---

[1]TWB 221.

[2]MJ 322; MBI 90; CF 16.

[3]MJ 321.

[4]Marcel's early thinking on the judgment of
existence is in MJ 23-26. Cf. above, pp. 49-50.

> Given normally signifies presented to a
> subject. Now here I would not like to
> insinuate anything of the kind . . . .
> This assurance appears to us as though
> constitutive of what we habitually call
> the subject. It is not added to it or
> provided for it; without this assurance
> the subject ceases to be anything; it
> disappears or at least is reduced to a
> logical shadow of itself.[1]

To say "I exist" should not be taken to refer to
any objective datum whatsoever; nor is it a means
of distinguishing the I from something else that
does not exist, for again that would imply a
criterion by which the predicate of existence is or
is not applied, bringing us back into the realm of
judgment. "But . . . when the I exist is thus
cleared of private meaning, it tends to merge with
an affirmation such as 'the universe exists' the
universe itself also being the negation of 'something in particular' without thereby necessarily
being reduced to the general and abstract."[2] Marcel
has consistently avoided identifying the existential
indubitable with the sense of "I exist": "To say 'I
exist' is to say 'I am in the world,' I belong to a
certain 'concert,' I am involved in a consensus."[3]
And in another context:

> The property of the existent is to be
> involved or inserted, that is, to be in
> a situation or in communication. Conse-
> quently, if, when claiming to posit it,
> one abstracts not only from such a situa-
> tion but from every situation whatsoever,
> one substitutes for it, if not a pure
> fiction, at least an idea.
> There is no point contesting the

---

[1] MJ 323, italics Marcel's.

[2] Ibid.   [3] PI 194.

existence of the external world, let us
say, things, if at the same time my own
existence is not denied to me who not
only perceives them but is in communication with them.[1]

Marcel contrasts this view with Descartes'
cogito, another instance in which existence is used
as the indubitable point of departure for philosophy. But what Descartes discovered, Marcel claims,
is not the existential subject but rather the subject of knowledge juxtaposed against a field of
objects of knowledge, hence the subject as universal, not singular or concrete. "The cogito introduces us into a whole system of affirmations and
guarantees their validity. It guards the threshold
of the valid . . . . But it certainly does not
follow from this that the objective world to which
access is opened up to us by the cogito coincides
with the world of existence . . . ."[2] The cogito
is the precondition for objective, hence verifiable
knowledge; in contrast, Marcel argues that existence
can in no sense be an object of knowledge.

The most suggestive interpretation of this
contrast is provided by Paul Ricoeur:

Descartes dit: plus je doute, plus je pense,
donc plus je suis . . . . Je m'assure de moi
dans le recul du monde . . . . Par ce mouve-
ment centripète qui me déduit moi-même au
pur sujet de connaissance, je me constitue
comme être délié du corps et transparent à
lui-même. G. Marcel dit: plus j'adhère,

---

[1]PI 143. Cf. CF 16-17; MBI 88-90; 109-110;
MJ 323; TPE 16.

[2]MJ 325, italics Marcel's. See also ibid.
40 ff., 182, 261, 288; BH 170-171; TPE 16-17; CF 65-
66; TWB 227. In the last of these he concedes that

> plus je suis participant à l'existence et
> moi-même existant. Je m'assure de moi-même
> dans le mouvement centrifuge de l'ex-ister
> par lequel je m'expose aux autres dans
> l'épaisseur vivante de mon corps. A la
> dialectique cartésienne de raréfaction
> réflexive qui a pour terme le sujet poncti-
> forme de la connaissance intellectuelle, G.
> Marcel oppose sa dialectique d'épaississe-
> ment existentiel qui a pour terme la pléni-
> tude de l'existence totale, rayonnant autour
> de mon corps existant.[1]

Descartes' centripetal dialectic ends up in an
impasse: from a self-enclosed consciousness there
is no passage to existence, whether of the other or
of the external world, for existence can never be
demonstrated.[2]

In a deliberate attempt to contrast his own
thought with Descartes' impasse, Marcel will stress,
as the key to his epistemology, that my situation
has to be understood as open or "perméable" as opposed to self-enclosed. This permeability extends
throughout the range of possible experiences in
which I am involved both through incarnation and
intersubjectivity. In fact, it can be said that
Marcel's account of existence as "the global sense
of the world as existent" is but the first stage in
his definition of the range of permeability

---

he may have been guilty of reading Descartes as a
Kantian.

[1]Paul Ricoeur, Gabriel Marcel et Karl
Jaspers, philosophie du mystère et philosophie du
paradoxe (Paris: Editions du temps présent, 1947),
p. 107. Italics Ricoeur's.

[2]MJ 32. On the cogito as "impasse," see in
particular ibid. 182 and 288. On the reality of
the external world, see TPE 117.

available to the self.[1]

Symbiotic to man's permeability is what Marcel calls the "exclamatory" sense of existence:

When I say, not that I am, but that I exist
. . . I glimpse more or less obscurely the
fact that my being is not only present to
my own awareness but that it is manifest
being. It might be better, indeed, instead
of saying "I exist," to say "I am manifest."
The Latin ex--meaning out, outwards, out
from--in as much as to say: I have something
to make myself known and recognized both by
others and by myself, even if I wear bor-
rowed plumes.[2]

Existence has this quality of calling attention to itself; it has radiance or revelatory power; thus it can not be "posée," nor "conçue" nor "connue" but only "reconnue à la façon d'un terrain qu'on explore,"[3] or, in a later term, "discovered" as opposed to the sense in which, among the idealists, it is invented.

I am inserted into "the existent universe" through "my body." To confront "my body" is to confront an ambiguity. From one point of view, my body is simply another object; it can be used,

---

[1]MBI 144-145.

[2]Ibid. 90-91. Cf. CF 17. This passage is identified as an entry from Marcel's diary dated 1943 but it is not to be found in the published extracts for that year in PI. Passages expressing parallel notions are ample. See PI 184-215, especially 184-185 which is dated January 17, 1959 or some sixteen years after the entries among which it is published.

[3]Journal métaphysique, p. xi.

maintained, repaired, and ends up by being scrapped. From another point of view, however,

> . . . my body does not reveal itself as a tool which I could do without because I can find another for it, or because I can exercise some other activities for which I have no need for it. It is given to me as the absolute condition of all possible instrumentality--and also of all possible enjoyment; in this sense it is given to me as being my all, with this reserve, however, that it retains--or rather that I retain, by means of it, the possibility of sacrificing myself.[1]

In other words: ". . . it is of the essence of my body that it can and must be considered in turn as 'I,' and as 'not I.'"[2]

Marcel's critique of the sense of my body as object is directed primarily against the view of body as instrument. To identify my body exclusively as an instrument launches an infinite regress. An instrument is an extension of something else; a human instrument is an extension of a human body. But if the body is an instrument, of what further bodily self is it in turn an instrument? More important, the view of body as instrument in no way captures the sense in which what transpires to my body transpires to me for my body can not be seen as detachable from who I am. "Hence the protest . . .: 'I do not make use of my body, I am my body.'"[3] What is felt most primitively is the

---

[1] PI 137.

[2] Ibid. 139; cf. BH 12.

[3] MJ 332-333; BH 12; PI 234. The formulation "I am my body" first appears in MJ 243.

indispensability of my body to my sense of self. To ignore this is to deprive my body of that ". . . absolute priority in virtue of which my body is posited as the center in relation to which my experience and my universe are ordered. Thus my body only becomes an occasion for a problem under conditions such that the very problem that we intended to state loses all meaning."[1]

At the other extreme, to say that I am only my body reinstates the notion of body as simple object. It is to avoid this materialistic interpretation of the self that much of philosophy and religion have taught contempt for the body. But neither of these does justice to the full implications of "my body." My body is neither identified with me nor distinct from me; both identification and distinction are operations that have significance only in the realm of objects.[2]

The one phenomenon which suggests that I can dispose of my body as if it were a possession is suicide. But once I commit suicide, I have renounced any further claim to disposing of my body. In other words, I can dispose of my body only in an absolute way; this suggests again the inseparability of my body and my self. My body's death is my death and I cannot anticipate what will become of me after my body's death. It is only at death that my body becomes a body.[3]

---

[1]MJ 334-335. Marcel's critique of the instrumentalist view of the body can be found inter alia in ibid. 332-335; MBI 99-102; CF 16-19. The earlier inquiries on which these conclusions are based are in MJ 231-275 passim.

[2]CF 20. On the rejection of the materialist implications of this claim see EBHD 46; MBI 100-101; CF 19.

[3]BH 82. Cf. Marcel's further exploration of the implications of this view in BH 137, 142, 156. Martyrdom, as contrasted with suicide, is

This understanding of "my body" is central to Marcel's view of man's situation.

> Long ago I realised that every existent
> must appear to me as prolonging my body
> in some direction or other--my body inas-
> much as it is mine, that is to say, inas-
> much as it is non-objective. In this sense,
> my body is at one and the same time the
> prototype of an existent and in a still
> deeper sense a landmark for existents.
> The world exists in the measure in which
> I have relations with it which are of the
> same type as my relations with my own
> body--that is to say inasmuch as I am in-
> carnate.[1]

It is my body which makes possible my insertion into the existent universe; more, every other existent has to be understood as tied to me as my body is tied to me.

---

discussed in BH 148. An intriguing extension of Marcel's thought on the sense of the "body-subject" is in Jacques Sarano, The Meaning of the Body, trans. by James H. Farley (Philadelphia: The West-minster Press, 1966). Sarano is primarily inter-ested in the implications of this view for illness and the practice of medicine. See also: Martin J. Lonergan, "Gabriel Marcel's Philosophy of Death," Philosophy Today, Vol. 19, No. 1 (Spring 1975), pp. 22-29 and in particular the illuminating dis-cussion of the distinction between "body-object" and "body-subject" in the "Dialogue entre Gabriel Marcel et Mme Parain-Vial" published in the "Extraits des Entretiens qui eurent lieu à Dijon les 17 et 18 mars 1973 sur la pensée de Gabriel Marcel," Revue de Métaphysique et de Morale, 79e année, No. 3 (July-September 1974), pp. 383-397.

[1]MJ 269.

To state the existence of a being or of a
thing would be to say: This being is of the
same nature as my body and belongs to the
same world; only this homogeneity doubtless
bears less on the (objective) essence than
on the intimacy that the word my, my body,
involves . . . . In the fact of my body
there is something which transcends what can
be called its materiality, something which
cannot be reduced to any of its objective
qualities. And the world only exists for me
inasmuch as I think it (this expresses it
badly) inasmuch as I apprehend it as bound
up with me by the thread which also binds me
to my body.[1]

It is in this sense that Marcel will identify incarnation as the central given of metaphysics[2] for the assurance of incarnation includes
the assurance of the existence of the so-called
"external" world.

Marcel's theory of incarnation suggests
that whereas in the empiricist tradition, the paradigmatic sensory experience is sight, for him it

---

[1]MJ 315. Cf. BH 11; EBHD 46-47. It is
worth noting that Marcel has come full circle in
his understanding of existence. At the outset of
his career, he identified existence with objectivity
and spatiality (MJ 14-18); now it is the very model
of presence. But to assert that existence is
homogeneity (however qualified) with me raises the
spectre of spatiality which Marcel never really un-
tangles but which figures less and less in his
writings after MJ. My body is the prototype of the
existent, less in its materiality than in its being
peculiarly mine; all existents are similarly mine
in that sense.

[2]BH 11.

will be touch.[1] This is amply born out by his discussion of sensation.

What Marcel, in the early pages of the
Journal, identified as "experience-limit"--"contact
between a body bound up with a perceiving consciousness and an external datum"[2]--he now identifies as
sensation. Sensation is "affection, not information."[3] It is the impact of the existing universe
on the perceiving consciousness; but even this
formulation is too suggestive of a subject-object
model. There is no independent sense datum which
impacts upon a perceiving consciousness. Rather,
we use the term "sensation" as simply one more way
to characterize our situation as incarnate beings
in the existent universe.

Marcel emphatically rejects any view of
sensation as a message emitted from one station,
received by a second and then translated into the
appropriate sensory language of sound, sight, smell,
etc. Marcel has consistently understood the message theory of sensation as tied to the instrumentalist theory of the body. Both lead to an infinite
regress; the instrumentalist view of the body
assumes a prior instrument to which this instrument
is an extension; the message view of sensation assumes that sensation begins as a datum transmitted
to the receiving station and then translated into
a sensation. Both assume the self-body dualism for
the body is seen as interposing itself between the
self and the world in order to fulfill its function
as the instrument of transmission. How then to
account for the experience of "my body?" Once the
self and the body are seen as distinct, there is no

_____

[1]Hence his reference to his "sensualistic
metaphysics" in MJ 316. Cf. the exchange in TWB
59-60.

[2]MJ 25-26.

[3]Ibid. 187.

90

way of closing the circuit again.[1]

The message theory of sensation assumes the independence of the self, the body and the world; in contrast, Marcel asserts that these are three inseparable components of one extended reality. My self/my body/the existent universe represent one extended adherence, or, to use Marcel's technical vocabulary, one extended "participatory" relationship with what we call "sensation" serving so to speak as the "hyphen" which binds the first two terms of this relation to the last.

> If sensation is to appear in some way intelligible, the mind must establish itself at the outset in a universe which is not a world of ideas. If it be possible to prove . . . that sensation is not susceptible of being conceived as a message, as a communication between different situations, it must involve the immediate participation of what we normally call the subject in a surrounding world from which no veritable frontier separates it.[2]

Human existence, then, is physical participation in the material universe with which it is in a pre-reflective relation and sensation is a momentary actualization of this coupling of our

---

[1]Marcel's critique of the message theory of sensation is found *inter alia* in MJ 257-259, 327-332; CF 24-26; MBI 104-110; EBHD 43-45.

[2]MJ 331-332. There is a suggestion in Marcel that just as sensation may be interpreted as the "hyphen" which couples the self/body components of the relation to the world, so "feeling" serves as the first "hyphen" that ties the self to the other two components. This might be a legitimate interpretation of passages such as MBI 101-104, 117-118 and CF 24-26.

bodily beings in the existent universe. It is one dimension of our mode of being in the world.

The Dimension of Intersubjectivity

Intersubjectivity is a prolongation of the participatory relation of incarnation. As body, I am co-immediate with the existent universe; as self, I am co-immediate with other selves. Incarnation denotes my presence through my body within the existing universe; intersubjectivity denotes my presence as self within a community of selves. In neither case does any privileged status accrue to the "I." Just as the existence of the "I" as incarnate is given within the existing universe, so the self emerges within the intersubjective experience.

> It is only insofar as I assert myself to
> be, in one sense, not merely a somebody
> that I can acknowledge two facts; firstly,
> that there is another sense in which I am
> a somebody, a particular individual (though
> not merely that), and secondly, that other
> somebodies, other particular individuals,
> also exist . . . . It is obvious that if I
> am a somebody, a particular individual, I
> am only so at once in connection with and
> in opposition to an indefinite number of
> other somebodies.[1]

Marcel goes even further:

> . . . I should be inclined to contend that
> existence can be attributed only to others,
> and in virtue of their otherness, and that
> I cannot think of myself as existing except
> in so far as I conceive of myself as not
> being the others: and so as other than them.

---

[1] MBI 86.

> I would go so far as to say that it is
> of the essence of the Other that he exists.
> I cannot think of him as other without
> thinking of him as existing.[1]

This extreme position serves to indicate Marcel's
consistent refusal to grant priority both to the
existence and to the metaphysical relevance of the
I. If anything is prior, it is neither the I nor
the other but rather the "we." "The 'we' reveals
itself undoubtedly as really more profound than the
'I.' Despite appearances, it is certainly more
stable . . . . What matters for me is the inde-
structibility of the 'we.'"[2] This sense of the "we
are" is as central a datum for metaphysics as incarnation.[3] It is, in fact, more primary than the
simple "thou" for the thou is itself an abstraction
out of the "we."

> I am obliged to admit that is absurd to
> speak of _the_ "thou" and thus to consider
> as a substantive what at bottom is the
> very negation of all substantiality. In
> reality, once I have singled it out, I
> objectivise a particular aspect of the ex-
> perience of intimacy. From the core of
> the _us_ I subtract the element that is _not-_
> _me_ and call it _thou_. This element has the
> automatic tendency to take on the character
> of the _him_. And it is only in the measure
> that I succeed in re-living this experience
> of intimacy after the event that I am able
> to resist this temptation.[4]

---

[1]_BH_ 104.   [2]_PI_ 201.   [3]_MBII_ 9.

[4]_MJ_ 303. Cf. Marcel's discussion of the
preposition "with" in _TPE_ 39 and _MBI_ 177, 181.
Marcel's use of "thou" as distinct from "him" dates
from 1918 (_MJ_ 158), long before, according to his
claim, he came across the writings of Martin Buber
(_EBHD_ 38-39). In one of his two published papers

The distinction between the "him" and the "thou" is just one instance of the distinction between object and presence in Marcel's thought. The "him" is the absent third-party about whom I talk to a real or imaginary interlocutor; he is essentially a "completed questionnaire," a bundle of characteristics exposed to my judgments.[1] The "thou" is beyond characterization, judgment, or criteriology of any kind. He can only be addressed or responded to. Pre-eminently he is the medium for the creation of the I as individualized subject.

---

on Buber's thought (I and Thou," The Philosophy of Martin Buber, ed. by Paul Arthur Schilpp and Maurice Friedman, The Library of Living Philosophers, 12 [La Salle, Ill.: Open Court, 1967], pp. 41-48), Marcel indicates that, as is clear from the above, he prefers to stress the over-arching community or felt unity created by the I and Thou rather than their relatedness; to speak of "relation" here, Marcel claims, is to transform the terms of the relation into things--however inevitable this transformation by the very fact of language. Buber's response to Marcel is on pp. 705-706 of this volume. Marcel traces his own awareness of the distinction between "thou" and "him" to his metapsychical experiments and his work for the Red Cross during World War I (CF 32; EBHD 41-43, 51-53, 140-141; TPE 122). Eventually this distinction evolved into the object/presence distinction with a much wider range of application. However, as will be shown below, the original "presence" was the other human being seen as "thou."

[1]MJ 326; CF 32-33. Cf. MJ 165, 219; CF 33-37; BH 106-107. Marcel acknowledges his debt to Royce for his characterization of the "him" as the "absent third party" (MJ 146, 326). Marcel's major opponent on this issue is, of course, Sartre who is incapable of seeing in the other anything but an antagonist (TPE 73-76, 99-100; MBII 9).

. . . The more my questioner is external to me, the more I am by the same token external to myself; in confronting a Mr. so-and-so I also become another Mr. so-and-so, unless I literally happen not to be a person any more--a pen which traces words on paper or a simple recording apparatus . . . . It can happen, however, that a bond of feeling is created between me and the other person . . .; hence a unity is established in which the other person and myself become we. . . . He ceases to intervene between me and myself.[1]

Characteristically, Marcel rarely discusses intersubjectivity in the abstract. Rather, his discussion centers upon its three fundamental concrete expressions--fidelity, hope, and love--which he understands as significant data for metaphysics. His perceptive phenomenological descriptions distinguish fidelity from conformism and sincerity, hope from optimism and desire, and love from appropriation--contrasting all three with betrayal, despair, fear, pessimism, egotism, and self-centeredness. Each of these three is far removed from an objective act of the intellect and hence none is open to the charge of being illusory, erroneous, illegitimate, or unjustified; hope, for

----

[1]CF 33. It is worth noting how this view developed out of Marcel's earlier views. At the outset, the individualized subject was created by religious faith; now it is the experience of intersubjectivity that creates the subject, not simply as the crowning point of a dialectic but as a concrete individual human being. Similarly with the "thou." At the outset, the "objects" of love and faith were ideal constructs; now, the "thou" exists pre-eminently, even prior to me. All of this results from Marcel's dissociation of existence from objectivity and his turning to experience in the concrete for his philosophical data.

example, is precisely the refusal to reckon on the probabilities which make it more or less warranted. Each bears its own warranty of certainty for the persons involved in the relation. Marcel concedes that these acts, in their purity, occur only at rare intervals; reflection is always tempted to reduce them to objective judgments, but it is the task of a freely exercised further reflection to refuse to accept this reduction as ultimate.[1]

The experience of intersubjectivity--like that of incarnation--is a mode of being in the world. It extends the experience of incarnation and provides another dimension to my situation. As instances of participation, neither can be understood as the exchange of messages; rather, they are, so to speak, internal relations where the polarities of the relation are created by and through the participatory experience. The experience of "my body" is ultimately a paradigm for the experience of the thou. The thou, like my body, is immediately present to me, adheres to me, in fact creates me as an individual subject. Just as "I am my body," Marcel can claim "I am the other." The other (and my body) is part of the existent universe that "shapes me as in a womb."[2]

---

[1]On fidelity, see *inter alia* BH 40-56; TPE 34-36; EBHD 54-74. On hope, see HV 29-67; MBII 158-172; EBHD 141-144. On love, see MJ 58-66, 146-159, 222-223, 303-305; MBII 151-157; TPE 20-23. The most suggestive unpacking of Marcel's treatment of intersubjectivity is provided by William Ernest Hocking, "Marcel and the Ground Issues of Metaphysics," *Philosophy and Phenomenological Research*, Vol. 14, No. 4 (June 1954), pp. 439-460. See also Gallagher, op. cit., pp. 22-29, 66-81.

[2]CF 29; MBI 182 and 207.

The Dimension of Being

Both incarnation and intersubjectivity are at the same time gateways into another participatory experience, this one with being. Marcel understands this not as a different or more abstract experience, but rather as another dimension to everyday experience, a dimension which he calls its "metaphysical tenor."

> The metaphysical is not the meta-empirical, that which transcends all possible experience . . . . Could we not say, in this sense, that all experience involves an extremely variable content of what we call, rather improperly, the metaphysical tenor? . . . This metaphysical tenor of experience-- it is precisely by starting from the everyday that we can see in what it consists. The everyday, pure and simple, disregards the metaphysical; the everyday as devaluated or depreciated denies it; the everyday as consecrated or regenerated affirms it.[1]

The crowning position which this theme occupies in Marcel's thought is hardly reflected by the treatment accorded to it in his writings.[2] Nowhere is his disdain for systematic presentation more conspicuous or its absence more telling. Our discussion here will simply attempt to complete the picture of the human situation in order to prepare

---

[1] PI 125-126.

[2] Only twice in his philosophical writings does Marcel provide us with an extended analysis of what he means by being. One is "On the Ontological Mystery" (in TPE) and the other is in the opening four chapters of MBII. The passage in BH 116-123 is apparently an early outline of "On the Ontological Mystery." A later and more systematic review of his position is in TWB 45-55. The exchanges

for the epistemological study which follows.

At the outset, a short programmatic statement:

My effort can best be described as an
attempt to establish a concept which pre-
cludes all equation of being with _Ding_
while upholding the ontological without
going back to the category of substance
which I regarded with profound mistrust.

. . . my aim was to discover how a subject, in his actual capacity as subject,
is related to a reality which cannot in
this context be regarded as objective,
yet which is persistently required and
recognised as real.[1]

Marcel speaks of being as a need, an
exigence, an appetite, or, more precisely, a demand:
"Il faut qu'il y ait ou il faudrait qu'il y eût _de
l'être_."[2] This is not a definition of being;
rather what Marcel seems to be claiming is that
being cannot be defined without reference to its
being demanded. It is precisely the _demand_ that is

_____

that follow (pp. 55-80) clarify but do not advance
his thought.

[1]_TPE_ 127.

[2]The English translation (_TPE_ 14) reads:
"Being is--or should be--necessary." But in _MBII_
37, Marcel clarifies his meaning in this way: "The
il faut or the _il faudrait_ refers to the exigence
that is seated in me. Elsewhere the translator has
used the word _need_, and this also distorts my
thought somewhat, as it implies something that is
wanted rather than something that is _demanded_."
See also _MJ_ 182, 188; _MBI_ 39, 152; _BH_ 114; _TWB_
227-228.

the most relevant datum and its fulfillment will
depend more on a freely exercised option of the
seeker in response to this demand, than on evidence
from the outside.[1]

Being then cannot be understood as an
"object" of knowledge; knowledge presupposes being.
Prior to any knowledge of being, prior even to the
awareness of a demand for being, there is an infra-
intellectual affirmation of being within the knower,
with the knower as the stage rather than the subject.[2] The task will be to recapture this original
affirmation on the level of consciousness through
an act of the will. This recapturing (through what
Marcel will call "secondary reflection") is the
fulcrum around which Marcel structures his two
primary views of being: first, the "hypoproblematic"
sense of being as "foundation" ("soubassement"),
the pre-reflective ground of all things which shapes
the individual qua individual through the dimensions
of incarnation and intersubjectivity; and second,
the "hyperproblematic" or consciously-willed sense
of being as "plenitude," the focus for the "exigence
for being" which, when realized in its fullest sense
through communion with others, creates the individual as person.[3] But however understood, the mind

-----

[1]TWB 227-228 where Marcel responds to the
charge that the demand for being is "wishful
thinking."

[2]TPE 17-18; BH 35-36, 115.

[3]The distinction is referred to in TWB 45-
55. Marcel concludes this statement with the
suggestion that still a third sense of being, "a
being," may serve as the "mysterious connection"
between being as foundation and being as plenitude.
What he seems to be saying is that the dimension of
intersubjectivity straddles both sides of the
fulcrum. The other is both part of "the existent
universe" and, when loved, a "thou." Thomas

can never see itself as standing outside of being
and creating objective forms which define or
delineate it. In Marcel's term, being--like knowl-
edge--is a mystery; if anything, it is the paradigm
of mystery.

Further, whatever the outcome of the quest
for being for the individual, that outcome is not
subject to verification; what will emerge at the
term of the quest ". . . infinitely transcends all
possible verification because it exists in an immediacy beyond all conceivable mediation."[1] The
recognition of being, then, in a claim that will
have to be examined at length, has the character of
testimony.

On the "hyperproblematic" level, being, as
that which is ultimately to be desired, dovetails
with value. To say that nothing is (to use but one
form of the denial of being) is to say that nothing
counts, nothing resists an exhaustive analysis
bearing on intrinsic value.[2] Marcel's many and extended descriptions of contemporary technocracy and
its reduction of man to a series of functions is
designed precisely to portray the contemporary
world-outlook as nihilistic and contemporary man as
having lost his awareness of being; it is a world
where the demand for being is dulled or even
actively denied.[3] Such a world not only counsels

Anderson's "Gabriel Marcel's Notions of Being,"
Philosophy Today, Vol. 19, No. 1 (Spring 1975),
pp. 29-49, largely an exegesis of this paper, is
a most imaginative attempt to systematize Marcel's
thought on this complex and subtle theme.

[1]TPE 15.

[2]Ibid. 14-27; BH 57-59, 102, 119; EBHD 77;
TWB 224-225.

[3]TPE 9-14. Cf. Marcel's portrait of the
"barracks man" (PM 17 ff.).

but even invites despair which is an affirmation
that: "There is nothing in the realm of reality to
which I can give credit--no security, no guarantee."[1] Such despair is, on the side of logic,
completely irrefutable.[2]

But despair is not imposed on us by the
structure of things. If being is denied, it is
denied solely by an option of the individual,
freely exercised.[3] Here the role of the will is
paramount; there can be no demonstration either
from logic or from experience. The denial of being
may take the form either of denying being itself or
denying the being of individuals; ultimately these
two are one. If we refuse to speak of an individual
as being, we are doomed to reduce him to a function
in act as well as speech. If, on the other hand,
we deny being itself, we are left with a generalized nihilism which will end in the denial of being
to the individual as well.[4]

It is possible, on the other hand, to cut
through this reductionism by means of a series of
concrete approaches to specific experiences where
man is seen to challenge nihilism and despair,
primarily fidelity (or religious faith), love, and
hope--all experiences of genuine intimacy with
other human beings.[5] The aim of these concrete
approaches is to expose the ontological reference
implicit in these experiences. This is what Marcel
means by his oft-quoted claim that his purpose is

---

[1]TPE 27.

[2]BH 104, 110-111, 119; TWB 227-229; TPE
30-32.

[3]TWB 228-229; BH 110-111; PI 171-172.

[4]MBII 54-59; CF 147-148; BH 28-29.

[5]BH 73-74, 119-120; TWB 228-229.

to restore the "ontological weight" to experience.[1]
Each of these three cardinal experiences is a recognition of perennialness which transcends the eva-
nescence of the other's existence. It is precisely
the death of individual beings that tempts me into
a generalized denial of being itself. But if love
of another human being has any meaning, it rests
precisely in this: "to love somebody is to say to
him, 'You will not die.'"[2]

---

[1] BH 103; EBHD 74, 79.

[2] This line is from one of Marcel's dramas,
Le Mort de demain (1931) (BH 95-96; MBII 61).
Marcel frequently acknowledges that his preoccupation with the "problems" of immortality and survival after death stems from the devastation he
felt upon the death of his mother shortly before
his fourth birthday. He recalls a conversation
with his agnostic aunt, a few years thereafter,
during which she claimed that no one could know if
the dead were annihilated or lived on in some way.
Marcel's response was: "When I'm older I'm going to
find out!" (EBHD 25). In 1937, this issue led to
a dispute between Marcel and Brunschvicg. To
Brunschvicg's comment that ". . . the death of
Gabriel Marcel seemed to preoccupy Gabriel Marcel
much more than the death of Léon Brunschvicg preoccupied Léon Brunschvicg," Marcel responded: "the
only thing worth preoccupying either one of us was
the death of someone we loved" (TWB 131). In an
exchange with Marcel shortly before his death,
Ricoeur questions whether Marcel can legitimately
insist both on the reality of survival after death
and on the indispensability of the body to the
sense of self. The former could be accounted for
more easily through a body/soul dualism and the
latter implies a view of death as final. Marcel
acknowledges the tension between these two positions but insists that if death is indeed final,
then Christ's promises are all false. He views this
possibility as "un écroulement effroyable." "Si

The exigence for being, then, is exposed as the exigence for perennialness. It is the inter-subjective dimension when fully realized on the level of consciousness that pre-eminently provides a gateway to being.[1] These concrete approaches to specific experiences, however, should in no way be understood as providing a demonstration; rather, they represent one's personal reading of reality from which one appeals to others to take up their own equally concrete and equally personal inquiry.[2]

Marcel's inquiry into "my being" contrasts this with the sense of "my life" or "my existence." Marcel holds that man uniquely has the power to withdraw from his life in order to evaluate it.

> I withdraw from (my life) in a certain way,
> but not as the pure subject of cognition;
> in this withdrawal I carry with me that
> which I am and which perhaps my life is not.
> This brings out the gap between my being
> and my life. I am not my life; and if I
> can judge my life—a fact I cannot deny
> without falling into a radical scepticism
> which is nothing other than despair—it
> is only on condition that I encounter myself
> within recollection beyond all possible
> judgment and . . . beyond all representation.[3]

---

cela s'écroule, tout s'écroule" (Entretiens autour de Gabriel Marcel, pp. 172-173). There is then a clear convergence of Marcel's ontology and his personal experience.

[1]MBII 9-10, 16-17, 33, 59-62; BH 167; CF 147-148; TPE 27-40 passim.

[2]TPE 43-44.

[3]Ibid. 24; MBI 136-137; CF 173; BH 109-110, 118-119. Compare MBII 30-31 on "my being" and "my existence." Marcel does not identify "my life" and "my existence" but much of what he says in con-

My life stands in relation to another dimension of
my self which acts as a standard against which my
life can be measured. Hence the possibility of my
sacrificing my life in the name of a higher sense
of self. That higher dimension is my being. Marcel
can then claim that my being is at stake in my life;
my life can either betray or fulfill my being.[1]

Marcel does discuss the distinction between
being and existence themselves but his method is
one of "concrete approaches" and he prefers to
study abstractions in their concrete embodiments.
In one extended discussion of this distinction,[2]
Marcel concludes that when existence is understood
most authentically, i.e. when it is seen as the
polar opposite of objectivity, it seems to be indis-
tinguishable from being because, again, it manifests
perennialness.[3] In other words, Marcel seems to be
saying of "the existent" in the dimension of incarnation what he says of "the other" in the dimension of intersubjectivity; both are manifestations
of being, and I am involved with both in an immediate, participatory relation.

But what Marcel says and leaves unsaid
about the distinction between being and existence
has other more important implications. Paul Ricoeur

---

trasting each of these with "my being" suggests
that such an identification would not be illegitimate.

[1]BH 196.

[2]MBII, chapter 2.

[3]Ibid. 27. Cf. BH 37. Anderson, ". . .
Notions of Being," suggests that "being" can be
identified with "existence" (both in the abstract)
on the "hypoproblematic" level. But when "the
existent" becomes "a being," we have renewed the
identification on the "hyperproblematic" level

suggests and Marcel concedes that his thought on existence and being constitute responses to two different preoccupations.[1] His study of existence developed out of his search for an indubitable point of departure for his philosophical search; hence its contrast with objectivity. His study of being, however (at least in his more mature period) developed after the war years out of his pre-occupation with the increasing functionalization of man in a technocratic age. Hence one of his most extended and coherent discussions of being in "On the Ontological Mystery" (1933) begins with ". . . a sort of global and intuitive characterization of the man in whom the sense of the ontological--the sense of being--is lacking."[2]

This may explain why Marcel's writings are considerably more explicit about the results of the absence of this "sense of being" than of its presence. It may also explain his insistence that being is not a thing, not an object, not a _quid_ garnished with predicates, not the _ens realissimum_, not "all

---

(pp. 35, 41, 42-46). The latter claim is Anderson's suggestive reformulation of the considerably more obscure passage in TWB 52-55. We will question this identification below (pp. 271-276).

[1]TWB 225 ff. In fact, Marcel's study of these two themes rarely coincides. His very earliest, i.e. pre-1915, writings are centered about being, but this theme is starkly absent from the pages of MJ where existence moves to center-stage. This phase reaches its climax in "Existence and Objectivity" (1925). Being returns to the forefront with the post-1928 journal entries published in BH (e.g. 28 ff.) and summarized in "On the Ontological Mystery" (1933). These entries were recorded very shortly after his conversion to Catholicism (BH 24, dated March 23, 1929).

[2]TPE 9

of reality," not static perfection and above all
not the ultimate abstraction, in fact not an abstraction at all but ineluctably concrete, and that,
consequently, there is only a nominal difference
between the denial or affirmation of being (itself)
and the denial or affirmation of being to individuals. It is not a symbol or reflection or modality
of being that one encounters in the individual; it
is rather simply being.[1]

It also explains his insistence that being
(in this context called "transcendence") can be
found within experience and not in some mystical
beyond.[2] There is an experience of transcendence
itself, or more precisely, the experience of transcendence denotes a transformation within "ordinary"
experience in the direction of recognizing its
"metaphysical tenor"[3] or its "ontological weight."[4]

Finally it explains Marcel's inability to
provide a coherent account of the relationship of
existence to being. That there is an interval
between these two primary themes in Marcel's work
will be confirmed below when we turn to a discussion
of religious knowledge itself. We will note then
that this interval is of major importance in understanding the structure and development of Marcel's
thought as a whole.

Appraisal

We have noted that Marcel's analysis of the
"fundamental metaphysical situation" has to be
understood as a reflection of his central concern
which is to avoid any semblance of dualism or discontinuity within the structure of the situation.
This explains Marcel's determined effort to under-

---

[1]MBII 59.   [2]MBI 45-46.

[3]PI 125-126.   [4]MBI 103.

stand the two primary dimensions of the situation--incarnation and intersubjectivity--in terms of one set of categories and one vocabulary, often at the price of forcing the data, and of giving rise to a number of alternate philosophical difficulties--a price which he is clearly prepared to pay.

Thus Marcel finds the sense of being--understood as a sense of perennialness or worth--achievable through an experience of genuine intimacy with another person, leading him to portray the person who is most capable of such intimacy as open or available to a call from the other. Parallel to this, in the dimension of incarnation, he portrays man in a similar relation of--he uses the same term--"intimacy"[1] with the existent universe--which has the same quality of calling attention to itself[2]--in which he is situated through his body which is both _his_ and _him_ and which serves as the hallmark of existence. To suggest a possible reconstruction of the direction of his thought, the unexceptionable claim that I can attain a sense of being in a relation of intimacy with other persons leads to the more perceptive claim that it is _my_ body, recognized as uniquely _me_, that opens vistas of relations with the rest of the existent universe. But this, in turn, leads to the forced and counter-intuitive claim that the rest of the existent universe is related to me as my body is related to me.[3]

Marcel's later qualification that this parallel is less one of essence than of feeling[4] suggests his own discomfort at the implications of this view. But this discomfort is clearly less acute than that engendered by any suggestion of discontinuity between myself and the rest of the existent

---

[1]_MJ_ 315. [2]_MBI_ 90-91.

[3]_MJ_ 269. [4]Ibid. 315.

universe[1] or--by implication--between intersubjectivity and incarnation. Thus, contrary to the
presentation in this chapter, intersubjectivity
seems to precede incarnation--not chronologically
(i.e. in the _development_ of his thought) but
structurally.

        In order to maintain this tightly unified
view of the situation Marcel is forced to accept a
number of alternate philosophical difficulties,
often without giving them the consideration they
deserve.

        Thus his rejection of a mind/body dualism
leads him to proclaim "I am my body." But his
arguments for this position are mainly a critique
of dualist or instrumentalist theories of the mind/
body relationship. The views which Marcel seems to
be most directly challenging here--as in much of
his thought--are medieval supernaturalism and
cartesian mechanism. Both are frankly dualistic;
supernaturalism dissociates mind and body in order
to leave room for the immortality of the former
understood as soul, thereby relegating the body to
an inferior status as that which for a time en-
velops the soul. Cartesian mechanism dissociates
extended substance and thinking substance, making
the· former totally explicable in terms of the laws
of mechanics and thus providing the philosophical
foundations for modern science and technology.

        Marcel faults both of these positions for
their failure to do justice to the felt intimacy
and integrity to _me_ of the sense of _my_ body. He
opposes medieval supernaturalism by identifying
being (and God) as personal, concrete and immanent
in "the existent universe." He opposes mechanism
by seeing my body as integral to my sense of self,
hence as "body-subject," the locus of being and of
value, and thereby irreducible to a purely

----

[1]_MJ_ 274.

functional, instrumental, technological or more
generally objective account. On this basis, and
despite his protests against supernaturalism, he
insists vigorously on the reality of immortality
and survival after death and takes the data of
telepathy more seriously than most philosophers.

But Marcel is clearly skirting a number of
philosophical positions which are difficult in
themselves. Pantheism and materialism are two
obvious examples. He is quick to concede "I am not
only my body" but he never satisfactorily clarifies
what constitutes this "non-body" aspect of the self
apart from identifying it with the other elements
which enter into the permeable situation, or how
all of these are integrated in a non-dualist way
with the body. He will concede that being is both
identified with and also transcends beings but
again he cannot really clarify how this is possible,
how being can be both concrete and personal, or, as
we shall see, how being becomes the personal God of
Christianity.

He avoids a self/world dualism by establishing the body--understood as my body--as a "landmark"
or "prototype" of existents and conflates the
problems of existence and of the status of the external world by demonstrating that the "existent
universe" is a totally primitive, indubitable given
which prolongs or extends the sense of "my body."
He disclaims the materialist implications of this
position by arguing that he is referring more to an
identity of feeling than of essence but again, he
does not deal with the equally powerful feeling
that there is a difference in quality or intensity
between the intimacy one feels to one's body on one
hand and to the rest of the existent universe on
the other.

To further fortify his position, he espouses
a realist view of perception modeled more on touch
than on sight, with the qualification that what is
perceived is not an object external to the perceiver
but somehow bound up with him in the larger

109

structure of the existent universe. But again his
arguments for realism are basically a critique of
the dualist implications of representationalism and
he never seriously takes up the equally formidable
problems which have led others to espouse the
latter position over his own.

Finally, of course, it is his abhorrence of
the subject/object dualism which leads him to a view
of metaphysical knowledge as participation. More
on this below.

Marcel's analysis supports his claim that
the central issue in metaphysics is the nature of
the self.[1] It also supports his rejection of any
view of that self as tightly confined between rigid
frontiers.[2] This is why, ultimately, he insists
that the self must be seen as embedded in a situation which _is_ him or which makes him what he _is_,[3]
for neither in relation to the existent universe[4]
nor in relation to other persons[5] does the self
have any precedence. It is in and through the
situation that the self comes to be.

This notion of "situation" is how Marcel
structures what he calls the "permeability"[6] of the
self; it defines and specifies that influx from the
outside that brings the self into being. In fact,
what we call the "ego," Marcel sees as only a point
of emphasis for mobilizing mechanisms of defense
within what should otherwise be considered not as
an isolated reality but rather as a "moving and
vulnerable enclave."[7] This "enclave"--elsewhere

---

[1]MBI 83-84.   [2]HV 16.

[3]BH 20; CF 26.   [4]MJ 325.

[5]MBI 86.   [6]Ibid. 145.

[7]HV 16; EBHD 102.

referred to as a "city which I form with myself"[1]--
is the self in its multiplicity of relations within
the situational structure. This provides Marcel
with a context within which he can explore experiences as varied as the sense of "my past,"[2] my
family,"[3] telepathy and metapsychical experimenta-
tion,[4] "the existent universe" and intersubjectivity both with other selves[5] and within the self.
That this enclave is also "moving" is Marcel's way
of portraying the effects of this influx from the
outside on the self-perpetually-in-creation.

This notion of the situation serves the
additional purpose of delineating the realm of the
mysterious from that of the problematic. Whatever
is within the situational structure has to be
understood as a presence which raises mysteries;
whatever is outside is an object which raises
problems.

Essentially the situation defines the self;
it is the self--or, more precisely, the self is its
situation. The various components that go into the
situation bring the self into being and make it
what it distinctively is. But Marcel's insistence
on viewing the situation as "open" and "moving"
raises the question of identity. Whatever else I
feel about myself, I surely feel the presence of
some solid thread of identity--however defined--
which is stable, relative to the influxes that are
at work in influencing my make-up and to my sense
of growth which is the mark of the self-in-creation.
Surely this felt ego is much more than a mere defense mechanism. Marcel is clearly less disturbed
by his inability to account for this sense of felt
identity within the situation than by any suggestion

---

[1]HV 61.   [2]MBI 183 ff.

[3]HV 71.   [4]ECVQE 100-114; EBHD 41-42

[5]MBI 182-183.

111

of insularity.

In his many discussions of the situation as "open," Marcel likes to quote these lines from his play <u>Quartet in F Sharp</u>: "Yourself, himself . . . . Where does a personality begin? It was really you after all; don't you believe that each one of us is prolonged into whatever he creates?"[1] Whatever one may think of the possibilities for genuine intimacy or community between two human beings, one must characterize these lines as hyperbole. If anything, common wisdom suggests--and Marcel himself would seem to agree[2]--that what happens in moments of genuine intimacy is a sharpening of personality and individuality and not a blurring of the lines of personality. It is usually the person with a poorly developed sense of identity who is most incapable of intimacy with another human being. One must conclude, then, that here again Marcel prefers to emphasize the unity within the situation at the price of sharpening the reality of its components.

We have stressed, in these last pages, the first in a series of ambiguities that are to be found in Marcel's conceptual scheme. We shall pursue this theme in our critique of Marcel's epistemology in the chapter following and we shall see it emerge even more vividly in Marcel's discussion of religious faith at the end of this study. Here, the ambiguity stems from Marcel's view of the self as the paradigmatic mystery, or, in his own formulation, as <u>the</u> metaphysical issue. Marcel understands the self as "permeable" or open, and in motion, or progressively constituted by the ensemble of influxes that feed into it along the

---

[1] <u>CF</u> 35.

[2] "It is obvious that if I am a somebody, a particular individual, I am only so at once in connection with and in opposition to an indefinite number of other somebodies" (<u>MBI</u> 86).

dimensions of incarnation and intersubjectivity. In other words, the self comes to be through what he calls its "participation" in the existent universe, other persons and being--the other paradigmatic mysteries. Yet because all of this makes possible the integrated self with its felt identity, Marcel insists on characterizing it with one conceptual scheme. Hence the wide range of application of his primary categories and hence their inherent ambiguity.

If the difficulty with Marcel's understanding of the self is its inherent ambiguity, the difficulty with his treatment of being is its incompleteness. Our questions will become clearer if we try to locate Marcel's thought within the framework of the ontological tradition in philosophy.

Few concepts in philosophy have had as intricate a history as that of being. It has been variously understood as denoting the generic traits of everything that exists, as opposed to the particular traits that make anything what it distinctively is; as "reality as a whole," the unification --whether actual or mythical--of these generic traits into a single, all-embracing totality, as opposed to the diversity encountered in experience; or, as the ultimately real as opposed to the eternally changing appearances of the world as encountered.

More recently, though ontology has continued to play a central role in much of contemporary existentialism, other philosophical schools have dismissed the concept of being as neither designating nor referring to ". . . anything observable or discriminable in the world, as having neither a substantive nor attributive character."[1] That we _seem_ to be designating something when we

---

[1]Sidney Hook, The Quest for Being (New York: Dell Publishing Co. Inc., 1963), p. 164.

speak of being is the result of an unfortunate
peculiarity of language which does not permit us
to speak most generally of anything without first
substantifying these generalities and then abso-
lutising them.[1]

Marcel refuses to consider these latter-
day developments as worthy of serious philosophical investigation; he understands them as a
further symptom of the "broken-ness" of our func-
tionalised world and a result of the overweening
scientism of contemporary philosophical thought.
But it is more difficult--because of the incomplete, unsystematic and cryptic treatment this
already subtle theme receives in his writings--
to specify how Marcel would relate to the three
classical definitions enumerated above.

He would decisively reject the second of
the definitions as a throwback to idealism which
he devoted much of his mature philosophical
thought to opposing. He would be tempted by the
third definition as long as it did not identify
being with the traditional concept of substance
which he always viewed with suspicion because of
its excessively abstract quality. However he
would be intrigued with the first of the definitions; it suggests that being coalesces with
existence and Marcel, as we saw, was unable or
unwilling to distinguish too sharply between the
two as long as existence was identified with the
"existent universe" immediately participated in
by the individual. Understood in this way, it
leaves room for Marcel's view that existence reveals the face of being, or rather, in line with
Marcel's preference for the concrete, that the
existent as such can be grasped as being.

---

[1]F.J.E. Woodbridge, The Realm of Mind (New
York, 1926), pp. 33-34, quoted in J.H. Randall,
Jr., Nature and Historical Experience (New York:
Columbia University Press, 1958), pp. 126-127.

It is this last feature of Marcel's thought on being that is most striking. It reflects his ongoing preoccupation with avoiding abstractness and dualisms within the individual's metaphysical situation--this time between being and beings or between being and the world. Being is encountered precisely in beings and in the world--not as some new or extra entity beyond; being is encountered within experience--not beyond it. To love, hope in or be faithful to another--properly understood-- is to love, hope in or be faithful to being. Thus there is only a nominal difference between affirming or denying being and affirming or denying beings.

But if being is within both experience and the world, is Marcel not open to the charge that it does not in fact refer to any unique, observable or discriminable reality and should then be dismissed as superfluous? Can the situation not be described exhaustively without reference to being? Why then complicate the issue with the paraphernalia of a suspect ontology?

Marcel might respond by noting that what being refers to is not necessarily "a" distinctive reality, but rather to a different dimension of all of reality--that aspect of reality which escapes finitude or contingency, which resists functionalization or a reductionist analysis, which reveals the possibility of perennialness, which is ultimately desired or demanded, which becomes the ultimate value--and further, that what is needed beyond this listing is a way of referring to this dimension in a unified way. He would hasten to add that this unification should not be understood as an abstraction but rather as a "concrete totality" and to further clarify his thought, he would probably invoke one of his favorite metaphors, that of an orchestra playing a polyphonic work.

Each performer indeed plays his part in the ensemble; but it would be absurd to identify this ensemble with an arithmetical

sum of juxtaposed elements. But we can
very well imagine the process of thought
in the course of which the instrumentalist,
who in the beginning was conscious only of
the part which had been entrusted to him
. . . little by little becomes consciously
aware of the ensemble. And it is probable
that by that very fact the interpretation
of his own part will be transformed. It
is obvious that this concrete whole, namely,
the performance of the polyphonic work,
cannot be likened to an ideal. From the
viewpoint of the composer each part could
only be conceived as a function of the
whole. The whole precedes the parts, as
many philosophers, especially Kant, have
shown in the case of living organisms.[1]

This metaphor suggests the way in which an evolving
pattern can be seen as a unification in the process
of being created out of diverse elements--while
avoiding any suggestion of substantification or
abstraction.

That this does not represent all of reality,
Marcel would readily concede. But it is worth
noting that Marcel is completely consistent in re-
fusing to treat either being or its absence in anything but concrete or individual terms. Just as he
identifies being itself with its concrete manifestations, he avoids any attempt to substantify those
aspects of reality which do not reveal being.[2]
There is no hint in his writings that non-being or
the "nothing" constitutes a domain or has a distinctive power of its own. Both the presence and
absence of being are described in terms of their
felt quality within the individual situation. He
would also be the first to concede that not every-

---

[1] EBHD 78. Cf. MBII 187.

[2] TWB 73-75.

one is able to or willing to perceive the ensemble all the time. In fact, the entire enterprise is a highly precarious one and the momentary and evanescent glimpses that are afforded us should then be treasured above all.

Sidney Hook, one philosopher who dismisses the concept of being as neither designating nor referring to anything observable or discriminable in the world, nevertheless does not conclude that the term "ontological" cannot be consistently used. He proposes that we call "ontological," ". . . those statements . . . which we believe to be cognitively valid . . . and yet which are not found in any particular science . . . but which are obviously taken for granted by the sciences."[1] To the further question why philosophers select some features about the world for special attention, Hook replies that they do so

> . . . because of their belief that these
> features have special relevance to the
> career of human life on earth. Truths
> about them constitute what may be called
> philosophical anthropology . . . . Meta-
> physics in this sense gives us the kind
> of knowledge which, to indulge a fancy,
> a Platonic soul would like to have, after
> it has drunk the waters of Lethe, and
> before it descends, in answer to the ques-
> tions: What kind of a world am I going to
> live in? What is the life of man like on
> earth? The answers to these questions may
> be vague but they are significant. And it
> is arguable that to the extent that good
> literature as a vehicle of communication
> has a cognitive content what it says can
> be expressed as answers to such questions.[2]

---

[1]Hook, op. cit., p. 168

[2]Ibid., p. 170.

Marcel would undoubtedly agree.

Marcel claims that what holds the components of the situation together is a felt "intimacy." It is this intimacy, this "love"[1] that provides the situation with its circuits. But that task is traditionally assigned to knowledge. Marcel, then, has to define the conditions for an epistemology founded on love. He has emphasized that the traditional epistemology, bound as it is to the subject/object model, cannot understand love as anything but a subjective or contingent attitude of a subject toward an object.[2] His own early thought reflected the same inability to see love and knowledge as anything but antithetical.[3] His task then will be to provide an alternative to the traditional epistemology--one which will recognize the legitimately cognitive dimensions in love.

This, then, is the stimulus for Marcel's epistemology of the meta-problematical to which we now turn.

---

[1]". . . The domain of the meta-problematic coincides with love" (TPE 20).

[2]MJ 304.

[3]Ibid. 62-63.

CHAPTER IV

SACRED KNOWLEDGE

Marcel's Epistemological Categories

We have seen that Marcel's epistemological proposals are grounded in two distinctions: first, between "problem" and "mystery" and then, between "object" and "presence."[1] The first explicit formulation of the distinction appears in an extended journal entry dated October 22, 1932.[2] It reappears some pages later in an outline of an address later to be published as "Positions et approches concrètes au mystère ontologique."[3] All of his later writings refer back to these first two major formulations--often quoting them verbatim.[4]

---

[1]Marcel's use of a third basic distinction, between "being" and "having," is still a further recapitulation of much of what he has to say about problem and mystery. In general it may be said that an object can be "had" while a presence reveals being.

[2]BH 100-101.

[3]Ibid. 116. The address was published in 1933 as an appendix to Le Monde cassé and in English as "On the Ontological Mystery" in TPE.

[4]A portion of the first is quoted in EBHD 80 and of the second in MBI 211-212. Marcel suggests (Preface to MJ x) that the distinction clarifies and is anticipated in many of the entries in that work, e.g. p. 154, note 2 and pp. 288, 290,

Because of the significance of the October
1932 entry, it merits being reproduced here in its
entirety.

> . . . The phrase "mystery of being,
> ontological mystery" as against "problem
> of being, ontological problem" has suddenly
> come to me in these last few days. It has
> enlightened me.
> Metaphysical thought--reflection
> trained on mystery.
> But it is an essential part of a mys-
> tery that it should be acknowledged; meta-
> physical reflection presupposes this
> acknowledgment, which is outside its own
> sphere.
> Distinguish between the Mysterious and
> the Problematic. A problem is something
> met with which bars my passage. It is
> before me in its entirety. A mystery, on
> the other hand, is something in which I
> find myself caught up, and whose essence
> is therefore not to be before me in its
> entirety. It is as though in this province
> the distinction between in me and before me
> loses its meaning.
> The Natural. The province of the
> Natural is the same as the province of the

292-293. It is in fact anticipated even earlier
in Marcel's first philosophical writings, e.g.
PF 73-74. Further elaborations may be found inter
alia in TPE 18 ff.; HV 68-69; CF, chapter 1;
MBI, chapter 10. Gallagher, op. cit., pp. 30-31
traces the distinction to Royce. In support of
this, see MJ 326. The most sustained philosoph-
ical discussion both of this distinction and of
Marcel's entire epistemology is provided by
Jeanne Delhomme, "Témoignage et dialectique,"
Existentialisme chrétien: Gabriel Marcel (Paris:
Plon, 1947), pp. 117-201.

Problematic. We are tempted to turn mystery
into problem.

The Mysterious and Ontological are identical. There is a mystery of knowledge which
belongs to the ontological order (as Maritain
saw) but the epistemologist does not know
this, makes a point of ignoring it, and turns
it into a problem. A typical example: the
"problem of evil." I treat evil as an
accident befalling a certain mechanism which
is the universe itself, but before which I
suppose myself placed. Thereby I treat myself, not only as immune to the disease or
weakness, but also as someone standing outside the universe and claiming to put it
together (at least in thought) in its entirety.

But what access can I have to ontology
as such? The very notion of access here is
obviously inapplicable. It only has meaning in a problematic inquiry. If a certain
place has already been plotted out, the
question is then, how can I gain access to
it. Impossible to treat being in this way.

Presence and mystery equivalent--probe
further into this.

Predisposition for revelation. Whereas
in a world-picture constructed from a problematic point of view, revelation appears
as supererogatory.

It follows from my definition of metaphysical thought as reflection trained
upon mystery, that progress in this sort
of thinking is not really conceivable.
There is only progress in problematic thought.

It is a proper character of problems,
moreover, to be reduced to detail. Mystery,
on the other hand, is something which cannot
be reduced to detail.[1]

---

[1] BH 100-101. Italics Marcel's.

In regard to the object/presence distinction--apart from the claim that "presence and mystery (are) equivalent"--Marcel affirms that there is an "organic connection" between mystery and presence for ". . . every presence is mysterious . . . and it is very doubtful whether the word 'mystery' can really be properly used in the case where a presence is not at the very least making itself felt."[1] In general the realm of mystery is inhabited by presences, the realm of problem, by objects. More precisely, a problem is an issue posed by an object; a mystery is an issue posed by a presence.

On the basis of these texts and subsequent discussions in Marcel's writings, and following the schema suggested by Kenneth Gallagher,[2] Marcel seems to be suggesting that problems and mysteries differ in four ways.

1. They differ, first, in their intrinsic characteristics as perceived by a subject. An object is distinct from or external to me, totally exposed before me, with "handles" that permit me to "have" it, manipulate or transmit it to some other subject. Marcel emphasizes this "insular" character of the object: "The object as such is defined as being independent of the characteristics that make me this particular person . . . . Thus it is essential to the very nature of the object not to take 'me' into account: if I think it as having regard to me, in that measure I cease to treat it as an object."[3] Because of this insular character, an object is public and it poses problems[4] as

---

[1]MBI 216.

[2]Gallagher, op. cit., chapter 3.

[3]MJ 261. Italics Marcel's.

[4]Marcel notes the etymology of "problem" as connoting something which is "placed before me" (MMS 66). "Object lends itself to a similar etymological interpretation.

122

exemplified primarily in the subject matter of
science and related fields. In fact an immense
portion of the fund of human knowledge results from
man's dealings with problems because much of reality can be treated exclusively as object.

But there are portions of reality that do
not permit themselves to be treated _exclusively_ as
objects and there are even more significant portions
of reality which _in no way_ permit this treatment.
We refer to these as "presence." A presence involves me; it is part of me, or within me, or joins
with me in a larger whole. More generally, the
inner/outer dichotomy no longer applies. A presence poses a mystery. Marcel's classic characterization of mystery appears many times in his work:
"A mystery is a problem that encroaches upon the
intrinsic conditions of its own possibility
. . . ."[1] This is hardly a definition, suggesting
as it does that a mystery is a problem that is not
a problem. However, it does indicate the way in
which a mystery overflows the tightly-knit confines
of insularity of a problem.

To the extent that reality is progressively
less detachable from the self without annihilating
that very self, it partakes more and more of a mystery.[2] It also properly becomes the concern of
metaphysics which is "reflection trained on mystery."[3] Thus the central, or umbrella issue for
metaphysics is the nature of the self. But Marcel's
most illuminating discussions of the distinction
are reserved for those realities which can be
treated either as object or presence such as "_my_
body," which can be either _a_ body or _my_ body;
another human being, who can be either a problematic _him_ or a mysterious _thou_; or the so-called

---

[1]_BH_ 126. Marcel uses a similar formulation
in his first discussion of the "problem of being"
(_BH_ 117).

[2]_HV_ 138.   [3]_BH_ 101.

"external world"--i.e. what Marcel calls "the existent universe"--which can be treated precisely as "external" to me, or as he contends, integral to me and involving me as a prolongation of _my_ body-- though he concedes that within "the existent universe" there are realities which can be treated exclusively and legitimately as objects.

The self, being, and knowledge itself are paradigmatic instances of presence. Much of Marcel's writings are devoted to the ways in which we are "tempted" to turn presence into object and mystery into problem, how and why this occurs, and what results from this reduction. His central epistemological concern is to delineate those distinctive processes of thought appropriate to dealing with the mysterious.

One final note: In common parlance we use the term "objective" as synonymous with "detached" and opposed to "involved" to indicate that we are relatively free from emotion about a particular issue. Marcel would insist that this is a derivative meaning. We are free from emotion because we are _literally_ not "involved," i.e. "wrapped up" in the issue; it does not bear upon anything that is part of us.

2. Problems and mysteries differ in the kinds of activities they call forth from the subject. Problems call forth inquiries which lead to solutions. A problem is solvable--sooner or later-- because it lies exposed to the subject and can be grappled with by anyone who has or can acquire the necessary skill--i.e. by just about anybody. Both the inquiry and the solution participate in the "objective" character of the problem: each is detachable and transmissible to another subject without distortion.[1] Hence the cumulative character of scientific knowledge. Each solution to a scientific

---

[1]_MBI_ 213.

problem is a legitimate and more or less permanent
acquisition to the fund of knowledge.[1] Mysteries
permit of no such mastery by the subject.

> A presence is something which can only be
> gathered to oneself or shut out from one-
> self, be welcomed or rebuffed; . . . I
> cannot gather to myself or welcome what is
> purely or simply an object; I can only, in
> some sense, take it or else leave it. It
> goes without saying that the kind of taking
> or prehension I am thinking of is apprehen-
> sion by the intelligence, or, in a word,
> comprehension. In so far as a presence, as
> such, lies beyond the grasp of any possible
> prehension, one might say that it also in
> some sense lies beyond the grasp of any
> possible comprehension. A presence can, in
> the last analysis only be invoked or evoked
> . . . .[2]

We shall see how we go about invoking a
mystery. For the present, Marcel claims that what
makes a problem solvable is its public character;
this permits it to be accessible to transmissible
techniques, public testing and means of verification which insure that the solution is valid and
that the problem will remain solved. This is what
happens in science. But the history of philosophy
confirms that the central issues of philosophical
reflection have resisted solutions of this kind.
Hence Marcel's diatribes against the futility of
claiming to present final solutions to the "problems" of philosophy. Philosophical issues resist
this kind of resolution not because they are more
profound or more difficult; the mystery is not
simply an unsolved problem. It stems rather from

---

[1]TPE 123. For anticipations of these comments, see MJ 288, 292.

[2]MBI 208. Italics Marcel's.

the fact that the philosopher is "involved" in his data, not only because he cares passionately about the outcome, but because he _is_ the data, he is at the heart of the data, be it the nature or the self, being, knowledge, the ethical--whatever. This is why in philosophy ". . . the stage always remains to be set; . . . everything always starts from zero . . ." and this ". . . perpetual beginning again . . . is an inevitable part of all genuinely philosophical work."[1]

The philosopher, then, is left with two alternatives: he can turn mystery into problem and present his solution as objectively valid--which is futile; or he can acknowledge the mysterious character of the issue, trace the course of his reflection to his sympathetic audience as _his_ reflection, and appeal to others to take up their own.

3. Problems and mysteries differ in the status they accord to the subject. Because the object is accessible to anyone, the subject can be any one; he is anonymous, impersonal and hence interchangeable.[2] In face of a mystery, however, the subject is singular and his presence is indispensable, precisely because these various presences make him what he is in all his singularity. Thus the metaphysician is a witness, not an onlooker, and hence irreplaceable. As a corollary to this, evoking the mystery has the character of giving testimony.[3]

4. Finally, we speak of problems and mysteries in differing states of mind or with differing affect. Problems are confronted with a thirst

---

[1]_TPE_ 125.

[2]_MJ_ 208, 298, 314; _TPE_ 91-103, 120; _BH_ 120-121.

[3]_TPE_ 96-97.

for acquiring solutions and the control or power
that will result. There is a sense of confidence,
a feeling of mastery for with enough time and
effort, the inquirer will win out. We confront the
mystery, in contrast, with feelings of "wonder,"
"astonishment," "awe," "reverence" and "piety."[1]
It is with this in mind that Marcel will use the
term "sacred knowledge" to refer to the knowledge
of the mystery in contrast to the "profane knowledge" of the problematic, though he is careful to
point out that "sacred knowledge" need not have a
religious reference.[2]

Problems and mysteries differ then in their
intrinsic characteristics as perceived by the subject, in the activities they call forth from the
subject, in the status they accord the subject and
in the affect with which their distinctive questions are raised.

Marcel insists that these two realms demand
two separate epistemologies for the mystery, as we
have seen, is not the unknowable. Recognition of
the mystery ". . . is an essentially positive act
of the mind, the supremely positive act in virtue
of which all positivity may be strictly defined"[3]
anticipating his later claim that the certainty
conveyed by sacred knowledge far exceeds that of
scientific knowledge. Metaphysics is ". . . _reflec-_
tion trained on mystery";[4] the "unknowable" is

---

[1]These terms are from Marcel's monograph
"Peter Wust on the Nature of Piety," BH 213-236.
Peter Wust (1884-1940) was a German philosopher
one of whose works was entitled Naivität und
Pietät.

[2]The terms were suggested by Wust. BH 21,
189-190, 216.

[3]Ibid. 118.

[4]Ibid. 101. Italics mine.

simply the limit of the problematic.[1] The mystery
does not take us beyond experience ". . . for
beyond all experience, there is nothing . . . . It
would surely be much more true to say that what is
our problem here is how to substitute a certain
mode of experience for other modes."[2] More recently, he has identified his concern as to define
the conditions for a "reconstructive reflection"
and ". . . to bring it about in an intelligent and
intelligible way, and not by some kind of appeal to
purely subjective intuitions."[3] Reflection on the
mystery is simply another kind of reflection, an
adaptation of the intelligence to new kinds of
evidence. In another context, he claims that the
metaphysical unease which marks the beginning of
philosophy ". . . can only find peace in knowledge.
But of what knowledge is there a question here?
The metaphysician seems to deny his own vocation if
he does not proclaim that he is seeking 'truth';
but what is truth?"[4] The answer is a kind of
knowledge and truth that are distinct both from
science and from purely subjective intuition. The
distinction between problem and mystery is designed
to safeguard different ways of gaining knowledge,
not to circumscribe the field of knowledge itself.
To clarify these distinctive processes with as much
rigor as possible is the main purpose of his epistemology.

    That the traditional epistemology could not
account for knowledge of the mystery was clear to
Marcel long before the mystery/problem distinction
received its explicit formulation. An entry in the
Metaphysical Journal puts the question this way:

----

[1]Ibid. 118.

[2]MBI 47-48.

[3]TWB 229. Italics mine.

[4]HV 139.

The further I proceed, the more I am struck
by the fact that epistemological preoccupations tend to put our minds in a state in
which we can never resolve or even solve
the problem of love. For the theory of
knowledge has the essential task of at one
and the same time defining objectivity and
finding a basis for it. It gravitates
around the idea of the object, hence it
postulates that it is at least possible
for the subject to disentangle from the
heart of his concrete experience everything
that involves no personal contribution on
his part; and this though it sets aside the
metaphysical question of how an object can
be present to a subject. The subject-
object relation is presupposed in any epistemology whatsoever.[1]

In other words, the task is to define an epistemology that is liberated from the subject-object model
in order to be able to deal with the kind of knowledge involved in e.g.,the love of the lover for his
beloved. But as we shall see, that there is an
epistemological dimension to love is a claim that
Marcel substantiates not by any definition of
"knowledge" but rather by his phenomenological
descriptions of what happens when one loves another
as "person," i.e. as "presence."[2]

Reflection in Metaphysics

.The distinction between mystery and problem,
then, leads to a further distinction, this one affecting not _what_ we know, but rather _how_ various
aspects of reality are known, i.e. to a discrimina-
tion within the reflective process. The key to

---

[1]_MJ_ 304.

[2]As in e.g. _BH_ 105-107.

this further distinction lies in Marcel's claim
that reflection itself cannot be an object, external to the intelligence. It is not transparent
to itself; it cannot give a coherent account of
itself.[1] To the question: how can something which
cannot be reduced to a problem be actually thought?
he answers: "The contradiction implied in the fact
of thinking of a mystery falls to the ground of
itself when we cease to cling to an objectified and
misleading picture of thought."[2]

    Reflection can only be "grasped as such"[3]
so to speak in the process of its operation. But
that "grasping" is itself an act of the mind, itself a reflection, hence "a reflection at one
remove"[4] or a "reflection upon this reflection
(. . . a reflection 'squared'). By means of this,
thought stretches out towards the recovery of an
intuition which loses itself in proportion as it is
exercised."[5] This reflection which, at the very
least, consists in apprehending every objective
representation of itself as inadequate, is ". . .
the essential metaphysical step,"[6] where metaphysics is defined as the realm of the mysterious.

----

[1] BH 126, 215.

[2] BH 126. The French reads: ". . . la
contradiction . . . tombe d'elle même si l'on
cesse . . ." (Etre et avoir, p. 183).

[3] BH 126.

[4] Ibid. In Marcel's earliest writings, it
is referred to as a "later act reflection" (PF 75).
Cf. MJ 212.

[5] BH 118.

[6] Ibid. Marcel returns here to his earliest
epistemological critique of idealism (above, pp. 35-
38).

. 130

After many vagaries of terminology, Marcel finally characterizes this reflection upon a reflection as "secondary reflection." It stands in contrast to "primary reflection" which is the ordinary or objective reflection by which a subject comes to know an object. His classical statement of the distinction appears in The Mystery of Being: "Roughly we can say that where primary reflection tends to dissolve the unity of experience which is first put before us, the function of secondary reflection is essentially recuperative; it reconquers that unity."[1]

This formulation, with its reference to a "recuperative" reflection which "reconquers" a previous unity--and its various other characterizations such as "recollection" and "reprise" suggests that what we are dealing with here is a reflexive act of some kind, a return to or a recapturing of some intellectual act which pre-dates even primary reflection. Much the same is conveyed by Marcel's many references to secondary reflection as an act of relaxation, withdrawal, or abandonment of control over the intellectual process. This has to be understood in the context of his view of profane knowledge as a more or less permanent acquisition, an instance of "having" an object of knowledge which the subject thus controls and transmits. The knowledge gained by secondary reflection can in no way be "had"; it is achieved by allowing the mind to slip back in time to an earlier moment in the life of the mind, to swim against the tide of progressively controlling or acquiring profane knowledge.[2]

But if secondary reflection is a return to an earlier moment in the process of reflection, if

---

[1] MBI 83; cf. TWB 235.

[2] TPE 23-24; BH 113; MMS 68-69; EBHD 86-87.

131

primary reflection is <u>dis</u>-junctive, and secondary
reflection is <u>re</u>-cuperative, this suggests that
there must be three moments in our "awareness" (the
most vacuous term possible) of the world. The
third, as we have seen, is "secondary reflection";
the second is "primary reflection"; the first,
again after much uncertainty as to terminology, is
ultimately identified as "intuition aveuglée," or
"blinded intuition."[1]

      Marcel uses this characterization pre-
eminently to refer to the primitive affirmation of
being through me by the very fact that I am. It is
an ". . . affirmation that I <u>am</u> rather than an
affirmation that I <u>utter</u> . . . an affirmation . . .
<u>of which I am the stage rather than the subject</u>."[2]
In an earlier formulation, Marcel uses the phrase
"reflexive intuition":

> It seems to me that I am bound to admit
> that I am--anyhow on one level of myself--
> face to face with Being. In a sense I see
> it. In another sense I cannot say that I
> see it since I cannot grasp myself in the
> act of seeing it. The intuition is not,
> and cannot be, directly reflected in con-
> sciousness. But in turning towards its
> object, it sheds light upon a whole world
> of thoughts which lie beneath it.[3]

In another context, he expresses discomfort at the
term "intuition." This is not an intuition that
can be "given"; it cannot "figure in a collection,"
nor can it be "isolated" or "uncovered"; hence it
cannot be remembered or represented to myself. In
fact, "the more an intuition is central and basic

---

    [1]<u>MJ</u> x.

    [2]<u>TPE</u> 17; italics Marcel's.

    [3]<u>BH</u> 98. Hence the "blinded" intuition.

in the being whom it illuminates, the less it is capable of turning back and apprehending itself." Finally, he concludes: "Rather than to speak of intuition in this context, we should say that we are dealing with an assurance which underlies the entire development of thought, even of discursive thought; it can therefore be approached only by a second reflection . . . ."[1]

In other words, prior to any hold which the intelligence can have on being, there is an even more primitive hold which being has on the affirming or knowing subject which creates his reality as subject in the first place.[2] This is what leads Marcel to claim that cognition is itself a mystery for it is environed by being.

Though the pre-eminent instance of the blinded intuition is this pre-reflective affirmation of being in me, it can be said to be present whenever there is an encounter of the reflecting subject with a portion of reality that does not lend itself to be understood as totally other than that subject, i.e. with any instance of presence or mystery. Hence there is a blinded intuition of my body as _mine_, of the existent universe as encompassing me, and of other selves to the extent that they are "with" me in community. The second of these is apparently what Marcel, in other contexts, characterizes as sensation.[3]

---

[1]_TPE_ 25.

[2]"We are involved in Being and it is not in our power to leave it: more simply _we are_, and our whole inquiry is just how to place ourselves in relation to plenary Reality" (_BH_ 35).

[3]_CF_ 24-26; _MJ_ 327-332; _MBI_ 105-108. We have found no explicit identification of sensation as a blinded intuition. There are two possible reasons for this. First, the _locus classicus_ for

In each of these instances, the blinded intuition functions in two ways: first, it denotes the primitive, pre-reflective unity of the reflecting subject and what is to be known (not the "object" of knowledge), which unity, primary reflection is destined to sever into subject and object, and which secondary reflection, then, _may_ recapture. Second, it functions as an implicit criterion which highlights the inadequacies of any rendering of these experiences in terms of primary reflection and thus serves as stimulus for secondary reflection.

Finally, it should be emphasized that like the intuition of being in Marcel's earliest work, the blinded intuition itself does not constitute knowledge. It is pre-reflective, below the threshold of awareness, not even affirmable in speech. It only becomes knowledge when it is recaptured on a conscious level by secondary reflection. This is why Marcel uses the term "intuition" in these contexts, and immediately qualifies it as "blinded." In another context, it is an intuition which ". . . I possess without . . . knowing myself to possess it."[1] Significantly, though, he feels more comfortable with "assurance" than with "intuition." To the question: if the blinded intuition is pre-reflective or pre-cognitive, how can we "say" or "know" anything about it? Marcel would probably

---

Marcel's views on sensation is Part two of _MJ_ and "Existence and Objectivity," while the blinded intuition is first discussed some years later in _BH_. Second, Marcel usually reserves the blinded intuition for his discussion of being. However, ample justification for this identification can be found in the three references listed above.

[1]_BH_ 118.

answer: only indirectly,[1] by its serving as a
critique of primary reflection and a stimulus for
secondary reflection. In other words the disjunc-
tive effects of primary reflection and the recuperative effects of secondary reflection require
some prior stage in the life of the mind, if they
are to be intelligible.

Marcel rarely discusses primary or secondary reflection in the abstract but his work is
studded with examples of these processes at work.
His most illuminating discussions of the first deal
with the way in which primary reflection handles
the blinded intuition of "my body."

If I abstract from the index characterizing
my body--insofar as it is mine--if I con-
strue it as one body among an unlimited
number of other such bodies, I will be
forced to treat it as an object, as exhibit-
ing the fundamental properties of objectivity. It then becomes an object of scientific
knowledge; it becomes problematic, so to
speak, but only on condition that I consider
it as not-mine; and this detachment which is
essentially illusory, is the very basis of
all cognition. As knowing subject, I re-
establish or claim to re-establish that
dualism between my body and me, that interval which, we have learned, is inconceivable
from an existential point of view. A subject of this kind can be established only if
existence is first renounced; it is, it can
be said, only on condition that it considers
itself not to be. This paradox is fundamental for the object, for I can really
think about the object only if I acknowledge

---

[1]The intuition can ". . . grasp itself
only through the modes of experience in which its
image is reflected, and which it lights up by being
thus reflected in them" (idem.).

that I do not count for it, that it does not take me into account.[1]

Marcel elaborates the meaning of that last sentence:

> . . . the more I emphasize the objectivity
> of things, thus cutting the umbilical cord
> which binds them to existence and to what
> has been termed my psycho-presence to my-
> self, the more I affirm the independence
> of the world from me, its radical indif-
> ference to my destiny, to my goals; the
> more, too, this world, proclaimed as the
> only real one, is converted into an illu-
> sory spectacle, a great documentary film
> presented for my curiosity, but ultimately
> abolished simply because it disregards me.
> . . . What this amounts to is that the act
> of trying to break the nexus uniting me to
> the universe . . . is a purely abstract
> act.[2]

A number of points here merit discussion.

First, primary reflection is wedded to objectivity. One can only exercise primary reflection on an "object." This provides a criterion for
its legitimacy; primary reflection is legitimate
when and to the extent that what is known has the
qualities of an object and illegitimate when what
is known cannot be considered an object--either at
all or in part. Marcel's further identification
of objective knowledge as "scientific" is his way
of defining the distinctive scope and legitimacy of
that enterprise.

---

[1]CF 20. Cf. MBI 92-94 for another version
of the same discussion. Further examples of primary
reflection at work are: on sensation, MBI 105-108;
on faith, MBII 63-67; on prayer, MBII 106-107.

[2]CF 20-21.

Second, by virtue of the fact that primary reflection deals only with objects, it establishes the status of the subject that exercises that reflection as impersonal and hence interchangeable.

Third, primary reflection is likened to a technique which is transmissible from one impersonal subject to another. It eventuates in some piece of knowledge which can be "had"[1] and which is a more or less permanent acquisition to the fund of knowledge. Hence the cumulative character of scientific knowledge.

Thus far, Marcel has been simply echoing the implications of his distinction between object and presence. But the passage has more startling implications for the traditional dissociation of the object of knowledge from the subject. Note that the object is portrayed as "not taking me into account"; by emphasizing objectivity, I affirm "the independence of the world from me (and) its radical indifference to my destiny, to my goals."

This passage goes far to establish two central features of Marcel's thought: his conviction, first, that love is an epistemological category[2] and second, that there is an essential continuity between the dimensions of incarnation and intersubjectivity. If anything, it re-enforces our previous conclusion that Marcel's understanding of incarnation is patterned on that of intersubjectivity. For it is one thing to say of the one I claim to love that he "does not take me into account" or that he is "indifferent to my destiny, to my goals," but it is quite another thing to make that claim of the existent universe. That Marcel can ascribe this "indifference" of the world to

---

[1] BH 145-146.

[2] MJ 304; TPE 20; earlier (MJ 62-63) love and knowledge were antithetical.

primary <u>reflection</u>, i.e. to an act of the <u>mind</u>, suggests the very extended sense in which he understands cognition. We will return to this below.

The critique of the subject/object structure of epistemology is a common theme in existentialist literature. Marcel lends the discussion of this theme his own distinctive emphases which are mainly metaphysical and social: it falsifies the picture of man's "situation" as "being-in-the-world" (i.e. it is "illusory") and it leads to an excessively depersonalized and functionalized view of the human being. The first of these merits more extended discussion in this context.

Marcel's fundamental critique of primary reflection, as we have seen, is that it inevitably issues in a series of dualisms; this is why it is "illusory," for the separation once established, one or the other of the poles is absolutized and the most inventive mind cannot put them together again.

This is the basis for his critique of rationalism, particularly of Descartes. Descartes begins with the knowing subject as the indubitable point of departure for philosophy. But having isolated and absolutized the subject as thinker, he can no longer account for the subject's felt identity with his body--which becomes simply a portion of extended substance possessed by the subject; Marcel's description of the phenomenon of "having" or "owning" is designed to expose the limitations of that model as a satisfactory account of the relation between self and body.[1]

With the deprecation of the body as a constituent of the self, Descartes must play down the role of sensation in knowledge and hence erect another dualism, this time between the self and the

---

[1]<u>MBI</u> 95-102; <u>BH</u> 154-174.

world. In fact, the very existence of the latter is cast in doubt: at best, it becomes a "spectacle" arrayed before the knowing self, which hardly accounts for the way in which the self participates in the world, initiates action which affects the world or is in turn affected by the way in which the world is present to the self. Nor, finally, is it possible to make any sense of the fact that the self, understood as knowing subject, can love another person.

But neither does strict empiricism, for its part, do justice to "the unity of experience." Empiricism cannot distinguish any portion of experience as having a privileged status in that it affects or even constitutes me exclusively, which is just the way "my body" or the other selves that I love, hope in or am faithful to appear to me.

Marcel counters these dualisms with his theory of "the fundamental metaphysical situation" in which the self is embedded or which is the self. The "situation" pulls together a massive "unity of experience" which is conveyed in the blinded intuitions which lie just below the self's awareness of its situation, which primary reflection, in its knowledge-building operations, has to dissolve, and which secondary reflection tries to recapture.

Marcel most frequently defines secondary reflection in negative terms as the refusal to accept primary reflection as an exhaustive account of the cognitive process or its conclusions as ultimate: ". . . there is . . . an inverse movement, a movement of retrieval, which consists in becoming aware of the partial and even suspect character of the purely analytical procedure."[1] Secondary reflection manifests itself, then, in the refusal to treat my body as an object detachable

---

[1]TWB 235. Cf. CF 22 where primary reflection is identified as "fallacious."

from me, sensation as a communication of messages, the world as a spectacle arrayed before me, love as subjective, faith as arbitrary, prayer as an interior disposition or hope as unsupported by evidence.[1]

More positively, in the continuation to the above passage, the task of secondary reflection is to ". . . reconstruct, but now at the level of thought, that concrete state of affairs which had previously been glimpsed in a fragmented or pulverized condition."[2] Or, in another context which specifies the place of secondary reflection in the reflective process, he defines this reflection as

> . . . a reconstructive reflection grafted upon a critical reflection; a reflection which is a recovery, but only insofar as it remains the tributary of what I have called a blindfold intuition. It is clear that the apprehension of the ontological mystery as metaproblematic is the motive force of this recovery through reflection. But we must not fail to notice that it is a reflexive motion of the mind that is here in question, and not a heuristic process. The proof can only confirm for us what has really been given to us in another way.[3]

Or again, in the context of a discussion of interpersonal intimacy: "it is of the essence of genuine . . . intimacy, to lend itself to the decomposition to which it is subjected by critical thought; but

---

[1] MBI 92-93; MBII 62, 66-67, 98, 106; HV 66-67; CF 22.

[2] TWB 235.

[3] BH 126. The context is a discussion of the efficacy of proofs for the existence of God.

we already know that there exists another kind of
thought, a thought which bears upon that thought
itself, and is related to a bottled up yet effica-
cious underlying intuition, of which it suffers the
attraction."[1] Or finally, on the blinded intuition
of being:

> . . . we are dealing with an assurance which
> underlies the entire development of thought,
> even of discursive thought; it can therefore
> be approached only by a second reflection--a
> reflection whereby I ask myself how and from
> what starting point I was able to proceed in
> my initial reflection, which itself postu-
> lated the ontological, but without knowing
> it. This second reflection is recollection
> in the measure in which recollection can be
> self-conscious.[2]

In other words, and to summarize, secondary
reflection can be said to reflect on primary reflection, to be stimulated by the blinded intuition,
to be a self-conscious reflection and to be set in
motion by a deliberate act of the will freely
undertaken, i.e. by a _refusal_ to accept the conclusions of primary reflection as ultimate and
decisive.

It is understandable, then, why Marcel has
little more to say of a _positive_ nature about
secondary reflection. It is fundamentally an
attempt to _counter_ the conclusions of primary reflection and to allow the original blinded intuition to rise to consciousness and assume its full
weight. The many examples of secondary reflection
at work which dot Marcel's writings are usually
extended phenomenological descriptions of specific
experiences designed to demonstrate the inadequacies

---

[1]_TPE_ 39.

[2]Ibid. 25. "Recollection" is an earlier
formula for "secondary reflection."

141

of the various philosophical accounts of the experience from the traditional subject/object
perspective.

To continue the example of _my_ body, Marcel
discusses the various dualistic theories of the
mind-body relationship including psycho-physical
parallelism, psycho-physical interactionism, the
body as "owned" by the self, the body as "instrument" of the self--all designed to show the gap
between these accounts and the blinded intuition
which Marcel tries to convey by the claim "I _am_ my
body."[1] This polemical activity should be understood as a clearing of the ground for secondary
reflection.

The negative characterizations of secondary
reflection also reflect Marcel's doubt that this
reflection can ever be perfectly realized, or
"grasped"--these awkward formulations are the best
index of the difficulty here. If realized, it can
hardly be expressed in language which is even more
tightly bound to the subject/object structure.
Primary reflection constantly reasserts itself and
the intuition is pulverized once again. When
Marcel describes the lot of the philosopher as
doomed to a "perpetual beginning again"[2] he is
describing not only philosophical thought in its
technical form but secondary reflection as it manifests itself within life experience.

Secondary reflection lives off or is
"attracted" by the blinded intuition which persists
as an implicit criterion for measuring the conclusions of primary reflection and as a springboard to
go beyond these. Secondary reflection then differs
from primary in the _direction_ of the thought
process. Primary reflection moves towards greater

---

[1]_MBI_ 92-102.

[2]_TPE_ 125.

and greater abstractness, away from the immediately lived experience; secondary reflection focuses back on to the intuition in the direction of greater concreteness and immediacy. But again it is difficult to speak of secondary reflection in as "aggressive" a manner as this implies; hence Marcel's preference for seeing it as a form of relaxation, a moving away from the controlling features of primary reflection thus allowing the intuition to rise to consciousness--the ground having been cleared by the polemic against the conclusions of primary reflection.[1]

But what is most distinctive about secondary reflection is that it is set in motion by a

---

[1]Gallagher, op. cit., pp. 45-46 suggests the analogy of artistic creation. The influence of Bergson in all of this material, particularly his notion of intuition as developed in The Creative Mind, is striking. For example, Bergson writes that for the mind to grasp "flowing reality," ". . . it must do violence, reverse the direction of the operation by which it ordinarily thinks, continually upsetting its categories . . . . In so doing it will arrive at fluid concepts, capable of following reality in all its windings and of adopting the very movement of the inner life of things . . . . To philosophize means to reverse the normal direction of the workings of thought" (Henri Bergson, The Creative Mind, trans. by Mabelle L. Andison [Totowa, N.J.: Littlefield, Adams and Co., 1965], p. 190; italics Bergson's). More generally, Bergson's concluding summary to his "Introduction to Metaphysics," one of the papers in this collection, is rich in anticipations of Marcel's thought (pp. 188-200). On Bergson's influence on Marcel, see Etienne Gilson, "Un Exemple" in Existentialisme chrétien: Gabriel Marcel (Paris: Plon, 1947), pp. 1-8, and Marcel's contribution to The Bergsonian Heritage, ed. by Thomas Hanna (New York: Columbia University Press, 1962), pp. 123-132.

totally free act of the individual.

The participation which involves my presence to the world, however, cannot be affirmed, cannot be found again nor restored,
unless I resist the temptation to deny it,
i.e. to assume that I am a separate entity.

An objection may be raised: There is no
reason to use the term "temptation" here.
If your argument is valid we have no
choice. Can there be a choice between what
is reasonable and meaningful and what is
absurd: There can be, for the essence of
the absurd for a being like myself is just
its capacity to be preferred, usually on
the condition that it is not identified as
such. This reflection of the second degree
or philosophical reflection exists only for
and by means of freedom; nothing external
to me can force me to exercise it in this
respect; the very notion of constraint in
this context is devoid of content . . . .
My undeniable ability to pursue or not a
sequence of thoughts is, in the final analysis, only a mode of attention, and can be
immediately exercised; hence we can confirm
the fact that our freedom is implied in the
awareness of our participation in the universe.[1]

The "sequence of thoughts," here, is secondary reflection which is set in motion only if I refuse to
accept the conclusions of primary reflection as
final, complete and satisfactory. There is no
question of proof here, then, neither from logic
nor from experience, as would be appropriate in
primary reflection. Ultimately, the issue comes
down to an option--a "pre-philosophical" option, as

----

[1]CF 22-23. Hence his definition of metaphysics as a "logic of freedom" (ibid. 26).

144

Collins describes it[1]--for or against the kind of resolutions of secondary reflection.

At a number of critical points in his writings, Marcel dwells at length on the subtleties involved in the exercise of this option. One of the more recent (1951) of these discussions--climaxing an extended meditation on the "problem" of survival after death--is most revealing.

> I will add that for the being still not set free who I am, this invincible assurance (that the being whom I love remains present after death, N.G.) is reinforced _indirectly_ through facts which are evidences or more exactly breaches: breaches in the prison in which I enclose myself as soon as I hypnotize myself with what is objectively given. I said "reinforced," I did not say "grounded" . . . . This world of ours is so structured that I can find around me every reason for despairing, for seeing in death the annihilation and the miserable keyword of the incomprehensible existence into which I have been senselessly thrown. But to a deeper reflection, this world appears simultaneously as being so constituted that I can become conscious in it of the power I retain to withstand these appearances . . . . But I will add . . . that metaphysical reflection . . . permit(s) me to select signs capable of conferring on this free act a minimum guarantee which I need. I need this guarantee because despite everything I continue to remain the center of a critical and polemic reflection, which, if it does not overcome itself, is secretly attracted by despair and nothingness. These signs have a consistency just sufficient for doing their job; if they were proofs, my freedom

---

[1]Collins, op. cit., p. 166.

before death would be as it were annulled
and so . . . life as well as death would
find itself stripped of its seriousness,
the sacrifice shorn of its tragic and
ultimate grandeur.[1]

The single context in which Marcel submits
the notion of proof in philosophy to a serious
analysis is his discussions of the proofs for the
existence of God[2] which we will discuss below. But
the outline of what he has to say emerges from this
passage as well. He is clearly shying away from an
out-and-out voluntarism; the will may play a central role in the drama but it requires the clarify-
ing powers of the intellect, first to expose the
inadequacies of primary reflection, and second to
integrate on the level of consciousness and through
secondary reflection, those cardinal experiences
where man breaks out of the "prison" of objectivity.
On the other hand, these intellectual operations
can only "reinforce"; they cannot "ground," not
only because they are not intrinsically decisive
but more because they lack the ability to convince
either myself or another. They cannot convince
because proof as a function of objective thought
requires the interchangeability of the subject and
this does not apply in metaphysics. This distinction between the intrinsic force of an argument and
its ability to convince brings Marcel back to the
role of the will. Finally, were the proofs to be
decisive and convincing, they would assume a coercive power which would strip me of my freedom.

Ultimately, though, it is the individual as
a concrete unity--not the will nor the intellect
alone--who opts, and the exercise of this option is
a direct outgrowth of the degree of permeability
which permeates his situation and makes these

---

[1]PI 242-244. Cf. BH 110-111, 118-119; TWB
227-229.

[2]MBII 173-180; CF 175-183; BH 121.

146

decisive experiences possible. Thus the "pre-philosophical" locus of the option; it encourages or discourages permeability which is ultimately the ground-tone of all of Marcel's epistemology.

How then do we establish the validity of the results of secondary reflection? How are they to be verified? How can we be sure that they are not illusory? Marcel seems to deal with these questions in a categorical way:

> To think, or rather, to assert, the meta-problematical is to assert it as indubitably real, as a thing of which we cannot doubt without falling into contradiction. We are in a sphere where it is no longer possible to dissociate the idea itself from the certainty or the degree of certainty which pertains to it. Because this idea _is_ certainty, it _is_ the assurance of itself . . . .[1]

This is Marcel's most characteristic position on the issue of verification of sacred knowledge.[2] Here he understands verifiability as linked to primary reflection where conclusions are public, subjects interchangeable, and reflection linked to a transmissible skill. None of this applies to secondary reflection. According to this stance, the issue of verifiability in secondary reflection is dismissed as irrelevant. Consider, for example, this discussion of the possible illusory quality of hope:

> To hope against all hope that a person whom I love will recover from a disease which is said to be incurable is to say: It is impossible that I should be alone in willing this

---

[1] _TPE_ 22-23.

[2] But, as we shall see, it is not his exclusive position.

cure; it is impossible that reality in its
inward depth should be hostile or so much as
indifferent to what I assert is in itself a
good. It is quite useless to tell me of
discouraging cases or examples: beyond all
experience, all probability, all statistics,
I assert that a given order shall be re-
established, that reality is on my side in
willing it to be so. I do not wish: I
assert; such is the prophetic tone of true
hope.

No doubt I shall be told: "In the immense
majority of cases this is an illusion."
But it is of the essence of hope to exclude
the consideration of cases; moreoever, it
can be shown that there exists an ascending
dialectic of hope, whereby hope rises to a
plane which transcends the level of all possible empirical disproof . . . .[1]

By definition, then, authentic hope is not only not
open to verification, it does not require verification for the person who hopes does not require this
verification, and the person who hopes is the only
one we are concerned with in the first place. Here
again, the distinction between the intrinsic conviction of profane knowledge, and the felt conviction
of sacred knowledge. Marcel's central claim in
regard to the mystery is that reflection here does
not yield generally accepted conclusions but rather
creates the subject in all his singularity. The
fruits of secondary reflection are then offered to
a sympathetic audience as the testimony of a witness; the validity of testimony is established
squarely by the presence of the witness himself.

    In what sense is the knowledge yielded by
secondary reflection "true"? Characteristically,
it is much easier to specify how Marcel does not

---

[1]TPE 28; cf. HV 63-66.

understand truth in metaphysics than in formulating how he does. He is clearly not interested in what he calls "particular" or "finite" truths in contrast to truth ". . . in the philosophical sense of the word."[1] Particular truths--identified as truths of science--are "impersonal," hence anonymous, independent both of the subject and of the inquiry that brings them about. They are "possessions" and are transmissible to others impartially. Particular truths reflect the characteristics of primary reflection. To restrict truth to the sense implied by "particular truths" is to confuse truth with validity. To apply this concept of truth to philosophical reflection is to degrade philosophy.[2]

In contrast, Marcel identifies truth "in the philosophical sense of the word" as the kind of truth for which we are prepared to die, which we can serve, or betray, or love--in other words, truth as "a value"; here truth becomes "something at stake."[3] Or, less dramatically, he is interested in the implications of such commonplaces as the fact that truth is something we can "face" or "shut out," something that can "mortify," "hurt" or finally, "liberate." In other words, Marcel, as is his wont, focuses on concrete situations when truth is at issue in the life of an individual.[4]

But in these instances, what is it that we "face" or "shut out" etc.? It is not simply "the facts" or "what is the case" or "the reality" understood as totally external to us. There are no "facts" outside us; it is the understanding self which lends them coherence and creates them as

---

[1]PI 16.

[2]Ibid. 16-21.

[3]MBI 58.

[4]Ibid. 63 ff. Cf. SEAR 15-23.

149

facts. What these commonplaces reveal to us, then, is a self made up of different dimensions that can be at war or brought into community with one another to the extent that the "situation" is open. In other words, we are led to two of Marcel's favorite themes: the self as "uncompleted structure" as determined by its "permeability."[1]

We are also led to intersubjectivity, either within the self or between the self and other selves, as the context out of which truth emerges. In fact, the search for truth can be said to <u>create</u> intersubjectivity as when two people are involved in ". . . a discussion about ideas in which both the conversationalists are so interested in their topic that each forgets about himself . . . ." Thus individuals that are involved in the search for truth enter into an "ideal community."[2]

In another context, Marcel reaches the same conclusions from an entirely different perspective. He likens our "knowledge" of reality to a "reading" of a musical score. The score itself is objective but there is no such thing as an "objective" rendering of the music; it does not impose itself on the interpreter with the ". . . compelling force of a physical text or law." But this reading is also clearly not purely "subjective," a "passing disposition." It is in fact a "creative interpretation" which can be more or less faithful to the reality of which it is an interpretation.[3]

This analogy has three implications. First, we must admit the possibility of a variety of such interpretations with no "objective" criteria for

---

[1]<u>MBI</u> 63 ff.

[2]Ibid. 73-74. The phrase "ideal community" is Royce's.

[3]<u>PI</u> 19-21.

determining which is true and which not. Second,
such interpretations admit of degrees of profundity;
there are hierarchies of meaning corresponding to
the depth of the demands that are brought to bear on
the score. Finally, and most important, these
interpretations emerge out of an intersubjective
experience, an "effective participation" between
the performer and the composer and between the performer and his audience which is not the impersonal,
anonymous, universal audience for whom "particular
truths" are true, but rather the audience of "connoisseurs"--those who have cultivated a certain
refinement of perception which can bring them into
"community" with the performer and the composer
because they are "open" to what is being expressed
in the music.[1] Again, then, we are led to a notion
of truth in philosophy as neither objective nor subjective but rather "personal" or "interpersonal" in
that it arises out of an experience of community.

      This discussion raises a number of ques-
tions. What precisely is the relationship between
truth and intersubjectivity? Is it "created" by or
"encountered" in intersubjectivity? But do these
not confuse truth itself and the search for truth?
Finally, what is the relation of truth to being?

              Sacred Knowledge as Participation

      The inter-relationship between truth, being
and intersubjectivity is established by Marcel's
characterization of sacred knowledge as "participation." This is how Marcel, in his later work most
frequently characterizes knowledge of the mystery.
Marcel's use of this term parallels almost exactly
his use of "being"; both are central to his
earliest (1910-1914) work,[2] disappear completely

_____

      [1]MBI 61-62.

      [2]PF 42 ff., 106 ff. This early use of

during the period of the _Journal_, begin to reappear
in _Being and Having_, and become central thereafter.
Marcel seems to have found in participation the
best way to characterize how man apprehends being
and this participatory experience becomes the
paradigm for the other participatory experiences
that go into the fundamental human situation.

Marcel understands participation as opposed
to "relation or communication"[1] or, in another context, as opposed to the attitude of the spectator,
with "contemplation" somewhere in between.[2] But
again, his most illuminating comments emerge out of
concrete examples. He traces a graduated scale of
participation ranging at one pole from objective
thought which is simply possession and where what
is possessed is totally detachable from the posses-
sor, through a number of intermediary stages to, at
the other pole, totally non-objective thought or
participation in its ideal form which establishes
my very reality as self.[3] It is in these latter
instances that the term has metaphysical relevance
and undercuts the subject/object dichotomy of
traditional epistemology. Participation, then,
marks the sought-after convergence of love and
knowledge. It is knowledge directed to mystery and
the task becomes to define how we think participation without "denaturing it, i.e. without turning
it into an objective relation."[4] The answer is
through secondary reflection.

---

participation is discussed in _EBHD_ 23 ff. and _CF_ 21.
For a prefiguration of participation, see Marcel's
distinction between "thinking" and "thinking of" in
_BH_ 31-32.

[1]_CF_ 21.

[2]_MBI_ 121 ff.; _BH_ 20-21.

[3]_MBI_ 111-117; _BH_ 114; _TPE_ 18.

[4]_CF_ 21.

The respective roles of the "blinded intuition" and "secondary reflection" are paralleled,
in this new terminology, by a distinction between
"submerged" and "emergent" participation. My
primitive pre-reflective awareness of being in the
existent universe is an instance of submerged par-
ticipation--participation not yet raised to the
level of consciousness or language. This experience,
reconstructed by the shaping powers of secondary
reflection, becomes an instance of emergent participation.[1]

Participation provides the circuits which
bind together the components of my situation. I am
my body through the participatory act of feeling; I
am in the existent universe through the participatory act of sensation; I am with others through the
participatory act of love; viewed from another
dimension, each of these is at the same time an
instance of my participation in being, personal and
concrete.

The extent of my participatory experiences
is a direct function of the degree of permeability
that I allow into my situation. But by identifying
permeability with the ability or will to participate, Marcel emphasizes that he understands each of
these as far more than passive undergoing or undis-
criminated receptivity. To participate implies to
"extend hospitality" suggesting a creative initiative on the part of the subject, an opening of
oneself or a giving of oneself to e.g. the other,
by allowing him to participate in my situation.
Marcel does not dwell on the distinction between
the infra-intellectual or submerged levels of participation and the more conscious or emergent
levels; this reflects his ongoing preoccupation
with stressing the continuity between the two,
though again the creative initiative would seem to
be much more appropriate to the latter than to the

---

[1]MBI 111-113.

former, to love than to sensation.[1]

Does this characterization of sacred knowledge as participation help us understand the nature
of philosophical truth?

> Let me say briefly that the truth toward
> which philosophical research aspires is
> essentially unpossessable; in any event, it
> cannot be considered or treated as a having.
>
> This is what I meant in the years 1910-1914,
> when I maintained that metaphysics is above
> all a philosophy of participation . . . . It
> is the participation of thought in being
> that we are here concerned with. Once the
> word participation is brought in, we are led
> to substitute the term being for the term
> truth. We must however, avoid all misunder-
> standing. Formerly I was hasty in affirming
> what I called the transcendence of being
> over truth. This is a dangerous and unac-
> ceptable way of speaking. Today I would
> prefer to say that being and truth are iden-
> tical, but on condition of pointing out, as
> I did above, the incommensurability of Truth
> with respect to finite truths to which
> .science gives us access, that is to say, of
> recognizing explicitly that the methods of
> verification in reference to which a truth
> is defined are here inapplicable. With
> respect to these methods and to these par-
> tial truths, the transcendence of being is
> the transcendence of truth.[2]

What Marcel seems to be suggesting here is
that once knowledge has been understood as participation, and every participatory act as ultimately

---

[1]CF 27-29; TPE 98-99; MBI 115-117.

[2]PI 18-19.

a participation in being, the truth of participatory
knowledge is determined by the extent to which what
is participated in is being--as opposed to anything
less than being (i.e. an object)--or more accurately,
to the extent that we are dealing with a thorough
act of participation as opposed to an act of primary
reflection. To "know" being, then, is to "know"
truth--with knowledge, in both cases, identified as
participation.

To participate in truth, in this sense, is
not to "have" anything in the sense that what is
"had" is transmissible, hence impersonal and objective. Obviously Marcel rejects any notion of
philosophical truth as correspondence; correspondence simply revives the dualism that participation
was designed to obliterate. The whole point of
distinguishing between object and presence was to
suggest that there are realities which cannot be
located wholly outside the knowing subject, and
these, the subject can "know" only by fully coming
to terms with their nature as "participated in"
realities.

This interpretation of "truth in the philo-
sophic sense" though hardly explicit in this passage, is born out by the analogy between knowledge
and the reading of a musical score. It is clear
how, from this point of view, there can be a variety of "true" readings of the world, each "personal," as opposed to objective or subjective, for
participatory knowledge is pre-eminently personal
knowledge, the knowledge of the concrete individual
subject in all his singularity. Second, there can
be a hierarchy of true readings depending on the
level of openness or penetration in the direction
of being that is achieved with the "blinded intuition" functioning as implicit criterion for the
secondary reflection which tries to recapture the
full-fledged, albeit submerged participatory relation.

Finally, truth, so understood, is encountered in intersubjectivity. Intersubjectivity is

pre-eminently the gateway to being. It is in participation understood as communion--either within
the "unstructured self" or with the other--that we
encounter being. In encountering being, we encounter truth; and our knowledge is "true" to the
extent that it is knowledge of "being," nothing
less.

Appraisal

Marcel's proposals touch upon a number of
issues in the theory of knowledge. Our evaluation
of these proposals will center about the two claims
that are the most far-reaching and central: that
participatory or sacred knowledge is indeed knowledge of a distinctive kind, and that this knowledge
is immediate and beyond verification.

The Issue of Participatory Knowledge

It is important to emphasize, at the outset,
how seriously Marcel regards his claim that participation is indeed knowledge. Unlike other versions
of this general approach, Marcel's critique of
objective knowledge issues neither in a general
scepticism nor in a deliberate subjectivism. He
insists that the mysterious is not the unknown but
a distinctive epistemological category; the alternative to epistemological objectivism is not
purely private and personal knowledge but the mutually enriching experience of intersubjectivity.
His highly defensive posture in regard to this
claim underlies its importance; he is by no means
prepared to accept the alternative that secondary
reflection yields only ". . . purely subjective
intuitions."[1]

Yet one wishes that instead of simply

----

[1]TWB 229.

articulating this claim, Marcel would have provided some definition of knowledge, or, in some other way, tried to vindicate or validate his use of this highly charged term. He does neither.

That knowledge can have something to do with an act of "participation" or union of the subject of knowledge with the object of knowledge--and that this union is identifiable with what we call love--is a tradition as old as philosophy. In Marcel's writings, this theme can be unpacked into the following claims:

1. that participation itself is an act of knowledge--not that it presupposes, includes or eventuates in knowledge--but that it is _itself_ knowledge;
2. that participatory knowledge is totally different from ordinary or objective knowledge;
3. that in their ideal manifestations, these two forms of knowledge are mutually exclusive;
4. that each is legitimate in its own sphere and becomes illegitimate only when it encroaches upon the other's;
5. that almost all of what has traditionally fallen within the scope of philosophical knowledge--including the knowledge yielded by metaphysics, ontology, epistemology, ethics and aesthetics--is participatory knowledge;
6. finally, that though participatory knowledge is not subject to the public testing that verifies objective knowledge, it nevertheless bears its own guarantee of certainty which at least to the knower and in its felt quality equals the certainty of publicly verified and consolidated objective knowledge.

To support these claims, Marcel's writings on epistemology provide us with: a delineation of the content or scope of objective knowledge, a justification of its claim to constitute knowledge, a polemic against its imperialistic encroachments into spheres not legitimately its own, a parallel delineation of the scope of participatory knowledge and finally, a claim that this too is knowledge, albeit of a distinctive character. What is clearly missing is a justification for this last claim.

It cannot be doubted that scattered throughout Marcel's delineation of the scope of participatory knowledge are elements that could be legitimately labeled as knowledge. But without Marcel's own working definition of knowledge, we are at a loss to isolate them. This leaves Marcel open to two charges:

1. participation may assume or issue in knowledge or it may be a complex experience which includes cognitive and non-cognitive components together;
2. whatever cognitive dimensions there may be to participation can be thoroughly accounted for in terms of ordinary, i.e. objective knowledge.

Let us use Marcel's approach and study a concrete example. Here is one of Marcel's many illustrations of a participatory experience of intersubjectivity:

When I stop somebody in the street to ask my way, I do not say to him, it is true, "Can you tell me how to get to such-and-such a Square?", but all the same I am making a convenience of him, I am treating him as if he were a signpost. No doubt, even in this limiting case, a touch of genuine intersubjectivity can break through, thanks to the magical powers of the tone of voice and the glance. If I have really lost my bearings, if it is late, if I fear that I may have to grope my way for hours through some labyrinthine and perhaps even dangerous warren of streets, I may have a fleeting but

158

irresistible impression that the stranger I
am appealing to is a brother eager to come
to my aid. What happens is, in a word, that
the stranger has started off by putting himself, as it were, ideally in my shoes. He
has come within my reach as a person. It is
no longer a mere matter of his showing me
the way as a guide-book or a map might, but
of his really giving a helping hand to somebody who is alone and in a bewildered state.
This is nothing more than a sort of spark of
spirituality, out as soon as it is in; the
stranger and I part almost certainly never
to see each other again, yet for a few minutes,
as I trudge homewards, this man's unexpected
cordiality makes me feel as if I had stepped
out of a wintry day into a warm room.[1]

In this example, two kinds of communication
seem to have taken place. There is, first, the
communication of concrete information in the form
of directions that will guide me home quickly and
safely. This is clearly objective knowledge--
precisely the kind of knowledge that would be fur-
nished by a guide-post or a map--and it is totally
verifiable by public testing. To the extent that I
know this stranger objectively, he serves the function of a signpost or a map.

But there is also a second-level communication conveyed by "the magical powers of the tone of
voice and the glance," in which the stranger gives
the impression that he is "eager to come to my aid"
or "really giving a helping hand to someone who is
alone and in a bewildered state." Marcel claims
that on this second level, the stranger and I know
each other but in a different way than on the first,
not simply as distinct subject and object, but
through a merging of our two selves into a larger
unity--call it a state of "intimacy" with each

---

[1]MBI 179.

other. Here I know him not simply as a source of
information but as a "brother" who is concerned
with helping me. This too is knowledge, says
Marcel. It is also beyond objective verification,
i.e. we know each other with absolute certainty as
being "with" each other or "present" to each other,
or, to use Marcel's favorite term, as "available"
or "permeable" to each other; there is no need to
confirm this for us and no one can intrude with
evidence that disproves it. Finally, in knowing
the stranger in this way, Marcel claims that I know
him as a person, or fully as a human being--as opposed to a merely functional source of information.

No one can dispute the cognitive nature of
the first level of communication, nor that it is
objective in any sense of the term. But what of
the second? Without Marcel's working definition of
participatory knowledge, it could be maintained
that what is being known here is that apart from
being an accurate source of information, this man
also makes an observable display of his eagerness
to help; thus the reference to "the magical powers
of the tone of voice and the glance." But this is
certainly objective knowledge as well--not as
precise or as clear-cut a matter as the first level
--but surely verifiable by others.

Further, this experience might have stemmed
from a cognitive experience--the man might have
been a policeman to whom I was directed--or it may
issue in knowledge--I will tell my wife that if she
is ever lost in that neighborhood, that particular
shopkeeper is a good person to ask for guidance.
But in both cases, the knowledge is totally objective by Marcel's own definition of objectivity.

If there is anything more to be said about
this second-level communication, it comes down to
something about the emotions and motivations that
accompany the giving of the information: he is
"eager to come to my aid," "really giving a helping
hand," he has put himself "in my shoes."

160

Now first, this dimension is clearly not objective; what is "eagerness" to one may be "mild interest" to another and the eagerness one perceives may be directly related to the "bewilderment" he feels. But second, it is difficult to understand--without further justification--how this reading of the other's feelings or motivations can constitute knowledge of _any_ kind; we are no longer on the level of observable tones and glances. Finally, it is patent that the possibilities for error stemming from a misreading of his feelings and motivations are rampant. In other words, we are confronting the complex of problems associated with the knowledge of other minds--a set of problems that Marcel hardly deals with, apart from pointing out the dualist implication of any analysis such as the above, and proposing instead that the mind-body relationship is a mystery--which is precisely the point that we are trying to understand.

It would be interesting to know how Marcel would handle this encounter if the objective level of the communication were proven to be wrong. He would doubtless want to claim that the participatory experience stands on its own. But one wonders if the glances, tones, eagerness to aid and readiness to help might not assume a different weight in retrospect and raise some question about the accuracy of his reading of the other's emotions and motivations. Would this not reinforce our suspicion that the only cognitive dimension to the encounter is actually the objective one?

Marcel of course would dismiss this entire analysis as an instance of objective reductionism of the most illegitimate kind.[1] He would claim that we have ignored two of the most fundamental assumptions of his epistemology: the claim that knowledge itself is a mystery which permits of no

----

[1]_TPE_ 20-21 provides an example of this kind of refutation.

objective representation,[1] and that secondary reflection yields nothing in the way of conclusions,
i.e. clear-cut, definable, isolatable units that
can be "had."[2] If secondary reflection has any
single role in Marcel's thought, it is precisely to
stand as a _rejection_ of the claim to adequacy of
any kind of knowledge with these characteristics,
at least when we are dealing with the mysterious.
A mystery can only be "evoked" i.e. recognized, not
"grasped," and participatory knowledge can never be
defined or justified in that sense.[3]

          We confront, here, the central difficulty
in launching any kind of critique of Marcel's
thought. Our claim is that Marcel has not made a
case for characterizing participation as a legitimate kind of knowledge because he has not presented a formal warrant for this claim. But Marcel
would surely counter that this verdict depends on
what we mean by "making a case" and "providing a
formal warrant." He would concede that he has not
made a Cartesian case for this claim but he would
immediately add that all of his philosophical assumptions are designed precisely to question the
adequacy and validity for philosophy of that kind
of case. He is asking us, in effect, to re-order
all of our expectations about what constitutes a
legitimate philosophical argument. If philosophy
is an attempt to resolve a sense of unease, if
philosophical method is a form of exploration within reality, if knowledge and reflection are mysteries, and if secondary reflection yields nothing
that can be likened to a permanent acquisition to
an expanding fund of knowledge, then it is impossible, by definition, to delineate the body of
sacred knowledge and provide a warrant for its
epistemological claims. Can we then fault Marcel
for not doing what he claims cannot and should not

---

[1]_BH_ 126.   [2]_CF_ 22.

[3]_MBI_ 208.

be done?

However this impasse should not be the final word on the issue.

First, "knowledge" is an honorific in philosophy. It should not be used indiscriminately without full appreciation of this honorific status. It is not simply a question of Marcel's failure to define a technical term; it is, rather, a matter of justifying his use of this honorific--which is an entirely different matter.

Second, from a pedagogical point of view, Marcel is proposing a departure from a commonly accepted use of a key philosophical concept. It is not sufficient, in such instances, to expose the inadequacies of the traditional use of the concept. Such a departure requires also a clear delineation of the new ways in which the concept will be used.

Finally, a paragraph from Hocking's study of Marcel's metaphysics is very much to the point here. Writing about Marcel's ". . . non-Socratic hesitance . . . toward conceptualized versions of reality," Hocking concludes:

> I am inclined to the thesis that all meanings . . . are destined to meet the relentless and ultimately successful assault of the concept. For, after all, the concept imposes no constraint on that which is conceived. Changeless as the concept is, there is a concept of change, quite as valid as the concept of the static; there is a concept of the conceivable, another of the unconceivable . . . and any lover of mankind must try to gain an orderly view of a public disorder and moral descent toward chaos, as Marcel does in Man versus Mass Society. Musical works, Debussy to the contrary notwithstanding, fail of their purpose if nobody cares to repeat them (and, I would add if they contain no repetition);

and whatever is repeatable is conceptu-
alizable.[1]

Marcel has not provided us with a clearly deline-
ated "concept" of sacred knowledge and his failure
to do so has little to do with the substance of his
thought; it remains an idiosyncrasy of his philosophical style.

Thus far, our questions have stemmed from
assumptions which are admittedly antithetical to
Marcel's. We may be prepared to concede that this
procedure is illegitimate but there can be no question about the legitimacy of taking Marcel's thought
on its own terms and evaluating it according to
certain internal criteria such as its clarity, its
coherence and its faithfulness to its own stated
purposes.

At the end of the previous chapter we
pointed to the fact that Marcel's attempt to eliminate any hint of dualism between the components of
the situation led him to understand the dimensions
of incarnation and intersubjectivity as essentially
parallel and continuous. We suggested then that
however desirable this continuity might be, it was
bought at the price of straining and even distorting the unique characteristics of each of these
dimensions and of giving rise to other philosophical

---

[1]Hocking, "Marcel and Metaphysics,"
pp. 441-442. One of Marcel's last published comments (Entretiens autour de Gabriel Marcel, p. 40)
echoes Hocking's conclusion here: ". . . il n'est
pas question de tomber dans cette erreur qui con-
sisterait à voir dans la philosophie simplement une
espèce de description du vécu. Ce serait absurde.
Pour moi, il doit y avoir une certaine conceptuali-
sation." But he adds that his protest is directed
against ". . . une certaine objectivation réaliste
du concept . . . ." The tension between these two
claims is central and inescapable.

difficulties. These problems emerge in a more
striking way in Marcel's epistemology and come to a
focus on the issue of the cognitivity of participatory knowledge.

The ground of Marcel's epistemology is his
distinction between presence and object, or mystery
and problem. The distinction is based on a spatial
metaphor. I am "within" the existent universe,
"within" a community with other selves and "within"
being; my reflection cannot be "outside" itself,
though a stone or a chair can. Nor, of course, can
I be "external" to myself.

Now all of these claims are true in a sense
--but they are not all true in the same way. I
cannot be "within" all of these realities in an
equally literal way, for the "self," "the existent
universe," "community" and "being" are very different kinds of realities. I may be "within" the
existent universe in a literal way but then I am
only metaphorically "within" a community. From the
opposite perspective, I may be literally in a relation of "intimacy" with other selves but only metaphorically can I be in a state of "intimacy" with
the existent universe.

The same confusion shows itself in Marcel's
identification of love and participation. Love may
be the most literal characterization of what binds
two people together in intersubjectivity but that
love should be ". . . the starting point for the
understanding of the mysteries of the body and
soul"[1] is again to resort to metaphor. On the
other hand, the best way to indicate the way in
which being affirms itself in me by virtue of the
fact that I _am_, even prior to any _conceptual_ grasp
of being, may well be to invoke the term "participation"; but to claim that when I "love" someone,
the lines of our distinctive personalities are

---

[1]_TPE_ 20.

blurred so that we "participate" in each other's being is, as we have held, to indulge in hyperbole.

The same ambiguities are present in Marcel's understanding of secondary reflection and permeability. In some contexts--notably in regard to our attempts to recapture the blinded intuitions of being, _my_ body, and the existent universe--secondary reflection is portrayed as an act of the mind, properly a reflective act, however tenuous.[1] In other contexts--notably in regard to the critical dissolution effected by primary reflection on love, fidelity and hope--it emerges as a highly charged, emotional, conversion-like experience which marks a dramatic turn-about in a specific interpersonal relationship and leads to a re-ordering of priorities and values.[2] The experiences are quite different yet they are both identified as secondary reflection.

"Permeability" suffers from the same ambiguity. Is it an epistemological category or a moral disposition? In some contexts, it is clearly the former; it denotes an openness to the impact of the existent universe in sensation, for example. In other contexts, permeability becomes "availability" to the call of another human being in trouble.[3] Marcel treats these two as identical but one has epistemological implications and the other does not.

The identification of participation and love as knowledge of a distinctive kind is the end result

----

[1]TWB 235-236; CF 22; EBHD 86; MBI 93; TPE 23-25.

[2]MBI 168-169 provides one striking example of this use of secondary reflection. See also the description of his feelings after his own conversion (BH 15, 20, 24).

[3]CF 27-29.

of these prior ambiguities. There is the objective
knowledge by a subject of an object distinct from
it, and there is a different matter--the love of an
individual for another human being. It is possible
for the knowing subject to experience a complex set
of feelings about an "object"--e.g. the artist for
the scene he is painting--and it is possible for
the lover to "know" a great deal about the one he
loves, though this knowledge may be verified objectively.

Marcel has taken a set of highly complex
experiences--in fact, the most complex and subtle
experiences available to man and attempted to fit
them into a single conceptual scheme in which the
key notions are "presence," "mystery," "blinded intuition," "secondary reflection" and "participation." He unifies all of this data through his
application of this single conceptual scheme to the
"situation." The situation must be a source of
unification because the situation defines the self
and the self--for all its permeability and ability
to grow--has to be held together. But the unification is precarious and one longs for the rigorous
analysis which would clarify the discriminations
that are so obviously present in the material.[1]

---

[1]This is the substance of Merleau-Ponty's
critique of Marcel in his review of Etre et avoir:
"Etre et avoir," La Vie intellectuelle, 8 (October
10, 1936), 98-109. See also the discussion in
Rabil, Albert, Jr., Merleau-Ponty Existentialist of
the Social World (New York and London: Columbia
University Press, 1967), pp. 63-67. It is also the
theme of a more generalized critique of existentialism by Mary Warnock, Existentialism (London,
Oxford, New York: Oxford University Press, 1970),
pp. 139-140. A similar challenge, directed
specifically against Marcel's concept of mystery is
in F.H. Heinemann, Existentialism and the Modern
Predicament (New York: Harper and Row, 1953),
p. 145.

On its own terms, then, Marcel's characterization of what we have called the "contours" of
the situation and its epistemological "circuits" is
ambiguous. Specifically: the self, the existent
universe, community with other persons and being
cannot all be univocally labeled as "mysteries";
nor can these realities be linked together by an
all-purpose theory of "participation" as articulated by "secondary reflection" which yields a
distinct "sacred knowledge." Or, in a more summary
way, Marcel has not established the structural
parallels between the dimensions of incarnation and
intersubjectivity or the identity of love with
knowledge, however conceived.

        In the final chapter of this study we will
indicate how this intrinsic ambiguity in Marcel's
understanding of the situation yields two antithetical views of religious faith and trace the
implications of this antithesis for our understanding of religious knowledge. For the present, the
problems in Marcel's epistemology may be sharpened
by a comparison of his thought with that of Paul
Tillich, the representative of contemporary existentialism who takes most seriously the epistemological issues involved in this style of philosophizing.

        Briefly, what Marcel calls "profane" and
"sacred" knowledge, Tillich calls "controlling" and
"receiving" knowledge. Significantly though, both
of these--indeed every instance of knowledge--in-
volve both objectivity and participation, or to use
Tillich's terms, detachment and union. In the first,
detachment predominates, and in the second, union--
but both are present in all knowledge. Controlling
knowledge is appropriate for the knowledge of a
thing:

        It unites subject and object for the sake of
        the control of the object by the subject.
        It transforms the object into a completely
        conditioned and calculable "thing." It de-
        prives it of any subjective quality . . . .
        Certainly, in every type of knowledge subject

and object are logically distinguished.
There is always an object, even in our
knowledge of God. But controlling knowledge "objectifies" not only logically
(which is unavoidable) but also ontolo-
logically and ethically.[1]

It is in this latter sense--the ontological and
ethical sense--that man "resists objectification."

A truly objective relation to man is determined by the element of union; the
element of detachment is secondary. It is
not absent; there are levels in man's . . .
constitution which can and must be grasped
by controlling knowledge. But this is
neither the way of knowing human nature
nor is it the way of knowing any individual
personality . . . including one's self.
Without union there is no cognitive approach to man.[2]

Receiving knowledge unifies the object with the
subject and includes the emotional element which is
absent in controlling knowledge. But though emotion is "the vehicle for receiving cognition,"
nevertheless ". . . the vehicle is far from making
the content itself emotional. The content is
rational, something to be verified, to be looked at
with critical caution. Nevertheless, nothing can
be received cognitively without emotion. No union
of subject and object is possible without emotional
participation."[3]

When union and detachment are united in
knowledge, we have "understanding"; to understand
"another person, or a historical figure, the life

---

[1]Paul Tillich, Systematic Theology, Vol. I
(Chicago: University of Chicago Press, 1951),
p. 97.

[2]Ibid. 98.   [3]Ibid.

of an animal or a religious text" we need both
"participation and analysis." In contrast, cognitive distortions occur when this polarity is dis-
regarded. In our day we have seen a tidal wave of
controlling knowledge--with results which Tillich
describes in terms remarkably similar to Marcel's
description of the "broken world."[1]

Existentialism has served as one of the
three main protests against this tidal wave of controlling knowledge but like the other two--romanti-
cism and the philosophy of life--it has failed
because it had no adequate criterion for distinguishing truth from falsity in receiving knowledge,
because it failed to see, in Tillich's words, that
the content of receiving knowledge is "rational,
something to be verified, to be looked at with
critical caution." Without verification, our judgments would be simply expressions of the subjective
state of a person ". . . but not acts of cognitive
reason."[2] The safest means of verification is the
repeatable experiment but it is not the exclusive
method. There is another kind of verification
which takes place "within the life-process itself."

Verification of this type (experiential in
contradistinction to experimental) has the
advantage that it need not halt or disrupt
the totality of the life-process . . . .
The verifying experiences of a nonexperi-
mental character are truer to life, though
less exact and definite.[3]

This experiential verification is appropriate to
receiving knowledge.

Receiving knowledge is verified by the
creative union of two natures, that of

---

[1]Ibid. 99.   [2]Ibid. 102.

[3]Ibid.

knowing and that of the known. This test, of course, is neither repeatable, precise, nor final at any particular moment. The life-process itself makes the test. Therefore the test is indefinite and preliminary; there is an element of risk connected with it. Future stages of the same life-process may prove that what seemed to be a bad risk was a good one and vice-versa. Nevertheless the risk must be taken, receiving knowledge must be applied, experiential verification must go on continually . . . .[1]

Putting aside the issue of verification for the moment, there is much to comment upon in this material. Note, first, Tillich's distinction between the ways of objectifying: logical on one hand, and ontological and ethical on the other. By claiming that knowledge is always founded on the subject/object model--at least logically--Tillich is able to avoid some of Marcel's most tortuous problems. He does not have to invoke "secondary reflection" which remains a _reflection_ while undercutting the distinction between subject and object. Second, he does not have to divide the field of knowledge into two absolutely exclusive domains such as profane and sacred or objective and participatory knowledge.

Tillich's model discerns a dimension of detachment and union in all knowledge with the particular proportion determining in each instance whether we are dealing with controlling or receiving knowledge. There is a recognition here that we are never fully free of objectification, that at the heart of secondary reflection and participatory knowledge, there remains a core of verifiable objective knowledge and that in fact neither knowledge nor reflection is possible without the subject/object logic as its ground.

---

[1]Ibid. 103.

Tillich is quite consistent in this. In a
different context, describing the Augustinian or
"ontological" approach to the unconditional as distinguished from the Thomistic or "cosmological,"
Tillich formulates the ontological principle in
this way: "Man is immediately aware of something
unconditional which is the prius of the separation
and interaction of subject and object, theoreti-
cally as well as practically."[1] Tillich defends
his use of the term "awareness" here as ". . . the
most neutral term, avoiding the connotations of the
terms intuition, experience, knowledge." In regard
to knowledge, he claims that it ". . . presupposes
the separation of subject and object, and implies
an isolated theoretical act, which is just the
opposite of awareness of the Unconditioned."[2]

In the Augustinian framework, the unconditioned is _esse_, _verum_, and _bonum_; they are presupposed in every question and in every doubt and
hence are prior to the cleavage of subject and
object.

> Our mind implies _principia per se nota_ which
> have immediate evidence whenever they are
> noticed . . . . They constitute the Absolute
> in which the difference between knowing and
> . known is not actual. This Absolute as the
> principle of Being has absolute certainty.

---

[1]Paul Tillich, "The Two Types of Philosophy
of Religion," _Union Seminary Quarterly Review_, Vol.
1, No. 4 (May 1946). Reprinted in Paul Tillich,
Theology of Culture, ed. Robert G. Kimball (New
York: Oxford University Press, 1959), p. 22. A
comparative study of some themes in the philosophical theology of Tillich and Marcel is provided by
Daniel S. Robinson, "Tillich and Marcel: Theistic
Existentialists," _The Personalist_, 34 (Summer
1953), 237-250.

[2]Ibid. 23.

> It is a necessary thought because it is
> the presupposition of all thought . . . .
> The fact that people turn away from this
> thought is based on individual defects
> but not on the essential structure of the
> mind. The mind is able to turn away from
> what is nearest to the ground of its own
> structure.[1]

This passage captures in an uncanny way the essence
of Marcel's thought on how we participate--or
choose not to participate--in being. It is noteworthy, though, that Tillich concedes that our
"awareness" of being remains simply an awareness,
while Marcel insists on its being a matter of
knowledge of a distinct kind. Marcel also would
extend this immediate participatory knowledge to a
host of other experiences such as man's knowledge
of his self, his body, the existent universe and
the other-in-intimacy, all of which fall far short
of being "principia per se nota" in the way that
being is. On the other hand, Tillich's emphasis on
the "ontological and ethical" objectifying that
takes place in controlling knowledge catches accurately the social context out of which much of
Marcel's thought emerges, while eliminating the
ambiguity which persists in Marcel's wide-ranging
use of such basic categories as secondary reflection, permeability and participatory knowledge.

Tillich may have captured more of the complexity involved in knowing but we can ask of
Tillich, as we asked of Marcel, in what lies the
"knowledge" of receiving knowledge? No more than
Marcel does Tillich provide us with a formal
warrant for this claim. Like Marcel, he is open to
the charge that whatever knowledge is involved in
receiving knowledge can be thoroughly accounted for
by this dimension of objectivity. This charge is
buttressed by the fact that throughout his dis-

---

[1]Ibid. 15.

cussion of receiving knowledge the only distinctive feature of this knowledge--apart from the fact that it ". . . takes the object into itself, into union with the subject"[1] the import of which is precisely the point at issue--is the presence of emotion. But in what way does the presence of emotion transform controlling knowledge into a different kind of knowledge? Randall expresses the problem this way:

> After all, it is only by a metaphor that knowledge can be called a "union" or "participation." "Love" for the object of knowledge may in many types of knowledge be essential for any real "understanding"; but does that make the love itself knowledge? "Knowing is not like digesting, and we do not devour what we mean" is an aphorism of Santayana's still worth pondering. "Union" with another personality may well be a necessary condition of adequate knowledge of that personality. But union with a text--even a religious text--is hardly necessary to its proper interpretation.[2]

Without a formal justification for his use of knowledge in this context, Randall's question--directed both to Tillich and Marcel--stands unanswered.

Marcel is not wholly unaware of these difficulties; in fact, he recognizes them in the act

---

[1]Tillich, Systematic Theology, I, 98.

[2]John Herman Randall, Jr., "The Ontology of Paul Tillich" in Charles W. Kegley and Robert W. Bretall, eds., The Theology of Paul Tillich (New York: The Macmillan Company, 1961), pp. 149-150. This critique of Tillich is echoed by Bernard Martin, The Existentialist Theology of Paul Tillich (New York: Bookman Associates, 1963), pp. 72-73.

of dismissing them as stemming from primary reflection. They represent the price he is prepared to pay for certain clearly perceived philosophical gains. It is worth speculating on the nature of these gains.

First, like other existentialists, Marcel is trying to bridge the gap between philosophy (i.e. intelligence, reflection) and life. Early in his career, he indicted philosophical idealism as being excessively abstract, systematic and remote from the full reality of life as lived with its tragedies, its pain and its inconsistencies. Side by side with this, his more mature thought reflects his refusal to accept the fact that what he considers to be the cardinal experiences of life--love, hope and fidelity for example--which he claims to be crucial philosophical raw material, are purely passing, subjective dispositions, not worthy of serious philosophical treatment and by implication, not to be taken seriously. These two currents in Marcel's thought converge in the view of knowledge as participation.

Thus, philosophy differs from science in two ways: it has "redemptive" value,[1] i.e. it effects a transformation in the totality of the individual's "situation" (as opposed to remaining simply an intellectual game) and it is properly the task of every human being qua human being and not that of a special class of technicians. But for it to deserve the honorific "philosophy," it must deal with the equally honorific "knowledge."

Second, despite the confusions, distortions, and ambiguities, Marcel is fascinated by the parallels and continuities that the situational structure suggests to him. We noted earlier the parallels in his reading of incarnation and intersubjectivity; even more striking examples lie ahead.

---

[1]Collins, op. cit., p. 212.

Religious faith is modeled on fidelity and (in its immediacy) on sensation; the absolute thou is modeled on the contingent thous and both, as presences, reveal being.

Where there is continuity, where man confronts reality through one continuous chain of participatory relationships, the links in the chain inherit each other's strengths. Our discussion of religious knowledge will show that it is by virtue of his unified picture of the situation that he is able to ground the outward reaches of this situation--in this case religious faith--in what he perceives as the firm foundation of the participatory knowledge of my self, my body and the existent universe.

More specifically, by virtue of this conceptual scheme, Marcel is able to portray the individual self as presenting an integrated pattern of responses to the influx into the "situation" so that a response in one dimension of the situation will affect a response in the other. For example, if permeability and secondary reflection are operative throughout the situation then the self's permeability to other persons will influence his permeability to being and to God, or secondary reflection on the level of incarnation will make possible secondary reflection in regard to being. This linking together of the dimensions within the self helps account for its felt identity.

Finally, the "problem" of religious knowledge is not the problem of religious knowledge alone. Religious knowledge is now grouped with much of philosophy as yielding participatory knowledge in opposition to science. They stand--or presumably fall--together.

The Issue of Verification

We noted above that Tillich attributed the failure of various movements to stem the tidal wave of controlling knowledge to their inability to

176

solve the problem of verification, i.e. to provide a ". . . criterion of the false and the true."[1]   He acknowledges that receiving knowledge must have its own method of verification distinct from that of pragmatism and positivism. But the method that he settles upon--the _experiential_ "efficacy in the life-process of mankind"--sounds suspiciously like the kind of test that a good pragmatist could accept.[2]

Marcel deals with the issue of verification in sacred or participatory knowledge in two ways which are not easily reconcilable.

We have seen that his characteristic claim is that sacred knowledge requires no verification.

To think, or rather, to assert, the meta-problematical is to assert it as indubitably real, as a thing of which I cannot doubt without falling into contradiction. We are in a sphere where it is no longer possible to dissociate the idea itself from the certainty or the degree of certainty which pertains to it. Because this idea _is_

---

[1]Tillich, _Systematic Theology_, I, 99.

[2]The insight is Randall's in Kegley and Bretall, op. cit., p. 150 and Martin's, op. cit., p. 73. It is worth noting that Marcel could be shown to have implicitly accepted this pragmatic test as well. If, as he claims, philosophy can provide a resolution of the metaphysical uneasiness which provides it with its initial impetus, this sense of resolution is clearly a verification ex-perience. It is "experiential" instead of "exper-imental"; it takes place within "the life-process," and it is clearly "indefinite and preliminary" and fraught with risk. See Clyde Pax, "Marcel's Way of Creative Fidelity," _Philosophy Today_, Vol. 19, No. 1 (Spring 1975), 13.

certainty, it _is_ the assurance of itself.[1]

Or again:

> It will be asked: What is the criterion of
> true love? It must be answered that there
> is no criteriology except in the order of
> the objective and the problematical.[2]

What this amounts to is a dismissal of the
issue of verification as it applies to participatory knowledge. The need to verify depends on the
existence of a prior question about the veracity of
the knowledge; if there is no possible question,
there is no need to verify. The one who knows,
knows that his knowledge is not illusory or false
and because the knower is the only one who counts
in the first place, there is no further need for
verification. Verification is a public procedure;
it depends on the interchangeability of subjects.
Since this provision cannot be met, the entire
issue can be dismissed as irrelevant. Hence the
self-verifying nature of this kind of knowledge.

However, in other contexts, Marcel's position is not so much a dismissal of the issue but
rather a protest against an excessively stringent
expectation of what constitutes an appropriate
verificatory experience in this domain.

It is in these contexts that Marcel likens
our sacred knowledge of reality to the reading of a
musical score.[3] Verification does take place here
but it is far from the kind of public, "experimental" verification possible in objective knowledge. It is possible for a group of trained

---

[1]_TPE_ 22-23.

[2]Ibid. 20.

[3]_PI_ 19-20; _TWB_ 5-7.

musicians or music-lovers to agree that a specific interpretation of a musical score is a more or less faithful rendition of the composer's intent, is more or less "true" to the score. Authorities, in these instances, could point out with some precision just where and why the performance was "wrong," i.e. where the adagio was not sufficiently drawn-out or the pianissimo not sufficiently soft or the phrasing not in line with the melodic curve. A music teacher does this all the time and when the pupil plays the score a second time, the teacher may be able to claim--and other authorities present to agree--that the second rendition was more "true" than the first.

This is certainly not the universal verification of truth in science but neither is it totally private. It is a shared experience which requires a reference to other persons and so may be tentatively called "public"--though the testers are not completely interchangeable, and it may require certain innate qualities of taste and refinement as opposed to the training that is necessary for scientific verification--though it may require training as well. It certainly has the imprecision, tentativeness and risk that Tillich attributes to his experiential verification. But if the purpose of verification is to attempt to expose error and illusion, it can be said that this purpose is accomplished--with due reservation as to how "error" and "illusion" can be defined in these contexts. Further, it is certainly possible to specify a set of experiences which would "falsify" any one reading of a score. This suggestive analogy also leaves room for an element of "permeability" defined as an active-passive extending of "hospitality"[1] to the vision of the composer (or to the yield of experience) and for the fact that much of our permeability or lack of it is a matter of the will. However, this is hardly a dismissal of the

---

[1] CF 18-19.

issue of verifiability. If anything, it is not far removed from the kind of verifiability which Marcel has been trying to avoid.

We shall return to these positions on verification in far greater detail below when we consider the question of the verifiability of religious knowledge. We shall attempt to trace the sources for each of these positions in Marcel's thought and show how each has specific implications for Marcel's view of religious knowledge.

Intimately associated with the issue of verifiability is that of the immediacy of participatory knowledge. It is this immediacy, i.e. the fact that it is unmediated by any suggestion of inference, that is the source of the absolute certainty of participatory knowledge which, in turn, makes verification unnecessary.

But Marcel's discussion of immediacy suffers from the same kind of ambiguity which characterizes his portrayal of the situation. We can distinguish at least three uses of immediacy in his writings.

There is, first, the immediacy of our "awareness" of being. Here, Marcel is solidly in the Augustinian tradition as Tillich portrays it.[1] Being is encountered immediately by introspection as absolutely prior to the subject/object distinction and as "environing" reflection. Certainty, here, results from the fact that the denial of being itself presupposes being, thus establishing being. Being is the presupposition of the question of being, to paraphrase Tillich; or, to paraphrase Marcel, I am the stage, rather than the subject of the inquiry into being.

---

[1]Tillich, Theology of Culture, pp. 12-16 and 22-26.

180

Second, there is the immediacy of our
awareness of the existent universe. This is the
immediacy of sensation, or of direct "acquaintance"
as Russell uses the term, in contradistinction to
knowledge by description.[1] This kind of knowledge
by acquaintance may convey certainty but it is a
purely subjective or psychological certainty which
has no reference to anything beyond my own present
mental state. Marcel of course tries to avoid this
impasse through a realist theory of perception and
a metaphysical claim about the nature of existence
so that what is known immediately is not simply my
private mental state but "the existent universe"
which includes the subject of knowledge.

Finally, there is the immediacy of the
intersubjective encounter. Here Marcel seems to be
referring to the intensity of the emotional attachment between two human beings. The certainty, here,
comes from a deliberate refusal even to consider
any contrary evidence which may shatter the attachment.

These are three very different uses of immediacy; they can hardly be considered univocally
nor is the particular relation between immediacy
and verification identical in each case. The last
of the three, as we noted above, may have no epistemological relevance at all. The epistemological
issue is central to the first two but in each case

---

[1]Bertrand Russell, The Problems of Philosophy (London: Oxford University Press, 1943),
p. 46. That this kind of knowledge by acquaintance
is beyond doubt is questioned by A.D. Woozley,
Theory of Knowledge (London: Hutchinson's University Library, 1949), p. 182 n. The problem is
dealt with in Nicholas Capaldi, Human Knowledge:
A Philosophical Analysis of its Meaning and Scope
(New York: Pegasus Traditions in Philosophy,
Western Publishing Company, 1969), pp. 70-74.

it is beclouded by other considerations which may affect the legitimacy of the claim. In the first instance, the complication is the ontological claim; we have seen that there is a legitimate question about the possibility of speaking of being in the way that Marcel does. In the second instance, the complications rest in the uncritical acceptance of a realism of perception and in the metaphysical claim regarding existence--both of which are central to the issue.

Finally, to tie together these two broad issues of participatory knowledge and verifiability, it is worth pointing out that though certainty may be a necessary condition for knowledge, it is by no means a sufficient condition. One may be sure and turn out to be wrong; but one cannot turn out to be wrong if one knows.[1] More on this below.

Once again, then, we are forced to conclude that Marcel's primary categories are ambiguous. This time, the ambiguity pertains to the two features that most distinctively define sacred knowledge: its immunity to verification and its immediacy. But these are simply two further instances of the more general problem that cuts across Marcel's entire conceptual scheme. We found a fundamental ambiguity at the heart of Marcel's understanding of the self as situation. We saw that Marcel's major epistemological categories--presence, mystery, permeability and secondary reflection--were sometimes to be taken literally and sometimes metaphorically. We found, finally, a basic ambiguity in his attempt to identify love, hope and fidelity as well as sensation as a distinct kind of "sacred" knowledge.

There is a twin irony in all of this. First, Marcel's phenomenological descriptions which

---

[1]The point is Woozley's, op. cit., pp. 187-189.

serve as the raw material for his philosophical
scheme show a striking appreciation for the richness
and diversity of human experience. Second, Marcel's
own programmatic statements proclaim him to be the
arch-enemy of monism and system in philosophy. Yet,
despite the apparently directionless character of
his explorations, we find Marcel consistently reverting to a single conceptual scheme and philosophical
vocabulary in his attempts to structure his data.
We have, thus far, made no attempt to discern the
antithetical impulses which are at work in Marcel's
thought. This will be one of our tasks in the concluding chapter of this study.

     The epistemological issues on which we have
focused here will be central to our consideration
of Marcel's treatment of religious knowledge. This
is absolutely crucial for a philosopher such as
Marcel who roots faith and religious knowledge in
the more mundane and common expressions of fidelity
and knowledge as manifest in every-day life. God,
like being, is not located in some beyond, but
precisely in the existent universe and in the other
which it includes; our knowledge of God, like our
knowledge of being, is not some esoteric form of
knowledge devised solely for believing man. These
activities that form part of our daily functioning
are transformed by an awareness that discloses certain patterns to the one who wills to see them.
Marcel puts it this way:

     My deepest and most unshakable conviction--
     and if it is heretical, so much the worse
     for orthodoxy--is, that whatever all the
     thinkers and doctors have said, it is not
     God's will at all to be loved by us against
     the creation, but rather glorified through
     the creation and with the creation as our
     starting-point.[1]

_____

[1] BH 135

183

CHAPTER V

RELIGIOUS FAITH

Introduction

        The single theme which is always on Marcel's
agenda throughout the six decades in which he wrote
on philosophy is the nature of religious faith. It
is clearly the impetus for his earliest, recently
published philosophical writings;[1] it is the single
most pervasive issue in the first two volumes of
selections from his philosophical diary;[2] it is the
climax of his systematic presentation in The Mystery of Being;[3] it is the topic of a number of
closely argued monographs;[4] finally, it is omnipresent in his theatre. To no other single theme
did Marcel allot anywhere near an equal amount of

_____

        [1]PF 80-82, 106-125; cf. ECVQE 68-71. The
continuities between Marcel's early writings on
religion and his more mature thought are discussed
in Blain, "Marcel's Logic of Freedom," pp. 201-202.

        [2]It is noteworthy that apart from one brief
reference, it is totally absent from "Existence and
Objectivity" which is a summary of some of the main
themes of MJ. We will have more to say about this
omission below.

        [3]MBII, chapters 5, 6, 8, 10.

        [4]CF, chapters 6, 9, 10; also "Some Remarks
on the Irreligion of Today" and "Some Thoughts on
Faith" which are appended to BH, and two papers on
atheism in TWB.

attention. It is clearly one of the main impulses behind his philosophical quest.

Even when Marcel is not dealing with an explicitly religious issue, his characteristic philosophical vocabulary is studded with religious overtones. Two key terms--"mystery" and "sacred knowledge"--were noted earlier. Terms such as "revelation," "grace," "sin," "prayer," "witness," "martyr" and "salvation" dot all of his writings. It may be somewhat jarring for one trained in philosophy to find Marcel trying to define the "philosophical significance" of salvation ". . . without encroaching on the strictly theological sphere"[1] but it clearly causes <u>him</u> no discomfort at all. Examples of this kind can be easily multiplied.

The integration of religion and philosophy is not confined to vocabulary alone. We are dealing with an attempt to structure--on strictly <u>philosophical</u> grounds--a metaphysics which may prepare the ground for conversion to a specific revelational community. In one of Marcel's conversations with Paul Ricoeur, Ricoeur notes that the title of Marcel's monograph "On the Ontological Mystery" combines a religious reference with a philosophical one. He asks whether the resultant phrase, "ontological mystery," might speak more clearly to the philosopher than to the Christian since it implies no specific reference to Christ. Marcel replies by tracing his own journey to Christianity and concludes:

> I believe that even at the time I was writing those reflections on the ontological mystery I experienced the need to reach a level universal enough to make what I was saying acceptable or understandable by non-Catholics and even perhaps by non-Christians, so long as they had a certain apprehension

---

[1]<u>MBII</u> 180.

of what seemed to me essential.[1]

Then, speaking more generally of the main thrust of his work, he continues;

> I consider myself as having always been a philosopher of the threshold, a philosopher who kept himself in rather uncomfortable fashion between believers and non-believers so that he could somehow stand with believers, with the Christian religion, the Catholic religion, but also speak to non-believers, make himself understood by them and perhaps to help them. I don't think this kind of preoccupation is an apologetic one--that word would be completely inappropriate--but I do think that this fraternal concern has played an extremely important role in the development of my thought.[2]

Or, in still another context, concluding a discussion of his ontology, he adds: "An ontology with this orientation is plainly open to a revelation, which, however, it could not of course either demand or presuppose or absorb, or even absolutely speaking understand, but the acceptance of which it can in some degree prepare for."[3]

More striking still is the specifically Christian tone of much of this material, for example

---

[1]TWB 239.

[2]Ibid. 240. In a later comment ("Extraits des Entretiens . . .," p. 400) Marcel notes that as a "philosopher of the threshold" he speaks not only to the non-believers but also to "the non-believer in me."

[3]BH 120; cf. TPE 46; TWB 185-186; and Marcel's "Theism and Personal Relationships," Cross Currents, 1 (1950), 35, 42.

his choice of fidelity, hope and love as the three
cardinal intersubjective experiences and of incarnation as one dimension of the situation. Marcel
insists that Christianity plays nothing more than
the role of a "fertilising principle" in his work
and that the main outlines of his thought were conceived more than twenty years before his conversion
to Christianity. He does concede, however, that
the philosopher is located within a given historical
situation from which ". . . he is unlikely to abstract himself completely." He continues:

> . . . this historical situation implies as
> one of its essential data the existence of
> the Christian fact--quite independently of
> whether the Christian religion is accepted
> and its fundamental assertions are regarded
> as true or false. What appears to me evident
> is that we cannot reason today as though
> there were not behind us centuries of Chris-
> tianity, just, as, in the domain of the
> theory of knowledge, we cannot pretend that
> there have not been centuries of positive
> science.[1]

At isolated instances, Marcel goes beyond this
moderate position:

> . . . . I believe that the Christian who is
> also a philosopher and can dig under the
> scholastic formulas on which he is fluently
> nourished, would almost inevitably redis-
> cover the fundamental data of what I have
> called concrete philosophy (whereas he will
> certainly never find the idealism of
> Brunschvicg nor doubtless even that of
> Hamelin) . . . . I must say that . . . a
> concrete philosophy cannot fail to be

---

[1]TPE 44-45; cf. TWB 180-182 where he discusses the assumptions of his earliest thinking on
the dimension of incarnation.

magnetically attracted to the data of
Christianity . . . and I do not think that
this fact should shock anyone. For the
Christian, there is an essential agreement
between Christianity and human nature.
Hence the more deeply one penetrates into
human nature, the more one finds oneself
situated on the axes of the great truths
of Christianity.[1]

To the objection that these are not the words of a
philosopher, Marcel replies: "Here, I can only
repeat what I said at the beginning: the philosopher who compels himself to think only as a philosopher, places himself on the hither side of experience in an infrahuman realm, but philosophy implies
an exaltation of experience, not a castration of
it."[2]

There is then a reciprocal relationship
between philosophy and Christianity. The latter
provides the philosopher with a significant set of
experiences which form part of the data for philosophy and which philosophy ignores at the risk of
its own impoverishment. This data fortifies a
philosophical approach which in turn prepares the
ground for accepting a specific revelation. Thus
Marcel maintains a rigid distinction between
"natural" and "revealed" mysteries while insisting
that the latter can only be addressed to ". . . a
being who is involved--committed--that is to say,
to a being who participates in a reality which is
non-problematical and which provides him with his
foundation as subject. Supernatural life must,
when all is said and done, find a hold in the
natural . . . ."[3] We will return to this final

---

[1]CF 79. But Marcel also finds some forms
of Christianity to be a real obstacle to the
emergence of fidelity (HV 92).

[2]CF 80.   [3]TPE 46.

189

claim below.

From the age of thirty-nine (1929) Marcel
was a practicing Catholic. His conversion to
Catholicism was an overwhelming event.[1] When he
writes of the dynamics of conversion, of the movement from non-belief to belief, he writes out of
the impact of a deeply felt personal experience--
all the more significant for one who stresses that
faith is the act of a singular and concrete subject
and who emphasizes the role of personal witness in
bringing others to faith. Marcel had no formal
theological training and confesses to being hard-
pressed to handle the theological intricacies of
the texts he was using to prepare for baptism;[2]
thus his disdain for a religion based on "abstract
theological statements" as opposed to a "living
relation" with God.[3]

Similarly, the realities of his childhood--
Jewish mother, Catholic father, Protestant upbring-
ing--may account for the almost total absence of a
rigid Catholic or even Christian defensiveness in
his work.[4] He rails against the spirit of

---

[1]It is discussed in detail in ECVQE 136-145;
cf. BH 23-24.

[2]BH 23; ECVQE 140-141.

[3]This distinction clearly places Marcel in
conflict with Thomism (EBHD 81; BH 98; CF 36-37;
PM 54; SEAR 9). The tension is discussed by Leo
Sweeney, "Gabriel Marcel's Position on God," New
Scholasticism, 44 (1970), 105-124. See also Trois-
fontaines, op. cit., II, 209 and chapter 9 passim,
Collins, op. cit., pp. 165-166, Bagot, op. cit.,
pp. 155-164, and Ricoeur, op. cit., pp. 352-360.
See also our discussion of Marcel's views on prov-
ing the existence of God, below, pp. 202-206.

[4]EBHD 133-134; ECVQE 213 ff.; MBII 172. He
did consider conversion to Protestantism but

exclusiveness in religion and exudes sympathy and understanding for those who are "on the road" struggling with the obstacles that life raises against religious faith.[1]

To look ahead, the central issue in Marcel's treatment of religious knowledge will lie in the distinction between faith as "abstract theological statements" and faith as "a living relation" with God. From the outset Marcel insisted that this "living relation," while not reducible to "abstract theological statements" remains at the same time, a <u>cognitive</u> relationship. The only other alternative would be to reduce faith to an arbitrary and private psychic event. The attempt to escape this dilemma--i.e. to provide an alternative to abstraction and arbitrariness--is Marcel's central philosophical task.

Marcel's approach to this challenge lies in extending the category of "sacred knowledge" to the realm of religion. Religious knowledge--like the knowledge of being, of other persons, of my situation as being-in-the-world--is sacred knowledge, knowledge of the mystery attained through an immediate participation of subject and object, and hence inaccessible to the kind of public verification available to "profane," objective or scientific knowledge. As we have seen, what is at issue here is not simply the legitimacy of religious knowledge but that of an entire segment of what traditionally has passed as philosophical knowledge

---

rejected it because of his conviction that only Catholicism contains the Christian message in its plenitude (ibid. 138-139). On the other hand, he characterizes as "erroneous" and "incoherent" the identification of any religion as simply a set of doctrines or an ". . .isme" of any kind ("Extraits des Entretiens . . .," pp. 347-349).

[1] <u>BH</u> 200.

including metaphysics, ethics, ontology, aesthetics and social philosophy as well as epistemology itself--because cognition is a paradigmatic example of mystery.

The strengths and weaknesses of this general epistemological approach have been discussed in a general way above. What remains is to describe and evaluate its attempt to deal with the specific issue of religious knowledge.

Faith

The main thrust of what Marcel has to say about religious faith is formulated in this way:

> The verb to believe is commonly used in an extremely vague and fluctuating way . . . in our domain . . . we shall have to concentrate our attention not on the fact of believing that but on that of believing in. The idea of credit can put us on the right lines. We speak of "opening a credit"; and there, I think, we have an operation which constitutes belief as such . . . . But . . . we have to get rid of the material ballast . . . in this opening of a credit. If I believe in something, it means that I place myself at the disposal of something, or again that I pledge myself fundamentally, and this pledge affects not only what I have but also what I am. In a modern philosophical vocabulary, this could be expressed by saying that to belief is attached an existential index . . . .[1]

And he continues:

Again, we might put it that from this point

---

[1] MBII 77; italics Marcel's.

of view *to believe* is essentially *to follow*;
but we must not attach a passive meaning to
that word. The metaphor of rallying may very
profitably be used to fill out that of credit.
If I *believe in*, I *rally to*; with that sort
of interior gathering of oneself which the
act of rallying implies. From this point of
view one might say that the strongest belief,
or more exactly the most living belief, is
that which absorbs most fully all the powers
of your being.[1]

In these contexts, Marcel habitually contrasts faith with two other phenomena with which it
is often confused. First, faith is not opinion.
Opinion is characterized by a lack of knowledge
which is not admitted and which then becomes har-
dened into an aggressive claim.[2] Essentially,
opinion is an affair of believing *that*; one has
opinion when one lacks knowledge and the aggressive
tone emerges as a compensation for this lack of
knowledge. In another context, the "believing that"
nature of opinion is related to its "externality"
to the very thing to which the opinion refers.
"The more of a state of affairs concerns me, the
less I can say in the strict sense of the term that
I have an opinion about it."[3]

Faith, on the other hand, refers to a
reality which can in no way be considered external
to me. Nor can faith itself be likened to a possession which I "have"--popular usage to the contrary notwithstanding. It is the stance of a
concrete being toward that which involves him most
intimately, i.e. his being. Instead of "having"

---

[1]Ibid. 78; italics Marcel's; cf. CF
134.

[2]CF 121 ff.; cf. MBII 68 ff.

[3]CF 129.

faith, one "is" one's faith; it stems from, or is directed to, or "grounds" one's being. It is through one's faith that one becomes a subject, for the act of faith concretizes most specifically just who I am. It is because of this intimacy of faith that one's faith cannot be verified by someone else; no "someone else" can take my place.[1]

Second, faith is not conviction. Conviction is distinguished by its note of finality. Convictions are "unshakable"; a barrier has been erected and the case is closed. Convictions refer to the past; to the extent that they are future-oriented, they see the future as fundamentally like the past, hence as totally anticipated. Convictions are pretensions which involve either a delusion or the consent to an inner lie.[2]

In contrast, faith is marked by an <u>opening</u> of the self as indicated by the metaphors of "rallying to . . ." or "opening credit for . . . ." Marcel, here draws upon his study of the man who is available, permeable to the world, to others and to being. Faith is accompanied by a sense of assurance--which is why it can be confused with conviction--but this assurance is of a very different nature: ". . . it goes beyond what is given, what I can experience, for it is an extrapolation, a leap, a bet, which like all bets can be lost. The stakes involved are difficult to define--for the reason that it is I who am the credit which I extend to the other."[3] And when the bet is lost, when defeat and disappointment occur, it is my very being who is affected and diminished. Faith is a risk for, on this model, no objective verification of my act of faith is possible. Conviction then, like

---

[1]CF 171, 182-183; BH 206; TPE 120.

[2]CF 130-134; MBII 75-77.

[3]CF 135.

194

opinion, is marked by its externality to me; faith, by its intimacy, its ability to affect the inner core of my being.

There is a close relationship between fidelity and religious faith; the latter is an extension of the former and they are nourished from the same source. One who is incapable of being faithful to a human thou is incapable of believing in an absolute thou.

It is clear that Marcel sees this experience of fidelity-faith as the intersubjective experience par excellence. Thus a pregnant entry in his journal,

> Being as the place of fidelity . . . .
> Access to ontology.
> Betrayal as evil in itself.[1]

serves to introduce an extended meditation[2] which begins with the question: "How can I promise--commit my future?" and continues by showing that it is the fidelity revealed in my commitment which pulls me out of the flux of time and brings me in touch with that which is perennial and indestructible, i.e. with being. Hence: "Being as the place of fidelity." Just as Marcel is unwilling to distinguish between beings and being, he is unwilling to distinguish between fidelity (to beings) and religious faith (to God/being). Being or God is revealed in beings; faith, in fidelity.

But a difference does remain. Both the continuity and the difference are noted very early in Marcel's thought.

> I could be prepared to say dogmatically that every relation of being to being is personal and that the relation between God and me is

---

[1] <u>BH</u> 41.   [2] Ibid. 41-56.

nothing if it is not a relation of being
with being, or, strictly, of being with
itself. The bizarre expression that comes
to my mind for stating this is that, while
an empirical "thou" can be converted into
a "him," God is the absolute "thou" who
can never become a "him."[1]

The finite thou is infinitely capable of being ob-
jectivized, though this objectivization can be
countered each time by a recapturing of the immediate participatory relationship. Even more,
objectivization of the finite thou is at times
legitimate. Thus there is an inevitable ambiguity
in every relation between finite thous:

> . . . if I stay on the hither side of the
> ontological affirmation . . . I can usually
> call into question the reality of the bond
> linking me to some particular being; in
> this domain disappointment is always possible
> in principle . . . . But . . . the more my
> consciousness is centered on God himself,
> evoked--or invoked--in his real being . . .
> the less conceivable this disappointment will
> be . . . . Hence this ground of fidelity
> which necessarily seems precarious to us as
> soon as we commit ourselves to another who
> is unknown, seems . . . unshakable when it
> is based not . . . on a distinct apprehension
> of God as someone other, but on a certain
> appeal delivered from the depths of my own
> insufficiency ad summam altitudinem; I have
> sometimes called this the absolute resort.[2]

In another context, this appeal is recognized as
being possible only because ". . . deep down in me
there is something other than me, something further

---

[1] MJ 137.

[2] CF 166-167; cf. BH 45-46.

within me than I am myself--and at once the appeal changes its index."[1] Marcel recognizes--and characteristically rejects as illegitimate--the question that poses itself immediately:

> Into an appeal for whom, however? Can I
> be sure, have I any justification for
> thinking, that this appeal is understood
> and that there is a being--someone--who
> knows me and evaluates me? We must reject
> at the outset the postulate on which this
> question is based . . . . The transcendence
> of the One to whom I appeal is a transcend-
> ence of all possible experience as well as
> of all rational calculation, which is but
> experience anticipated and schematized.[2]

And he continues:

> "Who am I? You alone really know me and
> judge me, to doubt You is not to free my-
> self but to annihilate myself. But to view
> Your reality as problematic would be to
> doubt You and, what is more, to deny You."[3]

It is impossible by definition--i.e. no possible legitimacy could attach itself--to any object--centered approach to the absolute thou. Marcel makes that point in this oft-repeated claim: ". . . when we speak of God we should realise that it is not of God that we are speaking."[4]

It is not surprising that Marcel should emphasize the parallels between religious faith and

---

[1] BH 125.

[2] CF 145.

[3] Ibid.

[4] MJ 159; italics Marcel's.

fidelity. However, it *is* striking that he should
find a parallel between religious faith and sensation.

> "Realised" this evening with prodigious
> lucidity:
> 1. That sensation (immediate consciousness)
> is infallible, that there is no place in it
> for error.
> 2. That in this way faith *ought* to partic-
> ipate in the nature of sensation (the
> metaphysical problem here lies in redis-
> covering, by thought and beyond thought, a
> new infallibility, a new immediacy).[1]

This passage is one of the first entries in the
second part of the Metaphysical Journal. The theme
returns in the very last entry in the Journal in a
discussion of his emerging view of existence as
presence, which directly reflects his view of sensation:

> . . . I am wondering whether we cannot throw
> light on the nature of belief by setting out
> from this theory of existence. Is not belief
> always the act by which I skip over one of
> the continuous series which bind up my im-
> mediate experience to a particular fact, and
> treat this fact as if it were given to me in
> the same way as my own body is given to me?[2]

Marcel suggests some of the implications of this
view:

> There is no need to underline how much this
> conclusion strengthens what I would like to
> call my "sensualistic" metaphysics. For
> obviously the connection between existence
> and sensation is as close as it could be.
> Is the connection with the theory of the

---

[1]Ibid. 131.   [2]Ibid. 316.

thou equally easy to grasp? As I see things
at present, it is. We must set out from the
him, from the _that_. _That_ is that of which I
speak to someone else . . . . To treat a being
as not taking us into account is in some way
to disinterest ourselves from this being
. . .; it is to adopt an attitude which is
fundamentally opposed to the attitude implied
by love.[1]

Marcel is very much aware of the materialistic implications of this view, but, as we have seen, he
prefers to deal with this problem[2] than to open the
possibility of a dualism between man and the existent universe.

> Although I have explicitly repudiated every-
> thing resembling or in any way connected
> with materialism, I would not be surprised
> if my complete rejection of dualism seems
> to some as necessarily establishing ties
> between man and his earthly environment
> which are so strong that the doors which
> open on the transcendent are thereby closed
> to him.[3]

Faith, then, is like sensation in its immediacy and hence in its infallibility. But in
recognizing this parallel, Marcel acknowledges that
"the metaphysical problem" lies in trying to redis-
cover--by and beyond thought--a new immediacy and
infallibility after the originals have been dis-
sipated by reflection--what he would later term
primary reflection--which dulls the immediacy of
faith and deprives it of its infallibility. Thus
is raised the central issue in Marcel's discussion
of religious faith: its status as knowledge.

---

[1] Ibid.

[2] Ibid. 315.

[3] CF 169.

In a brief retrospective note, Marcel suggested that the difficulty with which he had to cope in his earliest--i.e. ca. 1912--writings on faith was that of ". . . conceiving an order which, while irreducible to any objective constituents, would in no way be tainted by an arbitrariness commonly believed to prevail on the level of subjectivity."[1] It is a dilemma which was to haunt all of his work. In the Metaphysical Journal it appears as the choice between God as object or as ". . . the conceptualised expression of a particular manner of being or feeling which is properly mine," i.e. as a "personal disposition."[2] In The Mystery of Being, the choice lies between seeing faith as ". . . an incommunicable psychic event, which implies the end of any sort of theology, and that means of all universality" or else finding a way of ". . . framing something resembling a proof of the existence of God."[3]

That religious faith may be seen as arbitrary, subjective, a personal disposition, or an incommunicable psychic event is a position with which Marcel was intimately familiar. This was the "tragic" problem of Palais de sable (1913) which catches the sense of futility which Marcel himself felt at that period regarding his investigations into the intelligibility of religious faith.[4] Moirans, the protagonist of Palais de sable articulates the position very clearly:

La foi véritable surmonte l'illusion de l'objet; elle sait qu'il n'est pas de roc tangible auquel les hautes pensées se

---

[1] EBHD 25.

[2] MJ 261.

[3] MBII 173-174.

[4] MJ 133; ECVQE 82-88; cf. above, pp. 67-69.

200

heurtent. Nos pensées sont à elles-mêmes
leur seule réalité, elles se refusent à
se suspendre aux terrasses interdites du
monde.[1]

And he continues:

Il n'y a que des images qui passent au
fond d'une chambre obscure et qu'acclament
au passage les enthousiasmes humains . . . .
Mais parmi ces images, s'il en est d'ignobles
. . . il en est d'autres qui sont divines et
qui méritent d'être adorées . . . . Il faut
les aimer pour elles-mêmes, ces images
adorables et fugitives. La croyance ce
n'est que cela, l'adhésion de toute l'âme,
l'adhésion fervente à un beau rêve qu'on
sait n'être qu'un rêve.[2]

In another context, he suggests that the problem of
Palais de sable can only be solved by providing
some form of verification for religious faith.[3]   In
other words, the issue that this subjectivism poses
is that of the refutability of religious faith.   If
faith cannot be refuted, ". . . cannot even be refuted, . . . it is negligible" and should be dismissed by "a healthy man."[4]

Marcel does not dwell on a repudiation of
this position. If anything, Le Palais de sable is
as powerful a repudiation as any purely philosophical statement could be. In writing of the faith
of Moirans, Marcel characterizes it as dilettantish

---

[1]Palais de sable, p. 263; cf. Troisfontaines,
op. cit., II, 222-223.

[2]Palais de sable, p. 264.

[3]MJ 238.

[4]Ibid. 314.

and fraudulent.[1] The conclusion of the play shows Moirans rediscovering the concrete reality--not of his God--but of his daughter as a being worthy of being loved. Moirans discovers a finite thou and the implication is that one who is capable of loving another person may be capable of believing in a personal God. In a later discussion of the play, Marcel characterizes Moirans--and, by implication, the subjectivist--as blind:

> . . . his blindness is that of the idealist whose thought obscures communication with other people by preventing him from even imagining them in their concrete reality. Thus, we come upon one of the basic ideas of my work, and one to which we shall return . . .: self-consciousness, far from being an illuminating principle, as traditional philosophy has held, on the contrary shuts the human being in on himself and thus results in opacity rather than enlightenment.[2]

The metaphors of "sight" and "blindness," the role of openness to others and this evaluation of self-consciousness will play a significant role in our further discussion of the cognitivity of faith.

The alternative pole to subjectivism--if the dilemma is to be taken seriously--is that of objectivism. Marcel finds it exemplified in the enterprise of proving the existence of God. Whether or not God can be said to "exist" in the first place merits independent discussion. For the present, what can be said of the attempt to "prove" anything about God?

Marcel devotes an entire monograph to the subject and returns to his conclusions again and again. The core of his position is that for any

---

[1] EBHD 31-34.   [2] Ibid. 34.

202

kind of proof to succeed, there has to be what, in
different contexts, he calls a shared "field of
apperception," or a "minimum of agreement about
ends, about the supreme value," or a "minimal
assertion" apprehended as "necessarily true," or
finally, a shared "concrete situation" which implies the presence of a common ground or "vinculum"
--all of which can serve as the point of departure
for the proof.[1] The demonstration, then, should
move from this area of agreement to a further area
where agreement is not present at the outset.

     But paradoxically, when this sharing is
present, the proofs show themselves to be superfluous. Hence, "the proofs are ineffectual precisely when they would be most necessary, when,
that is, it is a question of convincing an un-
believer; conversely, when belief is already
present and when, accordingly, there is the minimum
of agreement, then they seem to serve no useful
purpose."[2] Marcel elaborates on the meaning of
this "minimum agreement":

     If a man has experienced the presence of God,
     not only has he no need of proofs, he may
     even go so far as to consider the idea of a
     demonstration as a slur on what is for him a
     sacred evidence. Now, from the point of view
     of a philosophy of existence, it is this sort
     of testimony which is the central and irre-
     ducible evidence. When, on the other hand,
     the presence of God is no longer--I shall not
     say felt, but recognised, then there is
     nothing which is not questionable . . . . The
     truth seems to be that there is room for only
     one thing here, and that is a conversion
     which no creature can flatter himself he is

---

[1]CF 175, 177, 180; MBII 176. On Marcel's
notion of proof, see Collins, op. cit., pp. 165-166.

[2]MBII 176; cf. CF 179.

capable of bringing about.[1]

In other words, the proofs seem to lack the power
to convince, whatever their intrinsic force.[2] When
they do convince, it is because, to use Marcel's
phrase, the "presence of God" has been "recognized."
The proof is simply a rendering in discursive or
conceptual form of an understanding previously arrived at in some other way. But then the demonstration is properly superfluous.

The proofs conceal another assumption which
Marcel finds wanting: they postulate "natural man"
as an a-historical constant. True to his situational approach, Marcel claims, in contrast, that
"natural man is a historical reality." He "evolves"
and he "disintegrates" and this disintegration

> . . . explains not the impossibility--it
> would be inappropriate to use this word--
> but the relative ineffectiveness on the
> apologetic level at least, of so-called
> rational theology . . . . In the final
> analysis, it is because the unity of man
> has been shattered, because his world is
> broken--that we confront this scandal of
> proofs which are logically irrefutable but
> .which in fact exhibit a lack of any per-
> suasive power.[3]

---

[1]MBII 176-177.

[2]The distinction is Collins', op. cit.,
p. 166.

[3]CF 180. A critique of Marcel's disparage-
ment of this "objective" approach may be found in
Blain, "Logic of Freedom," pp. 203-204. Marcel's
Thomist critics focus their objections on his
denial of God as creator: Sweeney, "Marcel's Position on God," pp. 122-124; Rudolph J. Gerber,
"Marcel and the Experiential Road to Metaphysics,"

The proofs are ineffectual because man
lives in a "broken world," and the shared understanding which renders the formal conceptual demonstration superfluous is the recognition of the
exigence of being by which man protests against his
broken world. That this is indeed Marcel's intent
becomes clear when he suggests what kind of proof
might be appropriate: "The proof can only consist
in a secondary reflection of the type which I have
defined; a reconstructive reflection grafted upon a
critical reflection; a reflection which is a recovery, but only in so far as it remains the
tributary of what I have called a blindfold intui-

Philosophy Today, 12 (Winter 1968), 274 ff.;
Gerber, "Gabriel Marcel and the Existence of God,"
Laval Théologique et Philosophique, 25 (1969), 9-
22; Gerber, "Difficulty with the Creative God in
Existential Phenomenology," The Personalist, Vol.
52, No. 4 (1970), 522-534. A more wide-ranging
critique is provided by Robert Osterman, "Gabriel
Marcel: Existence and the Idea of Being," The
Modern Schoolman, Vol. 32, No. 1 (November 1954),
19-38. The possibilities of reconciling Marcel and
Thomism are discussed by Mary Aloysius Schaldenbrand,
"Gabriel Marcel and Proof for the Existence of God,"
Studies in Philosophy and the History of Philosophy,
ed. by John K. Ryan, 1 (1961), 35-56; by Jeanne
Delhomme, "La Philosophie de Gabriel Marcel," Revue
thomiste, 44 (1938), 140-144 and by Clyde Pax, An
Existential Approach to God, pp. 73-104. Pax
(pp. 80-83) and Claude Bruaire, "Une Lecture du
Journal métaphysique," in "Extraits des Entretiens
. . .," pp. 343-346 suggest that his approach coincides with that of the ontological proof. (See
below, p. 219). Kenneth Gallagher, op. cit.,
pp. 133-157, presents a more forcefully argued case
for such a reconciliation. On the same issue cf.
Widmer, op. cit., pp. 139-145; Bagot, op. cit.,
pp. 155-164; Ricoeur, op. cit., pp. 352-360; and
Collins, op. cit., pp. 165-166.

tion."[1] Marcel specifies what this blindfold intuition consists of and how it functions:

> It is clear that the apprehension of the
> ontological mystery as metaproblematic is
> the motive force of this recovery through
> reflection. But we must not fail to notice
> that it is a reflexive motion of the mind
> that is here in question, <u>and not a heuristic
> process</u>. The proof can only confirm for us
> what has really been given to us in another
> way.[2]

The minimum of agreement, shared field of
apperception or shared concrete situation referred
to above now emerge in their true light as the
blindfold intuition of the ontological mystery, the
preconceptual awareness by the individual of his
participation in being. And the proof here is not
an objective demonstration of God's existence--not
a heuristic process--but a consciously willed recovery, on the level of secondary reflection, of
this preconceptual unity of man with being.

This is Marcel's way of avoiding the
dilemma of arbitrariness or objectivism. That the
dilemma seems so real to us is the function of
primary reflection. It is primary reflection which
attempts to reduce religious faith either to private
disposition or to the knowledge of an object-God
whose existence is or is not demonstrated. The
task of secondary reflection is first to challenge
the conclusions of primary reflection, i.e. to
question the image of faith implied in these alternatives, and then to recover the ontological dimension on a more conscious level.[3]

---

[1] <u>BH</u> 121.

[2] Ibid.; italics mine, N.G.

[3] <u>MBII</u> 67.

206

This is the basis for Marcel's ongoing protest that faith must be an affair of the intellect, that it must have a cognitive dimension. He characterizes his early work as an attempt to affirm ". . . the existence of a region beyond the verifiable which would be the province of religious thought" and he insists on the term "religious thought" because if religion is not to degenerate into pure sociology, ". . . it would have to remain thought."[1] In another context, he sets himself apart from Kierkegaard and Pascal in emphasizing ". . . the intelligible aspect of faith" for, he claims, the philosopher must emphasize ". . . the connection which binds together faith and the spirit of truth."[2] In this context, though he will emphasize the role of the will in faith, he denounces "the voluntarist error" which is based on separating the will from intelligence:

> A will without intelligence would be a mere impulse, and an intelligence which lacked will would be devitalized. But we shall only make it possible for ourselves, I shall not say to understand faith, but to discover some of its essential characteristics, if we establish ourselves at the ideal point of junction of these wrongly dissociated faculties.[3]

Marcel is aware of the way in which reflection seems to alienate man from his faith. He suggests that this reflection be understood as a test which can help the believer purify his faith the better to resist the attacks of objectivizing thought. But he also emphasizes that it is properly _reflection_ which ". . . confirm(s) the legitimacy of a faith which it grasps at first in its most abstract essence," with the understanding

---

[1]EBHD 25.   [2]MBII 177.

[3]Ibid. 178; cf. TWB 162.

that this reflection should lead steadily toward a more and more concrete reality to which faith refers.[1]

In an unpublished letter quoted by Trois-fontaines, Marcel protests against the misunderstanding which his approach has generated:

> Il devrait être évident pour tout lecteur attentif que la philosophie que je préconise est une philosophie de la réflexion. La réflexion seconde est plus profondément, plus essentiellement réflexion que la réflexion primaire. Certes elle s'apparaît à elle-même comme orientée vers ou, si l'on veut, comme aspirée par quelque chose qui la transcende et qu'elle ne peut avoir la prétention de comprendre, mais seulement de reconnaître . . . . Mais il n'y a absolument rien là qui puisse être taxé de fidéisme . . . il me semble que sur ce point ma position est très proche de celle de saint Augustin: Fides quaerens intellectum. Intellectus quaerens fidem.[2]

Marcel correctly isolates the issue of verification as having decisive importance in resolving this matter.[3] We saw above that he tends to understand verification in at least two ways which are not easily reconcilable. At times, he sees verification as implying the substitutability of subjects, hence as a depersonalizing of the subject of knowledge. This view of verification suggests that ". . . there is a set of conditions which are general in principle, i.e. are understood as normal or as applicable to any agent capable of

---

[1] MBII 127-128.

[2] Troisfontaines, op. cit., II, 235.

[3] MJ 314.

uttering valid judgements."[1]   But neither of these implications are operative in faith.   First, faith is the act of a whole person in his concrete singularity, and "no one can put himself _in my place_."[2] Again, "I am unable to take my friend's place for a number of reasons, of which the most striking is that he _is not distinct from his place_, that he is that very place itself . . . ."[3]

But in a different context, Marcel suggests that there are "infra- or supra-objective experiences, or levels of existence" where the "normal conditions of experience" are no longer applicable. Aesthetic experience is one such and it suggests a way in which miracles may be understood: "It is not inconceivable that there are beings who satisfy a set of spiritual conditions capable of modifying their apprehension of reality . . . . We can also concede that there are events which occur to such beings which have a maximum improbability from the point of view of our ordinary experience."[4]   In other words, there is a form of verification possible in the religious sphere but it is far from the universal verification afforded to scientific knowledge and hence not available to everyone indiscriminately.   There are religious--as there are aesthetic--connoisseurs, distinguished by refinement of perception, for whom this more tentative and limited kind of verificational process can take place.   We will have much more to say about these two approaches below.

Marcel's study of faith confirms what may

---

[1]_CF_ 6.

[2]_BH_ 206; italics Marcel's.

[3]_MJ_ 314; italics Marcel's.

[4]_CF_ 7.

be called his epistemological realism.[1] This is
spelled out most cogently in a series of entries in
Being and Having. He begins by establishing that
thought has to be seen as ". . . inside existence
. . . a mode of existence" which can abstract from
itself qua existence only at the price of falling
into a sort of lie or fundamental blindness; this
blindness, in turn, can disappear ". . . in proportion as it is accompanied by knowledge, which I
take to mean the return to being."[2]

     In this "return to being" thought discovers
itself as encompassed by being and hence as participating directly and without mediation, not in
the idea of being, but in being itself. "Thought,
far from being a relation with itself, is on the
contrary essentially a self-transcendence . . . .
Thought turns toward the Other, it is the pursuit
of the Other."[3] Understood in this fashion,
thought ". . . reaches Being itself past those intermediaries we call psychological (whose ontological nature remains, anyhow, impenetrable for us)."[4]
Again, a few pages later; "To assert the immanence
of thought in Being is to recognize with the

_____

     [1]Marcel's commentators prefer the phrase
"épistémologie personnaliste" (Ricoeur, op. cit.,
p. 49; Delhomme, op. cit., p. 139 and Widmer, op.
cit., p. 127) though the phrase is not Marcel's.
Bagot (op. cit., p. 150) understands it as identical with what Marcel means by participation,
i.e., ". . . un acte complexe, impliquant une noèse,
mais une noèse s'insérant elle-même dans une
dialectique vécue où appétit, désir, recherche
active d'une part, possession, saisie, contemplation de l'autre, ne cessaient d'interférer."

     [2]BH 27.

     [3]Ibid. 30.

     [4]Ibid. 32; italics Marcel's.

realists that thought, as soon as it is there, refers to something which transcends it and which it cannot claim to reabsorb into itself without betraying its true nature."[1] And still again, a few pages later: "I think, therefore, being is, since my thought demands being; it does not contain it analytically, but refers to it."[2] The same conclusion is reached from a different perspective: "Does our knowledge of particular things come to bear on the things themselves or on their Ideas? Impossible not to adopt the realist solution. Hence we pass to the problem of Being in itself. A blindfold knowledge of Being in general is implied in all particular knowledge."[3]

As we have seen, this immediate adherence to being itself is clearly Marcel's paradigmatic instance of sacred knowledge or knowledge of mystery. In this realm, subject and object adhere to or "participate" in one another. Further, participatory knowledge of this kind is absolutely personal or singular to the subject; in fact, it can be said to create the subject in all his singularity, for only this singular subject is involved in these participatory experiences. Finally, then, it is clear why this kind of direct adherence is beyond verification for what further experience could possibly verify such an absolutely singular and personal kind of adherence?

This train of thought is concretized into a distinction which is crucial to Marcel's epistemology and which is an extension of his distinction between "believing that" and "believing in."

Have been reflecting much on the difference between thinking (a thought) and thinking of (an object). Thinking is recognising

---

[1]Ibid. 36.   [2]Ibid. 38.

[3]Ibid. 28.

. . . a structure; thinking _of_ is something
quite different. German helps here: _denken_,
an etwas denken, _andenken_, _Andacht_. One
thinks _of_ a _being_ or even an _event_, past or
to come . . . . I may treat even an individual
person as an object of thought (I make this
transposition when I move from the Thou to
the He).[1]

He continues:

In brief, thinking does not come to bear on
anything but essences. Note that deperson-
alisation, while perfectly allowable in this
case, is impossible in the order of thinking
_of_. Only a _certain_ person can think _of_ a
certain being or a certain thing.[2]

How does this pertain to thinking--or thinking of--
God?

. . . we must try to understand how it is
that to pray to God is without any question
the only way to think of God, or more
accurately, a sort of equivalent raised to
a higher power of the action which would,
on a lower plane, be thinking of someone.
When I think of a finite being, I restore,
in a manner, between him and myself, a community, an intimacy, a _with_ . . . which
might have seem to have been broken . . . .
To ask myself how I can think of God is to
enquire in what sense I can be with Him.[3]

No single passage in all of Marcel's writings summarizes more strikingly the features of his
approach to religious knowledge:

---

[1]Ibid. 31. The French is "penser" and
"penser à."

[2]Ibid.   [3]Ibid. 31-32.

1. Faith is the intersubjective experience at its purest; it is an extension of the interpersonal relation between two human beings;

2. There is an inner tension within Marcel on the intellectual dimension to faith: faith is thinking, but not objective thinking; thinking _of_, not thinking that deals with _ideas_ of anything, not thinking that is tied to any intermediate psychological state, not thinking that is shut in by one's inner state of consciousness. The thinking that is appropriate to faith takes the form of direct participation in the reality to which faith refers, in God. Hence it is "being with," or attachment to God. Again, the materialistic implications are clear and again Marcel takes pains to deny them: ". . . do not forget that there is already, in the fact of _thinking of someone_, an active denying of space, that is, of the most material and also most illusory character of the 'with.'"[1]

3. Once again, however, we must ask in what sense this personal adherence to being or to any presence constitutes knowledge? Marcel is trying to avoid the dilemma of subjectivism or universalism. His dismissal of the "psychological intermediaries" with their "impenetrable" ontological status avoids the second of these alternatives. But if participation is in the reality itself--if it is a "being with" rather than a "thinking"--have we not, at the same time, done away with the epistemological dimension to the experience? We will have to return to this claim.

4. This view of thinking clearly stems from Marcel's primary emphasis on thought as "inside" existence, or as environed by being, i.e. as itself a mystery. This primitive awareness of blinded intuition of thought as within being functions in two

---

[1]Ibid. 32; italics Marcel's.

ways: it is the most important piece of data we have regarding the cognitive process itself within Marcel's broader metaphysical and ontological approach and it is, at the same time, the proto-act of faith, the primitive, pre-conceptual awareness that secondary reflection will recapture in bringing to full consciousness.[1]

5. Finally, most strikingly, this view leads Marcel to establish, if not the identity, then at least the parallelism or convergence of religion and metaphysics: "I am sure of this, anyhow: of the hidden identity of the way which leads to holiness and the road which leads the metaphysician to the affirmation of Being; also that it is necessary above all, for a concrete philosophy, to realise that here is one and the same road."[2] Thus the ultimate metaphysical act and the ultimate religious act are identical, as are, by implication, the metaphysical and religious absolutes. At the same time, he establishes the convergence of metaphysics and mysticism:

> . . . whether there is ultimately a precise boundary between metaphysics and mysticism is just what we are concerned to determine . . . . It is time that the metaphysician understands, if he wants once and for all to get out of the epistemological rut, that adoration can and ought to be a terra firma for reflection, a ground where he can find support, even though he is an empirical being and can participate in it only to the extent that his natural endowments permit.[3]

---

[1] Ibid. 55.

[2] Ibid. 84-85; cf. TPE 127.

[3] CF 146.

The infallibility, unverifiability, and
personal nature of religious faith are best summarized by Marcel's identification of religious
faith as testimony. Testimony requires the presence of an individual human being in all his
singularity and irreplaceability; his presence
makes him a witness and his presence is required
for testimony to be offered. Testimony must bear
on the historic, on an event that is unique and ir-
revocable, that cannot be reconstructed. The
giving of testimony implies--or at times requires--
the presence of an oath which consecrates both the
testimony and the witness; without a sense of the
sacred, testimony becomes meaningless. Testimony
commits the entire being of the witness; if the
testimony should prove false, it is not only the
word of the witness that has been annulled, it is
his entire person, his being that falls into question. The witness _is_ his testimony. The testimony
of the witness takes on an effectiveness that
transcends the life-span of the witness; in effect,
it bestows perennialness on the witness, which, in
Marcel's language means that it touches upon his
being. Finally, testimony always implies the
presence of another; in Marcel's language, testimony is "a-monadic" for we testify _to_ or in the
presence of some other person or persons, even if
no one _is_ physically present at the moment of testimony.[1]

Marcel refuses to accept the "false dilemma"
that we have a choice between serving as onlookers
or witnesses in our stance toward our lives. "By
adopting this standpoint, do we not forfeit all
chance of understanding the essential point of our
lives--the fact that we are witnesses and that this
is the expression of our mode of belonging to the
world?"[2]

---

[1]On faith as testimony, see _TPE_ 91-97; _BH_
210-212; _MBII_ 129-131.

[2]_TPE_ 97.

In the light of this, faith emerges as
". . . unceasing attestation"[1] which can only be of
". . . the living God,"[2] not the God whose existence
is demonstrated by rational theologies.

God

If faith is belief in, rallying to or extending credit to, what does this imply about that
reality to which faith refers? From what has gone
before, certain facts are clear. We have faith in
a reality who is personal, in a thou who is absolute, i.e. capable of bearing the weight of absolute recourse; who is living, i.e. historic or
capable of being encountered in an interpersonal
relation; and who is a presence, i.e. not external
to the believer but representing a depth within
himself in which he participates by virtue of the
fact that he _is_.

It is clear from this that what Marcel has
to say about God could be and in fact is said about
being. The overwhelming impression from Marcel's
work is that being and God are simply two ways of
referring to the same reality. What then, is the
relationship between the two? Why do we need these
two vocabularies? When do we use one term and when
the other?

Surprisingly, Marcel has little of an explicit nature to offer as an answer to these questions. There is one suggestive programmatic passage at the beginning of the second volume of The
Mystery of Being, but this passage raises more
questions than it answers. The context is a discussion of the exigence of being which is the point
of departure for metaphysics:

---

[1]BH 211.

[2]MBII 131.

. . . while we had then (i.e. in volume 1,
N.G.) to be satisfied with speaking of the
exigence of transcendence, we shall now be
led to examine the exigence of God. We
could say, I believe, in future that the
exigence of God is simply the exigence of
transcendence disclosing its true face, a
face that was shown to us before shrouded
in veils.[1]

He continues by describing how he plans to study
how metaphysics and religious philosophy are "inter-
locked" but then, in an apparent reversal he claims:

. . . we cannot lay it down as a principle
and a starting point that being as such
. . . is necessarily to be identified with
that which a believing consciousness gives
the name of God. Let us accordingly lay it
down once and for all . . . that it is only
the living witness, that is to say the
believing consciousness, which can decide
what can or cannot be regarded as God. I
shall lay it down as a principle . . .
that it is beyond the power of any philosophy
. . . to force a coup d'état which installs
as God something which the believing consciousness recognizes as such.[2]

Granted that it is not the philosopher who has the
right to identify being as God but only "the
believing consciousness," we are still no further
advanced regarding the how or why of this identification, nor the difference that such an identification would make.

These questions will have to be faced. For
the present, two prior issues regarding God.

---

[1]MBII 3.

[2]Ibid. 4.

First, can God be said to exist? The answer
to this question is necessarily complicated by the
evolution of Marcel's thinking about existence.
There is a central thrust to all of his writing on
this particular issue: the reality of God seems to
him to be inevitably compromised by talk of His
existence.[1] The problem then is to determine the
ground or motivation for denying God's existence so
that God's reality not be denied in the process.

This issue is raised at the very outset of
the Journal. He notes that God's existence can be
denied:

a. as self-contradictory (a squared circle);
b. as not in fact encountered in experience;
   or
c. as not in principle encounterable in experience in the first place.[2]

There are at least two ambiguities in this
scheme, one regarding the meaning of "experience"
and the other of "existence." The very last entry
of the Journal attacks the latter of these. "Thus
what is needed is the possibility of safeguarding
the existence of the absolute thou without attributing to it an objectivity that would ruin its
essence. It is at this point that my efforts to
dissociate existence and objectivity attain their
full significance."[3] Marcel may well have dissociated existence from objectivity but there is no
hint as yet of his possible distinction between
existence and being. The central thrust of all the
Journal entries on this issue, however, is directed
to distinguishing between the latter two of the
three original denials and of establishing that
when Marcel denies the existence of God, it is only
in the last sense that this denial must be under-

---

[1]EBHD 27.   [2]MJ 33.

[3]Ibid. 314.

stood. Thus, in the continuation to the earlier
entry in the <u>Journal</u> (and in the intricate vocabulary of Marcel's early philosophizing):

> To deny God as existing, in our sense, is
> to refuse absolutely to treat Him as an
> empirical object, and at the same time and
> in consequence to deny (and the negation
> is transformed into a negation of itself,
> that is, into the negation of a negation)
> that anything in experience, that anything
> in that which exists, can be <u>incompatible</u>
> with God, can <u>exclude</u> God. In this way the
> negation of the existence of God is con-
> verted into an affirmation of the power of
> God as transcendent as regards all that is
> empirically possible.[1]

Thus the denial of God's existence as
empirical object leads to the affirmation of His
"reality" as "transcendence," later to become
"being." Marcel recognizes in this formulation the
germ of the ontological argument, though he objects
both to what he calls the excessively "facile" form
of the argument--he refers to it as "playing with
words"--and to the fact that it is presented as an
argument in the first place.[2] Quite consistently,
if God's existence or non-existence cannot be
established on objective grounds, Marcel's refuta-
tions of atheism will move in an entirely different
direction as well.

----

[1]Ibid. 34; cf. 132, 154, 228, 261-262.

[2]MJ 33; BH 121, and his response to Claude
Bruaire, "Extraits des Entretiens . . .,"
pp. 350 ff. Paul Tillich shares Marcel's ambivalence about the ontological argument, retaining
the "nerve" of the argument in his "ontological
awareness of the unconditional" but like Marcel
rejecting it as an argument (<u>Theology of Culture</u>,
pp. 15-16).

But what of God's existence in the light of
Marcel's mature (i.e. post Metaphysical Journal,
Part one) thought on existence? We know that
Marcel reached the conclusion that existence, or the
"existential orbit" was tied to the sense of "my
body" so that "the existent universe" is a prolongation of the kind of intimacy (without materialistic implications) I feel toward "my body."[1] Does
God lie within this existential orbit? This question implies still another question, equally difficult to resolve: does being exist? what is the
relation between existence and being?

     Troisfontaines--who is rarely succinct--
summarizes everything that can be said about this
issue in four sentences:

> C'est l'existence "objectivité" (l'existence-
> première manière) que Marcel nie à Dieu.
> Quant à l'existence deuxième manière (i.e.
> what we have called Marcel's mature thought
> on existence, N.G.) inapplicable à Dieu lui-
> même, elle peut désigner notre "participation
> de fait" comme créatures; une relation
> constitutive avec Dieu est même incluse dans
> le donné immédiat d'où part toute pensée.
> Mais ce rapport immédiat, la pensée, ou bien
> l'altère en "l'objectivant" (réflexion
> première), ou bien le reconnaît en dépassant
> "l'objectivation" (réflexion seconde)--et
> alors nous accédons précisément au plan de
> l'être. L'existence (telle que l'entend
> Marcel) n'est jamais un demonstrandum, un
> point d'aboutissement; elle ne peut être
> qu'un point de départ, rien de plus.[2]

In short, Marcel's discussion of this issue is, for

---

[1]MJ 315.

[2]Troisfontaines, op. cit., II, 214; italics
Troisfontaines'.

the most part, devoted to a rejection of God's
existence as empirical "object." For the rest, the
existence of God is ruled out as an issue because
of Marcel's peculiar understanding of the "nature"
of God. To the extent that there is a blinded intuition of man's being-in-the-world within the
existent universe, there is an encounter on a pre-
conceptual level with God as existing, except that
on that level, it is totally inappropriate to
single God out as part of this undifferentiated
existential orbit.

Second, Marcel is similarly wary of conferring on God anything approaching the traditional
attributes. If God is absolute presence, we have
exhausted, by that phrase, all that we can say of
Him.

> . . . the absolute Thou is not merely unat-
> tainable but can only be thought apart from
> all those questions which the creature never
> ceases to raise: who is he? what does he
> want? what is he thinking? I have always
> had the conviction that the attributes of
> God as defined by rational theology:
> simplicity, immutability, etc., have value
> only if we succeed in discovering behind
> them the qualities of a Thou which cannot
> be construed as a him without being denatured
> or reduced to our absurd, human proportions.
> "When we speak of God it is not of God that
> we speak" I wrote not so long ago. I cannot
> overstress the fact that theological affirma-
> tions as such are a snare; for the "proper-
> ties" I have just mentioned, if construed
> as predicates, seem to be the most impover-
> ished that exist;[1]

God, as being, cannot be reduced to the realm of
"having" anything. He is best characterized by the

---

[1]CF 36; cf. BH 121-122; MJ 158.

biblical "I am that I am."[1] Parallel with his disdain for theology as a means of reaching God goes
an appreciation for worship: "God can only be given
to me as Absolute Presence in worship; any idea I
form of Him is only an abstract expression or in-
tellectualization of the Presence."[2] This goes
hand in hand with the claim that God is "living"
and that the only way to "think of" God is to pray
to Him, which in turn is to "be with" Him.

Marcel is extraordinarily sensitive to the
subtleties--both philosophical and psychological--
involved in the affirmation or denial of God. He
insists, first that it is not always clear who is
the believer and who the non-believer. Whose
evidence do we accept? Surely not that of the
believer himself. It is the responsibility of the
authentic believer to take account of the non-belief
that exists at the heart of his faith and thus
establish a bond with the so-called non-believer,
possibly realizing thereby that the latter may
embody the act of faith in greater purity than he
does.[3]

But granted that there is such a phenomenon
as the authentic non-believer--what makes him tick?
The dynamics of atheism is a topic to which Marcel
returns again and again.[4]

Atheism may come in a variety of forms.
There is an atheism that claims to base itself on
experience, either on the non-experience of God or
on the experience of facts that are incompatible
with what his concept of God would allow. Here,

---

[1]BH 147.   [2]Ibid. 170.

[3]CF 181; "Extraits des Entretiens . . .,"
p. 400.

[4]CF 120-139, 175-183; MBII 71-75; BH 199-
212; TWB 158-170.

atheism appears as a "hypothesis" which opposes the
equally "hypothetical" faith of the believer.
Marcel dismisses this as the least interesting and
important of the forms of atheism. He sees it as
completely misunderstanding the nature of faith.[1]

Second, there is an atheism which takes the
form of a simple claim ("revendication") as opposed
to an empirically based judgment--a definitive, unshakable, closed conviction that will not allow any
new data or question to intrude. This position is
a dogmatic one, a deliberate, willed closing-out of
the option for faith--in Marcel's vocabulary, a
lack of permeability.[2]

Third, if faith can be considered as a
response to an invitation, atheism can take the
form of a refusal--either through inattention or
out of pride. The atheist is telling the believer
that he does not wish to follow the believer's road
because it leads where he does not want to go--
either out of a fear that it would limit his freedom, or because belief is seen as an obstacle to
humanism, or finally because belief is identified
with an irrelevant and socially irresponsible
clericalism.[3]

Finally, there is an "existential" atheism
--what Marcel calls an atheism of revolt. He considers this to be the only form of atheism worthy
of serious philosophical consideration. When it is
based, for example, on a serious and sensitive appreciation of the reality of evil and suffering in
the world, it can become, paradoxically ". . . the
initial act in a purifying dialectic." It is the
responsibility of the philosopher and theologian to
deal directly with the conditions that call forth

---

[1]MBII 71-75; MJ 226-230; CF 127-130; TWB
158-162.

[2]CF 130-133.

[3]CF 178-179; BH 207-210; TWB 165-167.

this revolt so that it may indeed lead to a "decisive advance" in belief.[1]

The turn from atheism to belief is an act of secondary reflection. Like all acts of secondary reflection, it begins with a clearing of the ground, a critique of the views of faith propounded by primary reflection which understands faith as credulity, as an escape, as a hypothesis, as a private psychic phenomenon, as an internal disposition, or as an objective judgment on the world. It is set in motion by the will, by the exercise of a free option of the individual or of the soul ". . . as she wills or refuses to acknowledge that higher principle which momentarily creates her and is the cause of her being, and as she makes herself penetrable or impenetrable to that transcendent yet inward action without which she is nothing."[2]

The turn from non-belief to belief is "conversion"--". . . the act by which man is called to become a witness."[3] Conversion is to a "particular historical religion," i.e. to a particular revelational community.[4] Metaphysis does not bring about conversion; ". . . at its furthest extension metaphysical thought perceives the possibility of conversion, but perceives it as being dependent on conditions which it is beyond the power of freedom to bring about by itself."[5] In other words, freedom may be central to a philosopher's appreciation of ". . . the exigence of transcendence in its fullness" through secondary reflection, but this may still ". . . fall short of conversion to any

---

[1] TWB 168-170.   [2] BH 212.

[3] MBII 133; cf. TWB 185 where conversion is defined as ". . . acceptance of a specific creed in a certain specific ecclesiastical context."

[4] MBII 133.   [5] Ibid.

224

particular historical religion."[1] Conversion, then, depends on an interlocking of freedom and grace.

Metaphysical reflection may not bring about conversion but it provides the indispensable grounding which alone makes the welcoming of revelation possible.

> I would point out that no revelation is, after all, conceivable unless it is addressed to a being who is <u>involved</u>--<u>committed</u>--in the sense which I have tried to define--that is to say, to a being who participates in a reality which is non-problematical and which provides him with his foundation as subject. Supernatural life <u>must</u>, when all is said and done, find a hold in the natural . . . .[2]

And he continues:

> . . . I would say that the recognition of the ontological mystery, in which I perceive as it were the central redoubt of metaphysics . . . is perfectly well able to affect souls who are strangers to all positive religion of whatever kind; . . . this recognition, which takes place through certain higher modes of human experience, in no way involves the adherence to any given religion; but it enables those who have attained to it to perceive the possibility of a revelation in a way which is not open to those who have never ventured beyond the frontiers of the realm of the problematical and who have therefore never reached the point from which the mystery of being can be seen and recognised.[3]

Thus his understanding of his philosophical activity

---

[1]Ibid.   [2]<u>TPE</u> 46.

[3]Ibid. Cf. <u>TWB</u> 185-186.

as "the priming of a concrete spirituality" or as "a philosophy of the threshold" which can bring man to the point of conversion.[1]

The final step of conversion may be prompted by a variety of factors. Marcel emphasizes the role of an encounter with a genuine witness. One of the crucial steps on the road to belief is the stage of believing in the faith of others, the recognition that faith is a reality for the man who has it though the subject himself does not.[2] What happens in the encounter is nothing resembling a demonstration or the communication of objectively verifiable new information, but much as a flame kindles a flame, the witness calls to those who would, to travel their own roads from unbelief to belief.

Three final questions: Is participation in being identical with religious faith? Apparently not. Faith is not a metaphysical but a religious act; it acquires significance only within a communal, revelational structure.

Second, is being to be identified with God? The answer would have to be: not necessarily--for only the witness can make that identification when he is prepared to do so. But God should never be anything less than being, unless he is an idol.

But neither of these questions can be answered with complete confidence. Marcel uses two vocabularies: that of existential ontology and that of religion, without showing how and when the former is to be translated into the latter, or even distinguishing clearly when each can be used appropriately.

Paul Tillich, who also uses these two

---

[1]MBII 133; TWB 240.

[2]BH 202; MBII 138-139.

226

vocabularies, accounts for their inter-relationship though a theory of religious and theological symbolism. The religious absolute, God, is a symbol for the philosophical absolute, being. One has faith in the theological symbol, God, but one has an immediate self-evident awareness of being which provides the criterion of ultimacy by which we evaluate all concrete representations (i.e. symbols) which it assumes.[1]

There is no hint of this approach in Marcel. Neither does it appear in the thought of another contemporary philosopher of religion, Abraham Joshua Heschel, whose fundamental approach to these questions, conceptual scheme and vocabulary are strikingly similar to Marcel's. For Heschel, religion begins with a meeting between man--impelled by a sense of "radical amazement" (as opposed to intellectual curiosity)--and God--who is all "pathos," i.e. in an intimate, personal outreaching relation with the world. Both God and man are active in the relation, i.e. "in search" of each other. The meeting is momentary, personal, ineffable and self-verifying. It is also "preconceptual"; what we gain in the meeting is "awareness," not knowledge. Heschel is explicit in rejecting any attempt to provide an epistemological account of the experience. He sees all conceptualization and verbalization as an accommodation which may clarify the encounter but never capture its living reality or its immediacy. The assertion "God is" is an understatement, a feeble representation of the overwhelming reality of the presence of God to the believer.[2]

---

[1]Tillich, <u>Theology of Culture</u>, pp. 27-29.

[2]Heschel's most sustained analysis of the religious experience is in Part 1 of <u>God in Search of Man: A Philosophy of Judaism</u> (Philadelphia: The Jewish Publication Society of America, 1956), especially, pp. 101-124. His phenomenological analysis

But note that for Heschel, what is encountered is not being but rather God in His living
reality. Heschel emphatically rejects all theories
of theological or religious symbolism; a symbol is
a fiction or a substitute. He insists that any
theory of symbolism must provide a method for evaluating the validity or adequacy of the symbol,
which in turns requires a prior knowledge of what
it is that is being symbolized. However if we have
this prior knowledge, a symbol is superfluous; if
we don't, our symbolization becomes totally arbitrary.[1] Tillich, however--who is the implicit
target of this critique--does claim that we have at
least an awareness of what is being symbolized, i.e.
being. Heschel, on the other hand, has nothing to
say about being though he insists that God is immediately and unquestionably present to the believer.

Marcel's difficulty is that he insists on
the reality of both being and God but provides no
explicit account of how they are related. He conceives of the two vocabularies as flowing imperceptibly into one another and sees no possible
legitimate use of the vocabulary of religion without its prior grounding in the existential-ontolog-
ical scheme that he has propounded. The point of
contact between philosophy and religion cannot be

---

of the divine pathos is in The Prophets (Philadelphia: The Jewish Publication Society of America,
1955), especially chapters 12-14. The most in-
cisive and clearest exposition of Heschel's thought
is Fritz A. Rothschild's Introduction to Between
God and Man: An Interpretation of Judaism from the
Writings of Abraham J. Heschel, selected, edited
and introduced by Fritz A. Rothschild (New York:
Harper and Brothers, 1959).

[1]Heschel's critique of religious and
theological symbolism is in his Man's Quest for
God: Studies in Prayer and Symbolism (New York:
Charles Scribner's Sons, 1954), pp. 115-144.

pinpointed with accuracy, but, he seems to suggest that, if philosophical theism is in any way legitimate, if God can be attested to at all within a purely philosophical framework, such an attestation will remain highly precarious unless it merges into a formal religious affirmation within a revelational community.[1]

Finally, what then is religious knowledge? It is the conscious recovery, through secondary reflection, of our participation in being as translated into the vocabulary of a revelational community by one who thereby becomes a witness to God within that community. Our final task is to evaluate this position.

---

[1]This seems to be the thrust of one of his last statements on this question: ". . . the affirmation of God . . . comes into contact with philosophy . . . at the farthest limit of a philosophical inquiry (TWB 185-186). Cf. his description of how ". . . theism . . . melt(s) into Christianity . . ." in his "Theism and Personal Relationships" (p. 35), and of revelation as ". . . the crowning of an immense cosmic travail which at one and the same time calls it forth and implies it as its internal source" (ibid. 42).

CHAPTER VI

RELIGIOUS KNOWLEDGE: PROBLEM OR MYSTERY

The Unities in Marcel's Thought

There is no question that Marcel intends
his study of religious faith to stand as the pin-
nacle of his thought. It is no accident that every
major statement of his philosophical position
climaxes with a discussion of this issue. It was
his earliest philosophical concern, it is constantly in the forefront of his writings and it may
well be the single most important source of the
real unity which--his disclaimers to the contrary
notwithstanding--characterizes his work.[1]

Consider the following: man's situation is
characterized by two dimensions, that of incarnation (the self-body-sensation-existent universe
continuum) and that of intersubjectivity (the self-
body-love-thou continuum). Ultimately each dimension discloses being. But to the believer, being
is God; what is ultimately disclosed in the situation, then, both through the existent universe and
the thou, is God.

Hence, Marcel can write: "My deepest and
most unshakable conviction . . . is, that whatever
all the thinkers and doctors have said, it is not
God's will at all to be loved by us against the
Creation, but rather glorified through the Creation

---

[1]A perceptive analysis of the unity in
Marcel's thought is suggested by Roger Hazelton,
"Marcel on Mystery," pp. 163-167.

and with the Creation as our starting-point."[1]

But the linkage is even more narrow. We saw that faith (the participatory relation in religion) is modeled on sensation (the participatory relation in incarnation) in its immediacy, indubitability and unverifiability and is an extension of fidelity (the participatory relation in intersubjectivity). Fidelity is often described as identical to love which is Marcel's alternative to the traditional knowledge by a subject of an object distinct from it. Sensation, faith and love/fidelity are paradigms of participatory knowledge and each nurses from the other; each demands a certain permeability or openness within the situation of the individual and permeability in one dimension affects permeability in the other dimensions. Finally, each is achieved through secondary reflection.

Marcel uses each dimension of the situation to illuminate the others. An extended discussion of sensation leads imperceptibly into a discussion of what happens when one receives or welcomes an outsider into one's home with the active/passive nature of the latter welcoming illuminating the interactional character of the former.[2] Sometimes, key terms appear in startlingly varied contexts in one brief passage:

> It is an essential characteristic of the being to whom I give my fidelity to be not only liable to be betrayed, but also in some manner affected by my betrayal. Fidelity regarded as witness perpetuated; . . . Being is, as it were, attested. The senses are witnesses--this is important, and I think new; systematically ignored by idealism.[3]

---

[1]BH 135.   [2]CF 24-26.

[3]BH 96.

Here the theme of testimony appears in each of the three dimensions.

We saw above that much of the ambiguity in Marcel's thought stems from this disconcerting tendency to apply a univocal scheme to a wide variety of data. We must concede, however, that this also accounts for the unusually suggestive power of his phenomenological analyses which will remain as Marcel's enduring contribution to philosophy. The student who reads his work with "permeability" is struck again and again by the unexpected associations and imaginative perceptions that appear on every page. But the final impression is one of ambiguity and incompleteness--particularly in his philosophical treatment of religion. To a large extent this is the result of Marcel's philosophical style. All of these issues haunted him in one way or another for well over six decades; we find him continuously chipping away at different facets of the issues, often modifying his earlier views but never systematically bringing it all together. Merleau-Ponty's judgment that ". . . we do not have to do here with a fulfilled philosophy . . . (but rather with) suggestions"[1] may well serve as the most perceptive verdict not only on <u>Being and Having</u> but on his work as a whole, providing that we do not overlook the real unities and the genuine value that characterize these "suggestions" on a wide range of philosophical issues.

Marcel on Religious Knowledge

But the issue which this study is designed to clarify is Marcel's discussion of religious knowledge; it is on this issue that our final appraisal must focus.

---

[1] Maurice Merleau-Ponty, "Etre et avoir," p. 109.

Two claims are central to Marcel's epistemology: religious knowledge, as an instance of sacred knowledge, constitutes a genuine form of knowledge; and it is immediate knowledge, beyond doubt and verification. Each merits discussion.

As a point of departure, let us begin with an approach suggested by William T. Blackstone[1]-- of course without claiming that this approach is exclusive or conclusive. Blackstone's approach consists of four steps:

a. a delineation of the range of religious claims as a distinct class;

b. an investigation of whether these claims have cognitive significance (i.e. whether they can be true or false) which involves the elaboration of criteria for cognitivity and an evaluation of whether these claims meet this test;

c. a discussion of the epistemological issue, i.e. the elaboration of criteria for the application of the term "knowledge" and the vindication of these criteria;

d. an investigation of whether those religious claims that meet the test of cognitivity meet the further test for knowledge.[2]

The two crucial steps in this discussion are the elaboration of the two sets of criteria: for cognitivity and for knowledge. For the first of these, Blackstone proposes the test of falsifiability,[3] i.e. that some data be able to be found incompatible with the claim. For the second,

---

[1]William T. Blackstone, The Problem of Religious Knowledge (Englewood Cliffs, N.J.: Prentice-Hall, Inc., 1963).

[2]Ibid. 4.   [3]Ibid. 53.

234

Blackstone uses the three requirements set forth by
Ayer: ". . . first that what one is said to know be
true, secondly that one be sure of it, and thirdly
that one should have the right to be sure."[1] Ayer
insists, and Blackstone agrees, that all three
requirements must be fulfilled before one can be
said to know. But Blackstone distinguishes further
between knowledge in a pure sense and "justified
knowledge claims." The former applies when the
claim could never turn out to be false; the latter
". . . is a claim or belief for which one has 'good
grounds,' a belief which is strongly supported by
the evidence available."[2] Thus, Blackstone suggests that the task of epistemology is

> . . . to assist one in discovering which
> attitude (in a scale including belief, dis-
> belief, no opinion, etc.) is the appropriate
> attitude to adopt toward any given statement.
> Specifically in regard to sentences which
> perform the function which we have designated
> as religious, it is the task of the epis-
> temologist to assist us in discovering which
> attitude . . . is the appropriate attitude to
> adopt toward a given religious sentence.[3]

In conclusion Blackstone presents a set of vindicat-
ing arguments for the validity of his approach in
general and for these two sets of criteria in particular.

It is beyond question that Marcel is making

---

[1]Alfred J. Ayer, The Problem of Knowledge
(London: The Macmillan Co., 1956), p. 35. Blackstone, op. cit., p. 131. A substantially similar
proposal is made by John Herman Randall Jr., The
Role of Knowledge, p. 103.

[2]Blackstone, op. cit., p. 135.

[3]Ibid. 128-129.

epistemological claims for religion. He is not part of what Blackstone characterizes as the "left wing response" to the challenge of falsifiability, i.e. the response that concedes that religious claims do not meet the falsifiability test and are hence factually meaningless though they may accomplish other significant functions.[1] In fact, on at least one occasion, he explicitly accepts the falsifiability test.[2] He is equally explicit in insisting that religion yields knowledge. Negatively, he rejects any suggestion that religion is reducible to a "manner of feeling,"[3] "an incommunicable psychic event,"[4] an act of the will alone,[5] sociology,[6] or pure arbitrariness and subjectivity.[7] This is the Palais de sable syndrome and Marcel finds it totally unacceptable. Positively, his discussion of religious faith is studded with references to what he insists is its intellectual character. The apprehension of God is achieved through a secondary reflection or "reflexive motion of the mind";[8] the province of religion is a province of "religious thought";[9] faith has to be "intelligible";[10] the metaphysical problem surrounding faith is to try to recover a new immediacy and infallibility ". . . by thought and beyond thought."[11] He insists that religious knowledge is but one instance of sacred knowledge, knowledge of the mysterious which is reached by ". . . an essentially positive act of the mind";[12] it is similar to metaphysics which is ". . .

---

[1]Ibid. 75.

[2]MJ 314.

[3]Ibid. 261.

[4]MBII 173.

[5]Ibid. 178.

[6]EBHD 25.

[7]Ibid.

[8]BH 121.

[9]EBHD 25.

[10]MBII 177.

[11]MJ 131.

[12]BH 118.

reflection trained on mystery";[1] and finally the metaphysical unease which is the impetus for philosophy in the first place ". . . can only find peace in knowledge."[2]

But granted that metaphysical peace can only be achieved through knowledge, Marcel is at once constrained to ask: "But of what knowledge is there a question here?" It is a question that haunts all of Marcel's work; it reveals a fundamental tension that lies at the heart of his thought. For side by side with his insistence that it is knowledge that metaphysics seeks, and stemming from the most primitive anti-idealist and anti-rationalist roots of his thought, there lies a profound mistrust of the knowledge-seeking function of philosophy. It manifests itself in his oft-repeated denial that philosophy can provide an exhaustive account of reality in the form of knowledge. The universe into which we have been thrown ". . . cannot satisfy our reason";[3] the mind cannot objectively ". . . define the structure of reality and then regard itself as qualified to legislate for it."[4] This is an inevitable outcome of his view that cognition itself is a mystery, that it is implanted in and surrounded by being, that being transcends thought and thought can therefore never reabsorb being without betraying it,[5] and that the inquiry into being presupposes a prior, pre-conceptual affirmation of being through the subject of the inquiry as subject.[6] Finally, the impetus for philosophy is not primarily to explain or to understand but to try to transcend man's unease in

---

[1]Ibid. 100. [2]HV 139.

[3]TPE 124. [4]Ibid. 127.

[5]BH 36.

[6]Ibid. 115; TPE 17-18.

the face of his mortality.[1]

        This thrust finds its way into Marcel's writings on religion in his rejection of all rational theologies and in his more extreme claim that

> . . . God can only be given to me as Absolute Presence in worship; any idea I form of Him is only an abstract expression or intellectualization of the Presence. I must never fail to remember this, when I try to handle such thoughts; otherwise the thoughts will suffer distortion in my sacrilegious hands.[2]

It is further clarified by the distinction between "thinking" and "thinking of" and finds its ultimate expression in the identification of "thinking of God" with "praying to God" and "being with God,"[3] of the metaphysician's affirmation of being with "holiness"[4] and of metaphysics with mysticism.[5] But at this point, hasn't Marcel implicitly abandoned his preoccupation with religion as a source of knowledge?[6]

----

[1]MJ 288-293.   [2]BH 170.

[3]Ibid. 31-32.   [4]Ibid. 84-85.

[5]CF 146.

[6]Ricoeur identifies this tension as the fundamental difficulty in Marcel's existential ontology: "Si l'affirmation ontologique n'était aucunement un acte intellectuel, elle ne pourrait non plus être élevée au discours philosophique." Anticipating Marcel's objection, he specifies, further, that this problem does not stem from primary reflection, but rather from Marcel's own ontology (Entretiens autour de Gabriel Marcel, pp. 70-71). In a later exchange in the same volume (pp. 253-257) Ricoeur insists that the task of the

This tension confirms that at the heart of Marcel's thought lie certain experiences which are by definition individualistic and ineffable. This places Marcel into a double-edged conflict: with the strong social or intersubjective thrust of his own thinking on one hand and with the commonly held view of knowledge as a shared, social enterprise.[1] We will have to see in greater detail below whether it is possible for Marcel to maintain all of these impulses in equilibrium. For the present, it is sufficient to note that it is precisely this ir-resolution which accounts for the very precarious state of whatever knowledge Marcel does allow into religion.

Again, a comparison of Marcel's position on these issues with that of another thinker will help clarify the problem. Martin Buber shares with Marcel not only a basic approach and philosophical

---

philosopher is not necessarily to choose "exis-tence" over "objectivity" but rather to hold on to the link between the two and that the realm of the problematic is properly that of the specialist in philosophy. He adds: "Renoncer à la parole est un certain suicide du philosophe" (p. 257). Marcel, consistently, affirms that from his perspective, the philosophical specialist must be viewed with suspicion and that it would be easier for him to communicate with someone who has no philosophical training than with the professor of philosophy (pp. 249-250). This exchange took place two months before his death. The tension regarding the cog-nitive dimension in philosophy persisted to the very end.

[1]On knowledge as "a social product," see John Herman Randall Jr. and Justus Buchler, Philosophy: An Introduction, College Outline Series (New York: Barnes and Noble, 1942, revised edition, 1971), p. 117. It is worth noting that the context here is a critique of Bergson.

vocabulary but also an uncanny agreement on a host
of specific issues. But in a group of papers published as <u>Eclipse of God</u>[1] Buber meets head-on the
issue of knowledge in religion.

Buber's treatment of religious knowledge
differs from Marcel's in two ways:

a. Buber does not recognize any purely <u>philosoph-</u>
<u>ical</u> apprehension of being as <u>personal</u>, concrete,
imminent and transcendent; that takes place only
within religion;

b. consequently, Buber sharply minimizes the dimension of knowledge in the religious encounter between
the believer and God.

For Buber, as for Marcel, faith is "living in relationship" to being affirmed as eternal or absolute
Thou in "lived concreteness" (the relationship of I
to Thou); philosophy, in contrast, abstracts from
the concrete situation and dissolves the "lived
relationship" into a knowing subject and an object
distinct from and external to it (the relationship
of I to It).[2] Philosophy yields knowledge--even
knowledge of being itself:

> I-It finds its highest concentration and
> illumination in philosophical knowledge.
> In this knowledge the extraction of the
> subject from the I of the immediate lived
> togetherness of I and It and the trans-

---

[1]Martin Buber, <u>Eclipse of God</u> (New York:
Harper and Brothers, 1952). Buber also enjoyed a
long and productive career in philosophy and wrote
on all of these themes at various points in his
career. The position outlined here emerges specifically in this volume and does not claim to represent all of Buber's thinking on these issues.

[2]Ibid. 44-45.

formation of the It into the object detached
in its essence produces the exact thinking of
contemplated existing beings, yes, of contemplated Being itself.[1]

This does not imply a derogation of philosophy. On the contrary, knowledge is both a
"need" and a "duty" of man; the eating of the fruit
of the tree of knowledge led man into the world.
But on the other hand, "philosophy errs in thinking
of religion as founded in a noetical act, even if
an inadequate one . . . ."[2] Again,

That meaning is open and accessible in the
lived concrete does not mean it is to be won
and possessed through any type of analytical
or synthetic investigation or through any
type of reflection upon the lived concrete.
Meaning is to be experienced in living action
and suffering itself, in the unreduced immediacy of the moment.[3]

Like Marcel, Buber recognized the possible
claim that religion is an "intra-psychic" process
and that ". . . every alleged colloquy with the

----

[1]Ibid. 61-62.

[2]Ibid. 116. There are isolated passages in
Marcel's work where he seems to echo Buber here.
One striking instance is in TWB 14-15 where he
affirms that religion depends on faith only, and
philosophy, on reflection. But he immediately
modifies this claim by reminding us of the distinction between primary and secondary reflection. See
also BH 187 and his definition of "pure religion"
as ". . . a realm where the subject is confronted
with something over which he can obtain no hold at
all" and where he simply has to ". . . give himself
up." Here religion is reduced to worship alone.

[3]Ibid. 49.

divine (is) only a soliloquy, or rather a conversation between various strata of the self."[1] But
again like Marcel, Buber categorically rejects this:

> Actually, this proclamation means only that
> man has become incapable of apprehending a
> reality absolutely independent of himself
> and of having a relation with it . . . .
> For the great images of God fashioned by
> mankind are born not of imagination but of
> real encounters with real divine power and
> glory.[2]

In other words, no external criteriology can be
brought to bear on the living relationship itself;
the criticism is thus rejected as irrelevant. We
will return to this approach in our discussion of
verification below.

Buber does recognize, however, a dialectical
relationship between philosophy and religion.
Religion describes the encounter between the believer and the absolute Thou; but as the reality of
the encounter is attenuated, there arise concepts
of the Thou which ultimately become obstacles to
His presence.

> Then comes round the hour of the philosopher,
> who rejects both the image and the God which
> it symbolizes and opposes to it the pure idea
> . . . . This critical "atheism" . . . is the
> prayer which is spoken in the third person in
> the form of speech about an idea. It is the
> prayer of the philosopher to the again un-
> known God. It is well suited to arouse
> religious men and to impel them to set forth
> right across the God-deprived reality to a
> new meeting.[3]

---

[1]Ibid. 22.   [2]Ibid.

[3]Ibid. 63.

Thus the philosopher recognizes that

> . . . his idea of the Absolute was dissolving
> at the point where the Absolute lives, that
> it was dissolving at the point where the
> Absolute is loved; because at that point the
> Absolute is no longer the "Absolute" about
> which one may philosophize, but God.[1]

Thus the proper role of philosophy--and of
knowledge--is a critical one; it parallels what in
Marcel's thought is the negative or ground-clearing
role of secondary reflection in dismissing the improper representations of faith and God. But there
is no parallel in Buber's thought for Marcel's
"positive act of the mind" in which secondary reflection recaptures on a conscious level the immediately lived relationship with being of the
blinded intuition. Buber's "lived relationship"
with God does not lend itself to epistemological
accounting because it is not knowledge. Marcel
does attempt to find an epistemological dimension
to this further step; however, it is precisely this
further epistemological account that is fraught
with problems.

There is a genuine difference in the way
Buber and Marcel understand "religion." For Marcel,
the religious act seems to indicate conversion into
a specific revelational community; everything prior
to this is philosophy or metaphysics. Buber offers
a more generalized description of faith as it appears in any religious framework.

What is at issue here, however, is not
simply how these two thinkers use the terms "philosophy" and "religion"; there is a genuine difference of opinion regarding the point at which
knowledge and hence epistemological accounting
enters into and then departs from the dialectic

---

[1]Ibid. 69.

which produces the living relationship with God.
Buber sees the role of philosophy or knowledge as
essentially negative or critical; it dissolves
before faith. Marcel, in contrast, tries to establish faith as an act of knowledge, describable in
terms of its own distinctive epistemology.[1]

---

[1]Marcel published two monographs on Buber's
thought: "I and Thou" in The Philosophy of Martin
Buber, ed. by Paul Arthur Schilpp and Maurice
Friedman, The Library of Living Philosophers, Vol.
XII; and "Martin Buber's Philosophical Anthropology" in SEAR, pp. 73-92. Both touch upon some
highlights of Buber's thought and suggest some contrasts with Marcel's own formulations. More interesting for our purposes is Buber's clarification,
in this "Replies to my Critics" portion of the
volume, of the dialectic between I-Thou and I-It
from the perspective of epistemology: "Authentic
philosophizing originates ever anew from the fulgurations of the Thou relationship that still affords
no 'objective' knowledge . . . . Indeed, 'I-It
finds its highest concentration and clarification
in philosophical knowledge': but that in no way
means that this knowledge contains nothing other
than I-It, is nothing other than I-It. The fiery
track of the original fulgurations is inextinguish-
able . . . . An I-Thou knowledge that can be held
fast, preserved, factually transmitted does not
really exist. That which discloses itself to me
from time to time in the I-Thou relationship can
only become such a knowledge through transmission
into the I-It sphere. . . . Every essential knowledge is in its origin contact with an existing
being and in its completion possession of an enduring concept" (ibid. 692). The "fulgurations of the
Thou relationship" corresponds to Marcel's "blinded
intuition" of being; but consistently, there is no
recapturing of the intuition by a secondary reflection, nor is there any hint of a distinct kind of
"sacred knowledge." Significantly, Marcel's
"Martin Buber's Philosophical Anthropology" quotes

Marcel on Verification

There is then a real question, on the basis of the strictly _internal_ evidence mustered thus far, as to how seriously we should treat Marcel's claim that religion yields knowledge however defined; the comparison with Buber served to highlight this question. The question is sharpened, however, when we consider the issue of verification for this will determine the extent to which Marcel's account of religious knowledge can meet the criteria of knowledge suggested above.

We have noted above[1] that Marcel approaches the issue of verification in two contradictory ways, sometimes dismissing the issue as irrelevant to sacred knowledge which does not need and is beyond verification, and at other times, conceding the appropriateness of a more modest and imprecise kind of verificational experience while protesting against the far too rigid expectations of a scientifically-founded verificationism.

". . . as a motto for this lecture . . ." and with apparent approval, an earlier paragraph by Buber which makes the same claim as the above, i.e. that the I-Thou experience must be turned into an I-It, into concepts, for it to be transmitted to and valid for others as well (_SEAR_ 74). The Library of Living Philosophers volume on Marcel, announced some years ago, has not yet as of this writing (1979) appeared. In the absence of Marcel's own "Replies to my Critics" portion of this volume, one is grateful for the two extended discussions with other philosophers in which Marcel participated actively, and which have been published in recent years in _Entretiens autour de Gabriel Marcel_ and in _Revue de Métaphysique et de Morale_, 79e année, No. 4 (October-December 1974).

[1]Pp. 177-180.

The first approach is far more characteristic of Marcel especially in the area of religious
knowledge. He is aware of the possibility that the
appeal to being/God may go unanswered: "Can I be
sure, have I any justification for thinking, that
this appeal is understood and that there is a being
--someone--who knows me and evaluates me?"[1] But
the possibility is dismissed:

> We must reject at the outset the postulate
> on which this question is based . . . . In
> asking myself whether there is a being who
> hears my appeal and is capable of responding
> to it, I consider it as a hypothesis, a
> proposition which implies a possible veri-
> fication. It is clear, however, that if
> "by a miracle," I was in a position to per-
> form this verification . . . this Other,
> this empirically identifiable Receiver,
> neither would nor could be that absolute
> Resource to which I addressed my appeal.[2]

And he continues:

> Who am I? You alone really know me and
> judge me; to doubt You is not to free myself
> but to annihilate myself. But to view your
> reality as problematic would be to doubt You,
> and, what is more, to deny You.[3]

Not only is there no need for verification, then,
the very presence of a possible verificational experience must be mistrusted; what can be verified
is not God. In this vein, Marcel seems to be
identifying with the naive, unsophisticated man of
faith who asks: what kind of God would He be if I
can verify Him? The very posing of the problem of
verification is illegitimate, whether the purpose

---

[1]_CF_ 145.   [2]Ibid.

[3]Ibid.

be to expose error or to yield certainty. The felt
certainty of the believer is beyond any further
confirmation and the believer himself knows that
there can be no possibility of error. By implication, the critic who proposes the need for verification cannot obtain it for he is not open to God;
if he were, he, like the believer, would not need
it. Therefore neither the believer nor the critic
need verification and so the issue is dismissed.

In another context, Marcel grounds his dismissal of verification in the fact that verification implies ". ... that there is a set of conditions which are general in principle . . . as
applicable to any agent capable of uttering valid
judgments."[1] But this view implies the notion of
a "depersonalized subject" which is precisely what
sacred or religious knowledge rules out. There is
no concern for building up a progressively growing,
consolidated and shared body of knowledge. The
intermittent, incommunicable nature of sacred
knowledge eliminates the very legitimacy of public
verification.

Finally, the issue of verification is tied
to the issue of freedom. If religious knowledge
can be verified, then my act of faith would be
coerced by the evidence available and would lose
its value as the act which concretizes my freedom.[2]

In this vein, Marcel confronts head on the
proponents of the need to verify religious claims.
To the charge that he has no way to screen out
delusional, hallucinatory or inaccurate claims,
Marcel would reply that the believer <u>knows</u> that
none of these apply in his case, and that a critic
<u>could not know</u> what it is that the believer ex-
periences so that nothing that he could claim would
make any difference to the believer.

---

[1]Ibid. 6.   [2]<u>PI</u> 243-244.

The response of the verificationist to this position would have to be that Marcel's religious claims are thereby reduced to a series of purely autobiographical assertions regarding his private, subjective experiences alone, with no reference to anything beyond, to being or God however conceived. In other words, the verificationist would reaffirm the _Palais de sable_ position as the only legitimate one on Marcel's _own_ terms. To use Blackstone's criteria, Marcel's claims might be viewed as cognitive (because _some_ data is relevant to the truth or falsity of the claims) and even as knowledge. But the _extent_ of the knowledge would be reduced to a purely autobiographical claim that the believer has had that particular set of experiences.[1] And were Marcel to challenge these _criteria_, the verificationist would concede that all such criteria are proposals which need validation if they are to show themselves to be useful. But it then becomes Marcel's responsibility to propose alternate criteria and provide for their validation. Marcel does neither; he is torn between wanting to use the honorific "knowledge" while vigorously opposing any purely intellectualist stance in all of his philosophical analyses.

The issue here has been posed with clarity and succinctness by Emil Fackenheim who juxtaposes what he calls a "Buberian" view of faith and "subjectivist reductionism."[2] The subjectivist

---

[1]Blackstone, p. 58; Randall, _The Role of Knowledge_, pp. 94-95.

[2]Emil L. Fackenheim, "On the Eclipse of God," _Commentary_, 37 (June 1964), 55-60, reprinted in _Quest for Past and Future: Essays in Jewish Theology_ (Bloomington, Indiana and London: Indiana University Press, 1968), pp. 229-243. We have seen that Buber and Marcel do not agree completely on the range of these issues but Marcel's discussion of the nature of religious faith in e.g. "Some

reduces faith to private feelings accompanied by an illegitimate inference to a God who accounts for the feelings. The Buberian sees the man of faith in a real encounter with God who is a Thou over and above him. There is no way to judge between these claims, says Fackenheim, because to the Buberian, faith can only be known in an actual encounter which is just what the critic cannot or will not have. The critic cannot dismiss the believer's faith as a pseudo-faith because he, the critic, does not have a genuine relation to God to use as a standard to measure what is genuine or "pseudo" in a faith relationship. He can <u>decide</u> that there is no such thing as a real encounter, but he cannot <u>demonstrate</u> it.

> Buber's response to the challenge of sub-
> jectivist reductionism has disclosed that
> it does not refute Biblical faith, but
> rather that it opposes one faith to another.
> Biblical faith stakes all on man's primor-
> dial openness to the Divine . . . . The
> reductionist "faith" stakes all on the
> thesis that man is primordially shut off
> from God, and that all supposed openness
> is mere self-delusion.[1]

Thoughts on Faith" (<u>BH</u> 199-212), is strikingly similar to that of the Buberian man of faith as described by Fackenheim.

[1]Fackenheim, <u>Quest</u>, p. 242. Marcel agrees that the subjectivist position is indeed a postulate (<u>BH</u> 204-206; <u>TWB</u> 228). Buber's own formulation of his response to the charge of subjectivism is: "The experience for which I witnessed is, naturally, a limited one. But it is not to be understood as a 'subjective' one. I have tested it through my appeal and test it ever anew. I say to him who listens to me: 'It is your experience. Recollect it, and what you cannot recollect, dare to attain it as experience.' But he who seriously

But neither can the reductionist position be refuted:

> It cannot refute but only reject it; and it can testify against it. For the argument cuts both ways. The reductionist cannot use observable data--religious images and feelings--to demonstrate the subjectivity of faith. But neither can the believer use these same data to demonstrate the objectivity of faith.[1]

It is in this sense that Marcel describes faith as an "extrapolation" or a "bet" which can be lost; it is a risk on which the believer stakes his personal sense of being.[2] At this point, we also become aware of the critical role of the will; we opt for or we refuse, we declare ourselves open or closed, and a good deal of that decision is determined by the degree of openness which we have permitted into the other dimensions of our situation.

The crux of the argument revolves around what, if anything, is encountered in the encounter. The Buberian insists that the believer meets an actual Thou.[3] The reductionist counters that it is precisely the actuality of the Thou in the encounter that is in question. The believer suggests that if the reductionist would open himself to the encounter, he too would meet an actual Thou. The

---

declines to do it, I take him seriously. His declining is my problem" (Schilpp and Friedman, op. cit., p. 693). Marcel would agree.

[1]_Quest_, p. 242.

[2]_CF_ 135.

[3]"We must realize, I think, the truth of Plotinus' idea that God is veritably for us only in so far as we participate in him" (_MJ_ 35).

reductionist counters that no amount of simple
openness could yield certainty of an actual as opposed to an illusory Thou. There is no real clash
here; the two positions simply pass one another by
and no amount of demonstration or argumentation can
have any effect. The only hope for closing the gap
is through conversion.[1]

---

[1]In another discussion of the same conflict
(Encounters Between Judaism and Modern Philosophy
[New York: Basic Books, Inc., 1973]), Fackenheim
distinguishes sharply between the Buberian stance
on faith and any empiricist position, insisting
that for the Buberian, no possible experience could
verify or falsify faith. In order to appraise the
doctrine of encounter, then, ". . . a philosopher
must shed every trace of empiricism" (p. 27). It
is difficult, however, to hold Marcel to the
Buberian position on this issue. At times he
clearly echoes Buber: "We must notice that the object of faith is simply not manifested with the
characteristics which distinguish any empirical
person. It cannot figure in experience, since it
entirely commands and transcends experience" (BH
206). Also Marcel's denial of atheism is based at
least in part on the denial that God can be encountered in experience. In other contexts, however, he writes ". . . there must exist a possibility of having an experience of the transcendent as
such and unless that possibility exists the word
can have no meaning" (MBI 46; italics Marcel's), or
". . . it is a recourse to a certain type of experience which must be recognized first of all and
which in some way bears within itself the warrant
of its own value" (TWB 228-229). The passage from
BH is, as we have seen, in complete agreement with
Fackenheim's paraphrase of Buber; the second position conforms with Marcel's second approach to
verification to be studied below. Fackenheim
presents still a third version of this encounter in
Schilpp and Friedman, op. cit., pp. 273-296. A
survey of the strengths and weaknesses of the

From the perspective of this stance on the issue of verification, then, the most that Marcel can hope to emerge with is a stand-off. His position is unassailable by the reductionist but neither is the reductionist's by Marcel. From a broader perspective, however, Marcel's position is trivialized. The believer may well derive a heightened sense of personal meaning by virtue of his religious faith, but there is no way in which that meaning can be shared with anyone who is not within that identical frame of reference or what is more important, taken seriously by any one else. The irony in all of this is that Marcel takes the intersubjective experience very seriously indeed and locates it at the very center of his thought. It is not surprising then to find him in different contexts, moving toward a very different stance on this issue of verification.[1]

But what has been established here is that the two issues of verification and the status of religious knowledge are intimately linked to one another. To the extent that Marcel dismisses the issue of verification as irrelevant and identifies "thinking of" God as "being with" God, we must conclude that there is no intelligible way in which he can speak of acquiring knowledge--sacred or otherwise--of God. Ironically, on this approach, Marcel's conclusions here rejoin those of the end of Part one of the Journal. Faith (love) and knowledge are antithetical; faith is sensed as an obligation; demonstration and verification are absolutely ruled out, and God is only insofar as we

---

encounter approach to religious faith is in Fred Ferré, Language, Logic and God (New York: Harper and Brothers, 1961), chapter 8.

[1]Marcel's own hesitation regarding this first approach to verification emerges clearly in ECVQE 217-219.

participate in Him. In other words, he has reaf-
firmed the "tragic" _Palais de sable_ syndrome once
again.[1]

But throughout Marcel's mature work there
can be traced a second approach to this entire
issue. It can be pieced together from different
strands of Marcel's philosophical explorations on a
variety of issues.

This second stance emerges in his repeated
identification with the empirical tradition in
philosophy; in his early attempts to break with
idealism by seeking ". . . access to a higher empiricism,"[2] in his recollection of the holiday
world of his childhood where he ". . . allowed experience to proliferate without submitting it to
the control of thought,"[3] in his view of philosophy
as an "explicitation . . . of immediate experience"
so that he would remain creative as a philosopher
as long as his experience ". . . still contains unexploited and unchartered zones."[4]

It emerges toward the end of his career in
his reaffirmation of Schelling's "higher empiricism" which he characterizes as ". . . a recourse
to a certain type of experience" or as ". . . (a)
way of appreciating experience" so that he may
acknowledge certain ". . . cardinal experiences
. . . which effect . . . the retrieval of the
ontological aim and the criticism of the modalities

_____

[1]_MJ_ 133 and our discussion of this position,
above, pp. 67-69.

[2]_TPE_ 106; Hocking, "Marcel and Metaphysics,"
p. 441, refers to this as Marcel's "broadened and
heightened empiricism."

[3]Ibid. 116.

[4]Ibid. 128.

which conceal it from us."[1]   His method is "mining these experiences in order to recover there that reference to being . . ."[2]--what, in other contexts, he calls their "ontological weight"[3] or their "metaphysical tenor."[4]

It emerges, again, in one of his last published statements on the role of philosophy. ". . . Different philosophical (or artistic)experiences can enter into communication with one another. I would even say that a philosophical experience that is not able to welcome an experience other than itself in order to understand or if necessary go beyond it ought to be regarded as negligible."[5]

In regard to the role and nature of religion, it emerges in his claim that faith in God should have some sort of "universality,"[6] in his insistence that the word "transcendence" does not mean "transcending experience" for there must exist ". . . a possibility of having an experience _of_ the transcendent as such . . ." for ". . . beyond all experience, there is nothing";[7] in his claim that religious faith and the Christian fact are fundamental data which the philosopher ignores at the risk of his own impoverishment for philosophy is an "exaltation" of experience, not its "castration."[8] It is explicit in his claim that ". . . j'attache infiniment plus d'importance à l'élément empirique que bien des théologiens."[9]

It emerges, finally, in two striking

---

[1]_TWB_ 228-229.   [2]Ibid. 228.

[3]_BH_ 103.   [4]_PI_ 126.

[5]_TWB_ 7.   [6]_MBII_ 174.

[7]_MBI_ 46-47; italics Marcel's.

[8]_CF_ 79-80.   [9]_ECVQE_ 208.

passages, one dealing with miracles and the other with survival after death. In the first, Marcel claims that if we do away with the "postulate" of normal conditions of experience," we can illuminate the question of miracles. He continues: "It is not inconceivable that there are beings who satisfy a set of spiritual conditions capable of modifying their apprehension of reality . . . . We can also concede that there are events which occur to such beings which have a maximum improbability from the point of view of our ordinary experience."[1]

As to survival after death, he claims that

. . . metaphysical reflection . . . permit(s) me to select signs capable of conferring on this free act a minimum guarantee which I need. I need this guarantee because despite everything I continue to remain the center of a critical and polemic reflection, which, if it does not overcome itself, is secretly attracted by despair and nothingness. These signs have a consistency just sufficient for doing their job; if they were proofs, my freedom before death would be as it were annulled and so . . . life as well as death would find itself stripped of its serious-ness, the sacrifice shorn of its tragic and ultimate grandeur.[2]

There is, then, in Marcel's work, an ap-proach which sees faith as grounded in a wide range of public experiences, as verifiable in some tenta-tive way (which will have to be clarified) and most important, as eminently shareable with others so that the believer may call out to "other travel-lers" in the hope that ". . . certain other minds (will) respond--not the generality but this being

---

[1] <u>CF</u> 7-8.

[2] <u>PI</u> 243-244.

255

and that other . . . ."[1] Thus the effectiveness of
a witness in arousing the faith of another person,
or more generally, of philosophy as "an aid to discovery"[2] or "a flame arousing another flame."[3]

Characteristically, in these contexts,
Marcel uses the model of aesthetic appreciation.
To discern the presence of being or God in the
world is analogous to discerning beauty in a paint-
ing or order in a musical composition. In each
instance what is required is a refinement of taste,
a sensitivity to what is being presented, possibly
a certain education in the medium and above all a
certain openness to the experience.[4] Under these
circumstances the "postulate" of the strict verifi-
cationalists, namely that there are certain "normal
conditions of experience" which apply equally to
all men is clearly inapplicable.

A particular musical composition . . . seems

---

[1]TPE 44.

[2]MBI 2.

[3]MJ x.

[4]MBI 8-14; PI 19-20; EBHD 25-26; CF 4-8;
TWB 5-8. A perceptive elaboration of the parallels between religion and art concludes John
Herman Randall Jr.'s The Role of Knowledge in
Western Religion, pp. 123-134. Marcel would certainly concur with Randall's claim that religion
". . . teach(es) us to see what man's life in the
world is, and what it might be . . ." (p. 128),
though he would surely disagree that the "religious
knowledge" so gained is a "technique, a know-how"
(p. 133). He would, however, agree more with
Randall than with Tillich on maintaining a balance
between the "revealing" and "receiving" activity
in the religious transaction (n. 4, p. 124 and
n. 10, p. 131).

a pure chaos of sound to my neighbour while
I discern an order which completely escapes
him: shall we say that one of us is experi-
encing it under normal conditions while the
other is not? This is plainly an improper
way of speaking. It would be more appropriate to say that I am somehow in harmony with
the work while my neighbour is not. The
example is sufficient to indicate that there
are realms of experience which possess a
particular order or intelligibility subject
to conditions which cannot be properly
specified.[1]

Thus the question is not whether or not experience
is decisive, but rather of knowing which experience
is decisive and how that experience is to be
qualified. Significantly this apprehension takes
place only within the context of a real community:

One must be within the privileged world where
these events take place in order to discern,
appreciate or sanctify them. For this reason
miracles can only be acknowledged and authen-
ticated by the Church . . . . In evoking in
this context the role of the Church, I am
referring to a real community . . . A community is only possible when beings acknowledge that they are mutually different while
existing together in their differences.[2]

Marcel further specifies what makes real community
possible:

If we adopt the religious point of view, it
can be said that the universal is the awareness of participating together in a unique
adventure, in a fundamental and indivisible
mystery of human destiny. What brings me
closer to another being . . . is not the

---

[1]CF 6-7.   [2]Ibid. 7-8.

knowledge that he can check and confirm an
addition or subtraction I had to do for my
business account; it is rather the thought
that he has passed through the same difficulties I have, that he has undergone the
same dangers, that he has had a childhood,
been loved . . .; and it also means that he
is called upon to suffer, decline and die.[1]

All of this clearly suggests a very different kind
of approach to the challenge posed by the verifica-
tionist--but one that, as we can see, is very much
in line with some of the basic assumptions of
Marcel's thought as a whole.

A model for this approach to the verification of religious claims is suggested by John
Wisdom in his seminal paper "Gods."[2] Wisdom suggests that "the facts" that are discoverable by
experience and that can verify or fail to verify
religious claims need not simply be the kinds of
facts discoverable by a scientist and his micro-
scope; that to discern these facts may be analogous
to discerning a pattern when all the details of the
pattern are before the observers; that the pattern,
here, may be revealed by patient exploration,
sharpening and sharing of insight, by noting connections and disconnections that are not apparent
at first sight; hence, that disputes regarding the
existence or non-existence of the pattern are at
least in principle resolvable; and finally that the
procedure is similar to that used by two observers
trying to decide whether a work of art is beautiful
or not, or by men in a court of law trying to determine whether a defendant was or was not negligent.

---

[1] Ibid. 8.

[2] Proceedings of the Aristotelian Society,
London, 1944-45, pp. 185-206, reprinted inter alia
in Logic and Language (First Series), ed. Antony
Flew (Oxford: Basil Blackwell, 1952), pp. 187-206.

The Wisdom model illuminates the second
approach to verification in Marcel's thought. It
acknowledges that certain experiences can be more
or less revealing to men who are more or less able
to see or "open" to what they reveal; that one's
perception can be sharpened through a sharing of
the experience or blunted by an inability or refusal to look afresh; that what one sees or doesn't
see depends on a host of factors such as personality, education or cultivation (which by themselves have nothing overtly to do with religion)
yet still leaves room for a free act of the will;
that religious claims, then, are not purely autobiographical or subjective states of mind but
refer to "the facts" or "reality"--with this
reality both without and within the believer--and
that at least the more obvious cases of illusion
and hallucination can be weeded out; and finally,
that there is a sense in which religious disputes
are resolvable by a procedure which may be more
tentative and subtle than that used by science, but
which nevertheless shows itself to be effective <u>for
the purpose</u>.[1]

The basic similarity of approach between
Wisdom and Marcel may be seen--with due allowance
for differences in style and vocabulary--in these
two extracts. First Wisdom:

---

[1]A different perspective on the parallels
between Marcel and Wisdom is suggested by Jann
Benson, "John Wisdom and Gabriel Marcel on Proving
the Existence of God," <u>Philosophy Today</u>, Vol. 21,
No. 2 (Summer 1977), 194-200. Benson claims that
both Marcel and Wisdom implicitly reformulate the
traditional teleological argument for the existence
of God which he sees as neither completely <u>a priori</u>
nor completely synthetic. It does, however, confirm that questions of God's existence are not
beyond the scope of thought and reason. Benson's
reading of Marcel is based exclusively on one paper
in <u>CF</u> (175-183).

For when a man has an attitude which it
seems to us he should not have or lacks one
which it seems to us he should have then,
not only do we suspect that he is not influenced by connections which we feel should
influence him and draw his attention to
these, but also we suspect he is influenced
by connections which should not influence
him and draw his attention to these . . . .
Sometimes the power of these connections
comes mainly from a man's mismanagement of
the language he is using . . . . _Usually,_
however, wrongheadedness or wrongheartedness
in a situation, blindness to what is there
or seeing what is not . . . _is more due to_
connections which are not mishandled in
language, for the reason that they are not
put into language at all . . . . (It) is
certain that in order to settle in ourselves
what weight we shall attach to someone's
confidence or attitude we not only ask him
for his reasons, but also look for unconscious reasons both good and bad; that is,
for reasons which he can't put into words,
isn't explicitly aware of, is hardly aware
of, isn't aware of at all--.[1]

And now Marcel:

From the point of view of faith and of the
believer, unbelief . . . begins to look like
a refusal, refusal moreover which can take
on many different forms . . . . Perhaps most
often, it takes the form of inattention, of
turning a deaf ear to the appeal made by an
inner voice to all that is deepest in us
. . . . This inattention . . . is indeed a
kind of sleep, from which we can each of us
awake at any time. The inattentive man may
be awakened just by meeting somebody who

---

[1]_Proceedings_, pp. 198-199; italics Wisdom's.

radiates genuine faith . . . . The virtue
of such encounters is to rouse the inattentive to a reflection or return upon
themselves, to make them say "Am I really
sure that I don't believe"? This is
enough: . . . .[1]

On this second approach, then, how does
Marcel fare with regard to the tests for cognitivity and for knowledge?

In regard first to cognitivity (which now
becomes a far more pressing issue than on Marcel's
first approach to verification because of the more
"public" nature of these experiences), Blackstone's
very formulation of the criterion for cognitivity
as falsifiability is based on Antony Flew's
critique of Wisdom which has the sceptic asking:
"Just what would have to happen not merely (morally
and wrongly) to tempt but also (logically and
rightly) to entitle us to say 'God does not love
us' or even 'God does not exist'?"[2] Flew's answer
is that on Wisdom's model, nothing could possibly
count against God's love or God's existence and
Flew's conclusion is that "the religious hypothesis"
dies a death "by a thousand qualifications."[3] On
this basis both Flew and Blackstone would question
the very cognitivity of Marcel's assertions, let
alone his claim to provide for the possibility of
religious knowledge.

Marcel's and Wisdom's response to this
would involve two steps. Step one would be to

---

[1]BH 208-209.

[2]Antony Flew, "Theology and Falsification,"
New Essays in Philosophical Theology, ed. Antony
Flew and Alasdair MacIntyre (New York: The Mac-
millan Company, 1955), p. 99.

[3]Ibid. 97.

challenge Flew's formulation of the principle of falsifiability as excessively rigid, narrow and incapable of dealing fairly with the complexity and variety of all of man's knowing encounters with the world--and remodel it. Step two would be to answer Flew's formulation of the sceptic's question quite directly and show that it does meet the challenge of falsifiability in its new form. Both steps assume that the kind of experience that is relevant to the issue of cognitivity is not the private encounter of the believer with an Absolute Thou but rather a wide range of public experiences which cut across the believer's entire life span and which have to be assigned their proper weight.

Marcel and Wisdom would contend first that Flew's formulation of the principle of falsifiability is flawed by resting the case for whether what Flew, significantly, calls "the religious hypothesis" lives or dies as a meaningful assertion on an excessively simplistic view of experience as passive observation alone.

What they seem to be saying is that the way in which experience counts for or against religious assertions is a much more complex affair than a traditional empiricist would have it.[1] Marcel claims that all of experience has an interactional --or to use his term--a "participatory" character, that it is not a simple, passive undergoing but includes an active dimension which Marcel characterizes as a "welcoming," an "extending of hospitality" or a "giving of oneself," and that this active/passive character of experience extends throughout the range of participatory experiences from sensation (in the dimension of incarnation) through love (in the dimension of intersubjectivity) and to the experience of transcendence/being/

---

[1]See e.g. Marcel's comments on how he understands experience (TWB 228-229).

262

God.[1] How decisive the renderings of experience
are will depend on the _active_ side of the experience, on what the individual brings to the experience from himself, which may include conscious
conceptual schemes, education, basic character or
personality traits and a much more primitive set of
unconscious attitudes and feelings. All of these
factors will affect how the individual "reads" or
what implications he sees in his experience. In
particular, these unconscious factors will affect
what the individual _wants_ to experience and how _he_
wants to be influenced by it. Finally, both Wisdom
and Marcel insist that in religion all of these
factors are more apt to come into play than in
other areas of human behavior.

    This is what Marcel seems to be getting at
in his attempt to locate religious knowledge within
the broader category of sacred knowledge, to link
religious faith to a broad range of other activities such as loving, hoping, promising, to metapsychical experiences (which Marcel sees as a
"propadeutic" to religious faith[2]) even to the
believer's most primitive sense of _being_ a body _in_
the existent universe, and on this basis, to study
the various dimensions of the situation "which I
am" through _one basic set of organizing concepts_
which he applies univocally throughout the dimensions of the situation.

    And in regard to religious faith, this ap-
proach catches the way in which this particular

---

[1]Marcel's phenomenological description of
this active side of experience is in _CF_ 27-29.
Cf. Marcel's verdict that ". . . the error of
empiricism consists only in ignoring the part of
invention and even of creative initiative involved
in any genuine experience" (_TPE_ 128).

[2]_ECVQE_ 110, 218-219.

experience--more than any other--is rooted in the underlying intricacies of the character of the believer as a concrete individual. More than any other act, religious faith brings into focus every-thing that is significant and individual about the believer, everything that makes him who <u>he</u> is in all of his uniqueness. This is precisely why religious faith cannot be programmed and why its emergence is beyond prediction. Marcel and Wisdom have caught this aspect of religious faith most perceptively.

But even beyond this, on this model, Marcel can specify one further dimension within that which the believer brings to his experience "from himself" which exerts a powerful influence on the formation and formulation of religious claims: the force of tradition as embodied within a believing community.

We know how seriously Marcel takes the intersubjective fact. But in one of his most per-ceptive phenomenological descriptions--this one, of "The Mystery of the Family"--[1] Marcel sees the intersubjective experience as entering into the situation "which I am" not only on a "horizontal" dimension in the present, but also in a "vertical" dimension through history.

I have to recognize that behind the lighted but much restricted zone which I call my family there stretches, to infinitude, ramifications which . . . I can follow out tirelessly . . . . I can discern enough . . . to enable me to follow this umbilical cord of my temporal antecedents, and to see it taking shape before me yet stretching back beyond my life to an indefinite network which . . . would probably be coextensive with the human race itself. My family, or rather my lineage, is the succession of

---

[1] <u>HV</u> 68-97.

historical processes by which the human
species has become individualised into the
singular creature that I am.[1]

I am then formed by my individual lineage; it makes
me <u>what I am</u> in my concrete singularity. But at
the same time--and in another way--I am formed by
the traditions which this lineage gives birth to:

> . . . these traditions are to the inner man
> what the family setting is to the visible
> one. We cannot just say they are his en-
> vironment; they help to form him. Without
> them there is a risk of his becoming the
> plaything of every chance influence; his
> development is exposed to all the dangers
> of incoherence . . . they are first of all
> the records and examples which secure the
> bond between the generations.[2]

All of this gives added substance to what
Marcel is proposing as a third alternative to both
the Buberian approach to faith and its reductionist
alternative. The Buberian rejects any possible
experiential confirmation or repudiation of his
encounter with an Absolute Thou. The encounter
then remains personal, individualistic--and ultimately lonely; it cannot be shared with anyone else
for it has no meaning to anyone else. The reductionist, in turn, insists that at best, the
believer's claims are reduced to purely autobiographical reports of private experiences with no
reference beyond them, or at worst, are not even
cognitive (i.e. falsifiable) but rather mere expressions of emotion.

---

[1]Ibid. 71.

[2]Ibid. 78. Cf. Marcel's evaluation of the
role of the Church, in discerning, appreciating and
sanctifying miracles (<u>CF</u> 7-8).

In contrast, Marcel and Wisdom are proposing that the principle of falsifiability should
neither be dismissed out of hand nor accepted as
final in its suggested form. Rather, it has to be
remodeled to take account of the extraordinary complexity and variety of man's experiential encounters with his world. They claim that Flew's
formulation of the criterion is excessively simplistic in its understanding of experience and excessively narrow in its appreciation of "the facts"
that make for factual significance--especially as
both of these have to do with religion.[1]

The corrective that they would apply to
Flew's criterion is a more subtle appreciation of
the "participatory" character of experience, i.e.
the extent to which both the experiences that are
relevant to religion and the facts that they disclose are moulded by what the believer brings to
them "from himself." And in these last pages, we
have seen how Marcel expands this dimension of
"from himself" to include the decisive roles which
are played by tradition and community in shaping
these distinctive claims by confirming, repudiating
or modifying the formulations of these claims by
its representatives from generation to generation.

With the principle of falsifiability remodeled in this manner, we are ready for step two
in Marcel's and Wisdom's response to the challenge
posed by Blackstone and Flew. Given this understanding of experience as it pertains to religion,
is there some data that is incompatible with those
purported claims? Or as Flew's sceptic asks: "Just
what would have to happen not merely (morally and
wrongly) to tempt but also (logically and rightly)
to entitle us to say 'God does not love us' or even

---

[1]The limitations of the principle of
verification as it affects religious claims are
discussed in Ferré, chapter 4.

'God does not exist'?"[1]

To this Marcel would answer directly: the ensemble of experiences which go into creating what he calls the sense of "the broken world": a generalized sense of depersonalization where man is identified with his functions, an overwhelming sense of despair, of hopelessness, an inveterate pessimism, a nihilism in regard to the possibility of value, a feeling that "nothing counts."[2] In this context Marcel likes to quote Claudel:

> Nothing exists.
> I have seen and touched
> The horror of what is useless, adding the proof
>   of my hands to what is not.
> The Void does not fail to declare itself by
>   words which say: I am.
> This is my prey and the revelation I have
>   made.[3]

This too is a "pattern in time" and in Marcel's writings, it has, if anything, a more coercive impact on the individual than its opposite.

Are religious claims falsifiable then? In principle, certainly--by the experience of "the broken world." In practice, possibly--because which pattern an individual chooses to see, and how he reads or understands the patterns that he does see are affected by what he brings to his experience "from himself"--in all the ways which we have described above. The move from principle to practice is the move from the general to the concrete, to the individual in all his singularity and

---

[1]Flew and MacIntyre, p. 99.

[2]The best single description of this experience is at the beginning of "On the Ontological Mystery" (TPE 9-16).

[3]CF 172.

unpredictability. Thus, though we may be prepared
to make a flat statement about the falsifiability
of religious claims in principle, we must be much
more hesitant about any such proposal in practice.

On this second approach, then, Marcel can
be shown to be making cognitive, i.e. meaningful,
religious claims. To what extent, then, do they
constitute knowledge?

We maintained above that there was an
ambiguity in Marcel's delineation of a totally distinct realm of sacred knowledge, i.e. knowledge of
the mysterious. We saw that this approach blurred
significant distinctions and that Marcel nowhere
provides a warranty for referring to this distinct
kind of knowledge as constituting a legitimate kind
of knowledge. Finally, we attempted to show that
Marcel does not demonstrate that the same data
could not be accounted for just as adequately by an
approach which identifies the "knowledge" portion
of "sacred knowledge" as common, objective or
"profane" knowledge distinguished from other instances of profane knowledge because of the heavy
overlay of non-epistemological ingredients, both
conscious and unconscious, which come into play
here.[1]

The knowledge yielded by religion then is
not a totally distinctive kind of knowledge--for
knowledge is not susceptible to that kind of dis-
crimination; nor is it attained by a distinct kind
of reflection--for again reflection remains reflection whatever form it takes. But neither is
religious knowledge similar to the kind of knowledge
yielded by science. What are "the facts" of which
religion gives us knowledge? Wisdom's formulation
is ". . . patterns in human reactions which are
well described by saying that we are as if there
were hidden within us powers, persons, not our-

---

[1]See above, pp. 156-164.

selves and stronger than ourselves"[1]--patterns that
are essentially within us, that when disclosed
yield "exhilaration without anxiety, peace without
boredom," which war against "deadness and despair,"
which promote "oneness with one another," which
"release us from human bondage into human freedom,"
which yield, in a word, "salvation."[2]

Marcel would surely go along with all of
this. But his formulation would see in the unification of these patterns, the disclosure of "being"
--that reality within us, within the other and
within the existent universe which resists critical
dissolution, which removes us from the flux of
temporality and the fear of mortality--all understood as concrete and personal; to the extent that
experience discloses these patterns, it has "ontological weight" and it is the task of philosophy to
disclose this weight.

Both Wisdom and Marcel concede that it is
possible to speak of these patterns without using
the word "God," but both insist as well that at
certain times and for certain individuals this is
the only appropriate word to use.

Finally, can we legitimately refer to the
awareness of these patterns as "knowledge?" Ayer's
criteria for knowledge ultimately revolve around
the need for verification of whatever it is that we
claim to be knowledge. For only of that which can
be verified, tested and confirmed in some public
manner and by some specified set of procedures can
we legitimately claim truth, certainty and the
right to claim certainty.

Much of what we have found Marcel and
Wisdom to be suggesting, on this approach, is

---

[1] _Proceedings_, p. 204.

[2] Ibid. 205-206.

designed to show that there are verificatory procedures that are appropriate to the knowledge yielded by religion. They will insist--as they did regarding the criteria for cognitivity--that the requirements be adjusted to take into account the distinctive nature of the data; that "a pattern in time" or "being" is a much more subtle affair than the kinds of realities which the physical sciences have to deal with, that the process of verification cannot be as universal as that which science can demand precisely because so much of religious knowledge is affected by the character of the knower which is highly individualized and unpredictable; and that the knowledge yielded is more tentative, more difficult to formulate in language and surely less precise.

But with these qualifications, if the task of verifiability is to weed out illusion, hallucination and obvious error, and to assure that the facts that concern religion are more than simply personal, autobiographical claims, then enough has been said to show that believers have evolved procedures for doing just that, and that these procedures show a striking parallel to procedures that are used in other areas of human knowledge such as art.

And finally, if Blackstone is serious about his claim that the task of epistemology is not simply to dismiss the possibility of certain kinds of knowledge out of hand but rather to assist one in discovering ". . . which attitude (in a scale including belief, disbelief, no opinion, etc.) is the appropriate attitude to adopt toward any given statement . . .,"[1] then religious knowledge, as Marcel and Wisdom describe it, will find its proper place along that scale and they can be said to have helped the believer do just that.

---

[1]Blackstone, pp. 128-129.

Two Approaches to Religious Knowledge

We have traced two approaches to religious knowledge in the writings of Gabriel Marcel. They are clearly worlds apart. The former in effect leads to the elimination of knowledge from religion; the latter sees religion as yielding some kind of knowledge, however tentative. The former is frankly anti-empiricist; the latter assigns a significant role to certain experiences in confirming, repudiating or modifying the knowledge so gained. The former emphasizes the believer's isolation; the latter, his social orientation.

There is no reconciling these two approaches for they stem from two equally powerful but antithetical impulses in Marcel's thought as a whole. Each of these impulses emerges most clearly in one of Marcel's two most significant monographs-- "Existence and Objectivity" and "On the Ontological Mystery."

"Existence and Objectivity" is totally devoted to an unpacking of the dimension of incarnation. It deals with three themes: existence, sensation and the sense of _my_ body, and demonstrates ". . . the immediate participation of what we normally call the subject in a surrounding world from which no veritable frontier separates it."[1] The operative words here are "immediate" and "participation,"--the immediate participation of my self with my body, and my self/body with the existent universe and the absolute indubitability of any participatory experience which is immediate in this way.

"On the Ontological Mystery" on the other hand, begins with an extensive phenomenological description of man in the "broken world," centers on Marcel's most perceptive unpacking of the

---

[1]_MJ_ 331-332.

dimension of intersubjectivity and of the three
cardinal intersubjective experiences, fidelity,
hope and love, and climaxes with a discussion of
the way in which intersubjectivity discloses being
and, for the believer, God--precisely as a response
to the sense of "brokenness."

It is worth noting that the agendas of the
two papers are almost completely disparate; intersubjectivity is almost totally absent from the
first and incarnation from the second. It is also
worth noting that the first explicitly rejects the
possibility of any kind of verification, confirmation, empirical proof or disproof of the central
participatory experiences that it elaborates. The
second--though equally adamant in rejecting as
illegitimate the kind of verification that is
central to the technologically-oriented "broken
world"--nevertheless concludes with the claim that
there exists a middle ground between the alternatives of "excessive dogmatism" and simply allowing ". . . difficulties to subsist" and that is by
"calling out to other travelers . . .--not the
generality but this being and that other . . .
through love,"[1] in other words with the concession
that in some more limited, tentative way the individual can share and find support for his faith.

It is but a simple step from this to the
further conclusion that Marcel's first approach to
verification--the approach that dismisses the need
for verification as irrelevant--stems from his
thought on incarnation which seeks to root man
directly and immediately within the existent uni-
verse--from which no frontier can separate him--and
which must emphasize precisely the individuality of
man for ultimately it is through my body that I am
one with the existent universe. The second ap-
proach--which sees experience as verifying man's
participatory experience--stems from his thought on

---

[1]TPE 44.

intersubjectivity which sees man as realizing himself most fully through intimacy with other persons
with all that this implies for the possibility and
value of each individual's sharing his most meaningful experiences with his brothers.

Our conclusion here links up with and illuminates some of the conclusions reached earlier
in the course of this study. We noted that Ricoeur
suggests and Marcel concedes that his thought on
existence and on being constitute different responses to different preoccupations--the first, to
his search for an indubitable point of departure
for his philosophical explorations, and the second,
to his preoccupation with the increasing functionalization of man in a technocratic age; hence the
disparate agenda of the two major programmatic
statements in "Existence and Objectivity" and "On
the Ontological Mystery," and hence Marcel's inability to deal coherently with the relation of
existence to being.[1]

With this in mind, we may appreciate how on
the first approach to religious faith, Marcel sees
faith as modeled on sensation in its immediacy and
hence on man's immediate participation in existence
which is precisely what sensation designates according to "Existence and Objectivity."[2] On the
second approach faith is modeled on fidelity--of
which it is an extension--and fidelity, as we know,
is our access to being.[3]

Further, if the existential and empirical/
ontological thrusts in Marcel's thought are responses to two different preoccupations, it is
clear why his attempt to fit the dimensions of

---

[1]TWB 233-236 and above, pp. 104-106.

[2]MJ 131, 316, 327-332.

[3]BH 41.

273

incarnation and intersubjectivity into one mould should be a source of ambiguity. Much the same may be said about his treatment of the characteristics of sacred knowledge: immediacy, permeability and secondary reflection. Finally, it helps account for Marcel's wish to treat love, knowledge and participation as one. Each of these represents an attempt to reconcile the two impulses which ground his work as a whole.

Ricoeur sees these two thrusts in Marcel's thought as complementary. Marcel would agree. In fact, he tries to emphasize this complementarity by borrowing heavily from the vocabulary of each of these dimensions to clarify the other. But, in fact, they stem from two equally powerful and divergent impulses in his thought. That they are divergent is clearest in their implications for the verifiability of religious claims. Marcel cannot hold these two tendencies in equilibrium but he is clearly not prepared to abandon either one--and since he was not a systematic thinker, he was never forced to.

There is then no reconciliation of these two approaches but two final points should be made regarding the second approach. It is, first, profoundly Marcellian--even more Marcellian than the first--in its intersubjective emphasis, in its appreciation for the complexities and unpredict-ability of human behavior, in its respect for the individual as a concrete embodiment of a vast array of factors stretching far beyond his consciousness and in its regard for the decisive role of experi-ence, in the broadest sense, in moulding the stance of the individual.

Second, it is, in fact, much closer to what we know about the way in which religions develop and function, and hence is much more profoundly Christian--and certainly more Catholic--than the first approach. The believer, in western religions, rarely sees himself as alone in the presence of God; he is much more conscious of meeting God

274

through the mediating influences of tradition and community, i.e. for Marcel, through the Church.

Marcel's hesitation at accepting the "existentialist" label is well-founded. This second approach may well explain why.

Paul Ricoeur--who remains the most perceptive student of Marcel's thought--discerns in the ensemble of his work two irreducible tendencies which he labels the "orphic" or "lyric" and the "eschatological" or "dramatic."

Au niveau lyrique, la vie et la mort conspirent avec l'éternité, la présence de l'ami est en consonance avec la présence du Toi suprême, la liberté devient recueillement et réponse au don de l'être.

Au niveau dramatique la pensée est en combat avec les possibilités menaçantes du désespoir, du reniement, du suicide, la liberté est une option angoissante et non une réponse joyeuse, l'existence est affrontée au démoniaque qui assiège ses frontières.[1]

These two tendencies stand in tension--a tension best symbolized by the image of man as viator, itinerant, oscillating between fidelity and betrayal, hope and despair, invocation and refusal. Marcel's phenomenological description of this state of itinerance is his major contribution to philosophy. He is first and foremost a philosophical anthropologist, an extraordinarily perceptive student of man in the intricacies and varieties of his behaving and feeling. It is precisely this

---

[1]Ricoeur, Marcel et Jaspers, p. 405. Marcel's own treatment of what he calls the orphic and eschatological elements in his thought are discussed in HV 12 and 92 respectively.

stage of itinerance that is best illuminated by
Marcel's writings for the theatre, the philosophical significance of which has only been hinted at
in these pages. These plays display the full
range of Marcel's sensitivity tuned exquisitely to
the struggles within the individual as he tries to
discover some kind of resolution to the conflicts
that beset him. They portray best the "sociology
of shadows" to which "the metaphysics of light"
of his philosophical writings is the perfect
complement.[1]

---

[1] TWB 252-253.

SELECTED BIBLIOGRAPHY

A. Works by Gabriel Marcel

Marcel, Gabriel. "De la recherche philosophique." Entretiens Autour de Gabriel Marcel. Neuchâtel: Langages de la Baconnière, 1976.

_____. "De l'audace en métaphysique." Revue de Métaphysique et de Morale, 52 (1947), 233-243.

_____. Being and Having. Translated by Katharine Farrer. Boston: Beacon Press, 1951.

_____. Coleridge et Schelling. Paris: Aubier-Montaigne, 1971.

_____. Creative Fidelity. Translated by Robert Rosthal. New York: The Noonday Press, 1964.

_____. The Decline of Wisdom. Translated by M. Harari. Chicago: The Henry Regnery Company, 1955.

_____. En chemin, vers quel éveil? Paris: Gallimard, 1971.

_____. "Les Conditions dialectiques de la philosophie de l'intuition." Revue de Métaphysique et de Morale, 20 (1912), 638-652.

_____. "La dominante existentielle dans mon oeuvre." Contemporary Philosophy: A Survey. Vol. III. Firenze: La Nuova Italia Editrice, 1969.

Marcel, Gabriel. *The Existential Background of Human Dignity*. Cambridge, Mass.: Harvard University Press, 1963.

_____. *Homo Viator: Introduction to a Metaphysic of Hope*. Translated by Emma Craufurd. Chicago: The Henry Regnery Company, 1951.

_____. "L'Idée de Dieu et ses conséquences." *L'Age Nouveau*, January 1955, pp. 39-44.

_____. *Man Against Mass Society*. Translated by G.S. Fraser. Chicago: The Henry Regnery Company, 1952.

_____. *Metaphysical Journal*. Translated by Bernard Wall. Chicago: The Henry Regnery Company, 1952.

_____. *Le Monde cassé*. Paris: Desclée de Brouwer, 1933.

_____. *The Mystery of Being*. Vol. I: *Reflection and Mystery*. Translated by G. S. Fraser. Chicago: The Henry Regnery Company, 1950.

_____. *The Mystery of Being*. Vol. II: *Faith and Reality*. Translated by René Hague. Chicago: The Henry Regnery Company, 1951.

_____. "Notes pour une philosophie de l'amour." *Revue de Métaphysique et de Morale*, 59 (1954), 374-379.

_____. "Notes sur le mal." *Revue de Métaphysique et de Morale*, 79 (1974), 402-408.

_____. *Philosophical Fragments 1909-1914*. Translated by Lionel A. Blain. Notre Dame, Ind.: University of Notre Dame Press, 1965.

_____. *The Philosophy of Existentialism*. Translated by Manya Harari. New York: Citadel Press, 1961.

Marcel, Gabriel. <u>Presence and Immortality</u>. Trans-
    lated by Michael A. Machado. Revised by Henry
    J. Koren. Pittsburgh: Duquesne University
    Press, 1967.

_____. "Le Primat de l'existentiel: sa portée
étique et religieuse." <u>Actas del Primer
Congreso Nacional de Filosofia</u>. T. I.
Menendoza, Argentina, 1949, pp. 408-415.

_____. <u>Problematic Man</u>. Translated by Brian
Thompson. New York: Herder and Herder, 1967.

_____. <u>Le Quatuor en fa dièse</u>. Paris: Plon,
1925.

_____. <u>Royce's Metaphysics</u>. Translated by
Virginia and Gordon Ringer. Chicago: The Henry
Regnery Company, 1956.

_____. <u>Searchings</u>. New York: Newman Press,
1967.

_____. <u>Le Seuil invisible</u>. Paris: Grasset,
1914.

_____. "Solipsism Surmounted." <u>Philosophy
Today</u>, 10 (1966), 205-211.

_____. "Some Reflections on Existentialism."
<u>Philosophy Today</u>, 8 (1964), 246-247.

_____. "Testament philosophique." <u>Revue de
Métaphysique et de Morale</u>, 74 (1969), 253-262.

_____. "Theism and Personal Relationships."
<u>Cross Currents</u>, 1 (1950), 35-42.

_____. Three Plays: <u>A Man of God</u>, <u>Ariadne
The Funeral Pyre</u>. Translated by Rosalind
Heywood and Marjorie Gabain. London: Secker
and Warburg, 1952.

Marcel, Gabriel. Tragic Wisdom and Beyond, including Conversations Between Paul Ricoeur and
Gabriel Marcel. Translated by Stephen Jolin
and Peter McCormick. Evanston: Northwestern
University Press, 1973.

_____. "Truth and Freedom." Philosophy Today,
9 (1965), 227-237.

B.   Secondary Works

Bagot, Jean-Pierre. Connaissance et amour. Paris:
Beauchesne et ses fils, 1958.

Blackham, H. J. Six Existentialist Thinkers. New
York: Harper and Brothers, 1959.

Breisach, Ernst. Introduction to Modern Existentialism. New York: Grove Press, Inc., 1962.

Cain, Seymour. Gabriel Marcel. London: Bowes and
Bowes, 1963.

_____. "Gabriel Marcel's Theory of Religious
Experience." Unpublished Ph.D. dissertation,
University of Chicago, 1956.

Collins, James. The Existentialists: A Critical
Study. The Henry Regnery Company, 1952.

Copleston, Frederick, S.J. A History of Philosophy.
Vol. IX, Pt. 2. Garden City, N.Y.: Image Books,
1977.

Davy, M. M. Un Philosophe itinérant, Gabriel
Marcel. Paris: Flammarion, 1959.

Entretiens autour de Gabriel Marcel. Neuchâtel:
Editions de la Baconnière, 1976.

Gallagher, Kenneth T. _The Philosophy of Gabriel Marcel_. New York: Fordham University Press, 1962.

Gilson, Etienne, ed. _Existentialisme chrétien: Gabriel Marcel_. Paris: Librairie Plon, 1947.

Heinemann, F. H. _Existentialism and the Modern Predicament_. New York: Harper and Row, 1958.

Jolivet, Régis. _Les Doctrines existentialistes de Kierkegaard à J. P. Sartre_. Abbaye Saint-Wandrille: Editions de Fontenelle, 1948.

Keen, Sam. _Gabriel Marcel_. Richmond, Va.: John Knox Press, 1967.

Lê Thành Tri. _L'Idée de participation chez Gabriel Marcel. Superphénoménologie d'une inter-subjectivité existentielle_. Thèse présentée à la faculté de l'université de Fribourg, Suisse, pour obtenir le grade de docteur.

McCown, Joe. _Availability: Gabriel Marcel and the Phenomenology of Human Openness_. Missoula, Montana: Scholars Press for The American Academy of Religion, 1978.

Miceli, Vincent P. _Ascent to Being_. New York: Desclee Company, 1965.

Reinhardt, Kurt F. _The Existentialist Revolt_. Milwaukee: The Bruce Publishing Company, 1952.

Ricoeur, Paul. _Gabriel Marcel et Karl Jaspers_. Paris: Editions du Temps Présent, 1947.

Roberts, David E. _Existentialism and Religious Belief_. Edited by Roger Hazelton. New York: Oxford University Press, 1962.

Parain-Vial, Jeanne. _Gabriel Marcel et les niveaux de l'expérience_. Philosophes de Tous les Temps. Editions Seghers, 1966.

Pax, Clyde. _An Existential Approach to God: A Study of Gabriel Marcel_. The Hague: Martinus Nijhoff, 1972.

Sanborn, Patricia F. _Existentialism_. New York: Pegasus, 1968.

_____. "Gabriel Marcel's Conception of the Self." Unpublished Ph.D. dissertation, Columbia University, 1965.

Schaldenbrand, Mary Aloysius. _Phenomenologies of Freedom_. An Essay on the Philosophies of Jean-Paul Sartre and Gabriel Marcel. Washington, D.C.: Catholic University of America Press, 1960.

Shrader, George Alfred, Jr., ed. _Existential Philosophers: Kierkegaard to Merleau-Ponty_. New York: McGraw-Hill Book Company, 1967.

Spiegelberg, Herbert. _The Phenomenological Movement: An Historical Introduction_. Vol. II. The Hague: Martinus Nijhoff, 1971.

Troisfontaines, Roger. _De l'existence à l'être; la philosophie de Gabriel Marcel_. Vols. I and II. Louvain: Editions E. Nauwelaerts, 1953.

van Ewijk, Thomas J. M. _Gabriel Marcel: An Introduction_. Translated by Matthew J. von Velzen. Glen Rock, N.J.: Deus Books, Paulist Press, 1965.

Wahl, Jean. _Vers le concret_. Paris: Librairie Philosophique J. Vrin, 1932.

Widmer, Charles. _Gabriel Marcel et le théisme existentiel_. Paris: Les Editions du Cerf, 1971.

C. Journal Articles

Adams, Pedro. "Marcel: Metaphysicist or Moralist."
   Philosophy Today, 10 (1966), 182-189.

Anderson, Thomas. "Gabriel Marcel's Notions of
   Being." Philosophy Today, 19 (1975), 29-48.

Benson, Jann. "John Wisdom and Gabriel Marcel on
   Proving the Existence of God." Philosophy
   Today, 21 (1977), 194-200.

Blain, Lionel. "Marcel's Logic of Freedom in
   Proving the Existence of God." International
   Philosophical Quarterly, 9 (1969), 177-204.

Boutang, Pierre. "Le Souci de la transcendence."
   Revue de Métaphysique et de Morale, 79 (1974),
   315-327.

Bruaire, Claude. "Une Lecture du Journal Métaphysique." Revue de Métaphysique et de Morale,
   79 (1974), 343-346.

Bugbee, Henry. "A Point of Co-articulation in the
   Life and Thought of Gabriel Marcel." Philosophy
   Today, 19 (1975), 61-67.

Busch, Thomas. "Gabriel Marcel: An Overview and
   Assessment." Philosophy Today, 19 (1975), 4-11.

Collins, James. "Gabriel Marcel and the Mystery of
   Being." Thought, 18 (1943), 665-693.

Cromp, Germaine. "Le Rapport âme-corps chez le
   premier Marcel." Dialogue, 8 (1969-70), 445-
   459.

Delhomme, Jeanne. "La Philosophie de Gabriel
   Marcel." Revue Thomiste, 44 (1938), 129-144.

_____. "Le Jugement en 'je.'" Revue de Méta-
   physique et de Morale, 79 (1974), 289-307.

Dubarle, Dominique. "La Franchissement des
    clôtures de la philosophie idéaliste classique:
    la première philosophie de Gabriel Marcel,
    1912-1914." Revue des Sciences Philosophiques
    et Théologiques, 58 (1974), 177-212.

"Extraits des entretiens qui eurent lieu à Dijon
    les 17 et 18 mars 1973 sur la pensée de Gabriel
    Marcel." Revue de Métaphysique et de Morale,
    79 (1974), 328-410.

Gerber, Rudolph J. "Difficulty with the Creative
    God in Existential Phenomenology." The
    Personalist, 51 (1970), 522-534.

_____. "Gabriel Marcel and Authenticity."
    The Personalist, 48 (1967), 548-559.

_____. "Gabriel Marcel and the Existence of
    God." Laval Théologique et Philosophique, 25
    (1969), 9-22.

_____. "Marcel and the Experiential Road to
    Metaphysics." Philosophy Today, 12 (1968),
    262-281.

Hughes, H. Stuart. "Marcel, Maritain and the
    Secular World." American Scholar, 35 (1966),
    728-749.

Hazelton, Roger. "Marcel on Mystery." Journal of
    Religion, 38 (1958), 155-167.

Jarrett-Kerr, M. "Gabriel Marcel on Faith and
    Unbelief." Hibbert Journal, 45 (1947), 321-
    326.

Hocking, William Ernest. "Marcel and the Ground
    Issues of Metaphysics." Philosophy and
    Phenomenological Research, 14 (1954), 439-469.

de Lacoste, Guillemine. "The Notion of Participa-
    tion in the Early Drama and the Early Journals
    of Gabriel Marcel." Philosophy Today, 19 (1975),
    50-60.

Lonergan, Martin J. "Gabriel Marcel's Philosophy of Death." Philosophy Today, 19 (1975), 22-28.

Luther, Arthur. "Marcel's Metaphysics of the We Are." Philosophy Today, 10 (1966), 190-203.

McCarthy, Donald. "Marcel's Absolute Thou." Philosophy Today, 10 (1966), 175-181.

Merleau-Ponty, Maurice. "Etre et avoir." Review of Etre et avoir, by Gabriel Marcel. La Vie Intellectuelle, 8 (1936), 98-109.

_____. "La Philosophie de l'existence." Dialogue, 3 (1966), 307-322.

Murchland, B.G. "The Philosophy of Gabriel Marcel." Review of Politics, 21 (1959), 339-356.

Ostermann, Robert. "Gabriel Marcel: Existence and the Idea of Being." The Modern Schoolman, 32 (1954), 19-38.

_____. "Gabriel Marcel: The Discovery of Being." The Modern Schoolman, 31 (1954), 99-116.

_____. "Gabriel Marcel: The Recovery of Being." The Modern Schoolman, 31 (1954), 289-305.

Parain-Vial, Jeanne. "Dialogue entre Gabriel Marcel et Madame Parain-Vial." Revue de Métaphysique et de Morale, 79 (1974), 383-401.

_____. "Discovery of the Immediate." Philosophy Today, 10 (1966), 170-174.

_____. "L'Espérance de l'être dans la philosophie de Gabriel Marcel." Les Etudes Philosophiques (1975), pp. 19-30.

_____. "Notes on the Ontology of Gabriel Marcel." Philosophy Today, 4 (1960), 271-278.

Pax, Clyde. "Marcel's Way of Creative Fidelity."
    Philosophy Today, 19 (1975), 12-21.

_____. "Philosophical Reflection: Gabriel
    Marcel." The New Scholasticism, 38 (1964),
    159-177.

Robinson, Daniel S. "Tillich and Marcel: Theistic
    Existentialists." The Personalist, 34 (1953),
    237-250.

Schaldenbrand, Mary Aloysius. "Gabriel Marcel and
    Proof for the Existence of God." Studies in
    Philosophy and the History of Philosophy, 1
    (1961), 35-56.

Siewert, Donald J. "The Body in Marcel's Meta-
    physics." Thought, 46 (1971), 381-405.

Sweeny, Leo. "Gabriel Marcel's Position on God."
    The New Scholasticism, 44 (1970), 101-124.

Thévenaz, Pierre. "La Philosophie de M. Gabriel
    Marcel." Revue de Théologie et de Philosophie,
    26 (1938), 235-243.

Troisfontaines, Roger. "Le Mystère de la mort."
    Revue de Métaphysique et de Morale, 79 (1974),
    328-337.

Wisdom, John. "Gods." Proceedings of the
    Aristotelian Society, London, 1944-45, pp. 185-
    206.

Zuidema, S. U. "Gabriel Marcel: A Critique."
    Philosophy Today, 4 (1960), 283-288.

D. Complementary Works

Altizer, T. J. J., William A. Beardslee, and Harvey
    J. Young, eds. Truth, Myth and Symbol.
    Englewood Cliffs, N.J.: Prentice-Hall, Inc.,
    1962.

Ayer, A. J. The Problem of Knowledge. London:
     The Macmillan Company, Ltd., 1956.

Bergson, Henri. The Creative Mind. Translated by
     Mabelle L. Andison. Totowa, N.J.: Littlefield,
     Adams and Company, 1965.

Blackstone, William T. The Problem of Religious
     Knowledge. Englewood Cliffs, N.J.: Prentice-
     Hall, Inc., 1963.

Borowitz, Eugene B. A Layman's Introduction to
     Religious Existentialism. New York: A Delta
     Book, 1965.

Brown, James. Kierkegaard, Heidegger, Buber and
     Barth: Subject and Object in Modern Theology.
     New York: Collier Books, 1962.

Buber, Martin. Eclipse of God. New York: Harper
     and Brothers, 1952.

_____. I and Thou. Translated by Walter Kauf-
     mann. New York: Charles Scribner's Sons, 1970.

Bugbee, Henry G., Jr. The Inward Morning. State
     College, Pa.: Bald Eagle Press, 1958.

Capaldi, Nicholas. Human Knowledge. New York:
     Pegasus, 1969.

Copleston, Frederick. Contemporary Philosophy.
     London: Burns and Oates, 1955.

Diamond, Malcolm. Contemporary Philosophy and
     Religious Thought. New York: McGraw Hill,
     1974.

Fackenheim, Emil L. Encounters Between Judaism and
     Modern Philosophy. New York: Basic Books, 1974.

_____. Quest for Past and Future: Essays in
     Jewish Theology. Bloomington, Ind.: Indiana
     University Press, 1968.

287

Farber, Marvin, ed. L'Activité philosophique en France et aux Etats-Unis. Vols. I and II. Paris: Presses Universitaires de France, 1950.

Ferré, Frederick. Language, Logic and God. New York: Harper and Brothers, 1961.

Flew, Antony. God and Philosophy. New York: Dell Publishing Co., Inc., 1966.

_____ and Alasdair MacIntyre, eds. New Essays in Philosophical Theology. New York: The Macmillan Company, 1955.

Hanna, Thomas, ed. The Bergsonian Heritage. New York: Columbia University Press, 1962.

Heschel, Abraham Joshua. God in Search of Man. Philadelphia: The Jewish Publication Society of America, 1956.

_____. Man is not Alone. New York: Farrar, Straus and Cudahy, Inc., 1951.

_____. Man's Quest for God. New York: Charles Scribner's Sons, 1954.

_____. The Prophets. Philadelphia: The Jewish Publication Society of America, 1962.

Hick, John. Philosophy of Religion. Englewood Cliffs, N.J.: Prentice-Hall, Inc., 1965.

Hook, Sidney. The Quest for Being. New York: Dell Publishing Company, 1963.

_____, ed. Religious Experience and Truth. New York: New York University Press, 1961.

Hutchison, John A. Language and Faith. Philadelphia: The Westminster Press, 1963.

Kegley, Charles W. and Robert W. Bretall, eds.
  The Theology of Paul Tillich. The Library of
  Living Theology, Vol. I. New York: The
  Macmillan Company, 1961.

Merleau-Ponty, Maurice. _Sense and Non-Sense_.
  Translated by Hubert and Nina Dreyfus.
  Evanston, Ill.: Northwestern University Press,
  1964.

Molina, Ferdinand. _Existentialism as Philosophy_.
  Englewood Cliffs, N.J.: Prentice-Hall, Inc.,
  1962.

Rabil, Albert, Jr. _Merleau-Ponty, Existentialist
  of the Social World_. New York: Columbia
  University Press, 1967.

Randall, John Herman, Jr. _Nature and Historical
  Experience_. New York: Columbia University
  Press, 1958.

_____. _The Role of Knowledge in Western
  Religion_. Boston: Starr King Press, Beacon
  Hill, 1958.

_____ and Justus Buchler, eds. _Philosophy: An
  Introduction_. Revised ed. New York: Barnes and
  Noble Books, 1971.

Rothschild, Fritz A., ed. _Between God and Man:
  An Interpretation of Judaism from the Writings
  of Abraham Joshua Heschel_. New York: Harper
  and Brothers, 1959.

Santoni, Ronald E., ed. _Religious Language and the
  Problem of Religious Knowledge_. Bloomington,
  Ind.: Indiana University Press, 1968.

Sarano, Jacques. _The Meaning of the Body_. Translated by James H. Farley. Philadelphia: The
  Westminster Press, 1966.

Schilpp, Paul Arthur and Maurice Friedman, eds.
The Philosophy of Martin Buber. The Library
of Living Philosophers, Vol. XII. LaSalle,
Ill.: Open Court, 1967.

Schmidt, Paul F. Religious Knowledge. Glencoe,
Ill.: The Free Press, 1961.

Tillich, Paul. Dynamics of Faith. New York:
Harper and Row, 1957.

_____. Systematic Theology. Vol. I. Chicago:
The University of Chicago Press, 1951.

_____. Theology of Culture. Edited by Robert
C. Kimball. New York: Oxford University Press,
1959.

Troisfontaines, Roger. Existentialism and Christian
Thought. Translated by Martin Jarrett-Kerr.
London: Adam and Charles Black, 1949.

Wahl, Jean. Philosophies of Existence. Translated
by F. Merat. Schocken Books, 1969.

_____. Tableau de la philosophie française.
Paris: Fontaine, 1946.

Warnock, Mary. Existentialism. New York: Oxford
University Press, 1970.

Woozley, A. D. Theory of Knowledge. London:
Hutchinson House, 1949.

E. Bibliographies

Lapointe, François H. "Bibliography on Marcel."
The Modern Schoolman, 49 (1971), 23-49.

_____ and Lapointe, Claire C. Gabriel Marcel
and His Critics: An International Bibliography
(1928-1976). New York and London: Garland
Publishing, Inc., 1977.

Troisfontaines, Roger. De l'existence à l'être;
    la philosophie de Gabriel Marcel. Louvain:
    Éditions E. Nauwelaerts, 1953. Vol. II,
    pp. 381-425.

Wenning, Gerald G. "Works By and About Gabriel
    Marcel." The Southern Journal of Philosophy,
    4 (1966), 82-96.

Objective thought (objective knowledge) 35-39, 40,
    44-45, 51, 53, 57-58, 61, 66-67, 70, 83, 124,
    129, 136-138, 146, 152, 156-157, 159-162, 168-
    172, 178, 191, 202-206, 220, 239
Osterman, Robert 205
Other minds, problem of 161
Palais de sable 67-68, 69, 200-202, 236, 248, 253
Parain-Vial, Jeanne 88
Participation 36-37, 40-42, 44, 53, 63, 66, 91,
    96, 104, 110, 144, 151-176, 191, 210-211, 213-
    214, 232, 271
Pascal, Blaise 77, 207
Pax, Clyde 63, 177, 205
Permeability 20, 84-85, 110, 112, 146, 147, 150,
    153, 166, 176, 179, 223, 233, 250, 274
Phenomenology 2, 78, 129, 182, 275
Philosophy, assumptions for 6-28; _____, data
    for 21-22, 27, 175; _____, impetus for 6-
    14, 25, 162; _____, method in 14-21, 25-27,
    162
Plotinus 62, 250
Positivism 72
Presence 9-10, 51, 94, 119-129, 133, 216, 221-222
Problem 10, 34, 50, 119-129, 178
Prometheus, Myth of 75
Proof (demonstration) 81, 101, 103, 144-146, 202-
    206, 226, 249, 252, 255
Quartet in F Sharp 112
Randall, John Herman, Jr. 3-4, 114, 174, 177,
    235, 239, 248, 256
Realism, epistemological 69-70, 210-214
Reflection 24-27, 37, 50, 54-56, 57-58, 61-62, 74,
    96, 123, 127-128, 129-151, 171, 180, 207-208,
    236, 241, 255; _____, later act of 37, 40,
    70, 130; _____, primary 131-132, 134, 135-
    139, 140-143, 145, 147, 166, 175, 206, 208,
    238, 241; _____, secondary 5, 34, 50, 53-
    54, 131-132, 134, 139-151, 152-153, 161-162,
    166, 176, 205-206, 208, 224-225, 229, 236, 241,
    243, 274
Ricoeur, Paul 12, 14, 78, 83-84, 102-103, 104-105,
    186, 190, 205, 210, 238, 273, 275
Robinson, Daniel S. 172
Royce, Josiah 29, 31, 94, 120

ABOUT THE AUTHOR

Neil Gillman is currently Dean of Academic Affairs of the Rabbinical School and Assistant Professor of Philosophies of Judaism at The Jewish Theological Seminary of America in New York City. He has also served as Adjunct Assistant Professor in the Department of Hebrew Culture and Education at New York University.

A native of Quebec City, Canada, Professor Gillman was graduated from McGill University, Montreal, Canada, in 1954. He was ordained as Rabbi at The Jewish Theological Seminary of America in 1960, and completed his studies for the Ph.D. in Philosophy at Columbia University in 1975.